BLOOD, POWER, *and* BEDLAM

Jeffrey Ian Ross
General Editor

Vol. 2

PETER LANG
New York • Washington, D.C./Baltimore • Bern
Frankfurt am Main • Berlin • Brussels • Vienna • Oxford

Christopher W. Mullins *and* Dawn L. Rothe

BLOOD, POWER, and BEDLAM

Violations of International Criminal Law in Post-Colonial Africa

PETER LANG
New York • Washington, D.C./Baltimore • Bern
Frankfurt am Main • Berlin • Brussels • Vienna • Oxford

Library of Congress Cataloging-in-Publication Data

Mullins, Christopher W.
Blood, power, and bedlam: violations of international criminal law
in post-colonial Africa / Christopher W. Mullins, Dawn L. Rothe.
p. cm. — (New perspectives in criminology and criminal justice; v. 2)
Includes bibliographical references.
1. Criminal liability (International law). 2. Africa—Social conditions—1960–
3. War crimes—Africa. 4. Crimes against humanity—Africa.
5. Criminal liability—Africa. 6. International offenses—Africa.
7. Political violence—Africa. I. Rothe, Dawn L. II. Title.
K5301.M85   345.6'0238—dc22   2008002914
ISBN 978-0-8204-8842-4 (hardcover)
ISBN 978-0-8204-8841-7 (paperback)
ISSN 1555-3418

Bibliographic information published by **Die Deutsche Bibliothek**.
Die Deutsche Bibliothek lists this publication in the "Deutsche
Nationalbibliografie"; detailed bibliographic data is available
on the Internet at http://dnb.ddb.de/.

Cover design by Sophie Boorsch Appel

The paper in this book meets the guidelines for permanence and durability
of the Committee on Production Guidelines for Book Longevity
of the Council of Library Resources.

© 2008 Peter Lang Publishing, Inc., New York
29 Broadway, 18th floor, New York, NY 10006
www.peterlang.com

All rights reserved.
Reprint or reproduction, even partially, in all forms such as microfilm,
xerography, microfiche, microcard, and offset strictly prohibited.

Printed in the United States of America

For Arwen P. Mullins
and the hope you see a world without these crimes

For my children Christopher, Nathan, and Hahnna
who continue to give me the answer to why.
DLR

CONTENTS

	Foreword	ix
	Series Preface	xiii
	Preface	xv
	Acknowledgments	xvii
Chapter 1.	A Criminology of Violations of International Criminal Law	1
Chapter 2.	Whither Justice? International Law	23
Chapter 3.	The Pathology of Disorder: Postcolonial Social (Dis)Organization	51
Chapter 4.	Cutting the Tall Trees	79
Chapter 5.	The Unending War	107
Chapter 6.	Two Centuries of Horror	131
Chapter 7.	Again the World Stood by and Watched	167
Chapter 8.	Explaining Atrocity	191
	References	219

FOREWORD

The history of Africa has been one of some triumphs, and much tragedy. Early in the twenty-first century no continent seems more afflicted by its historical legacy, or more challenged in the quest for a good future. Some 300 million people in Africa live in a state of poverty. The average per capita income is about $600. Approximately nine out of ten people in Africa's poorest countries live on less than $2 a day, and most of these on less than $1 a day. A broad lack of essential skills, poor infrastructure, and bureaucratic red tape all contribute to relatively low rates of productivity in many African countries. Furthermore, it has been estimated that some 40% of Africa's wealth is held offshore, and that the annual cost of corruption in Africa is some $150 billion.

More than two million African children die annually in their first month of life. Some one million die of malaria alone. Over 28 million people in Africa have been infected with the AIDS/HIV virus, and well over two million Africans have died from this affliction. Millions of people in the southern part of Africa live with the enduring threat of drought. Many die of malnutrition and starvation. And millions more have died as a consequence of warfare and crimes, broadly defined.

The tragedies of Africa are intertwined with a range of state crimes, perpetrated over a period of centuries. The slave trade–promoted and facilitated by various states—is of course one part of this history. The long stretch of colonialism—exemplified in its most cruel and oppressive aspects by the Belgian Congo regime under King Leopold II—followed. From the middle of the twentieth century on the independence movement in Africa gained rapid momentum, ultimately driving out the colonial powers. But all-too-often the independent post-Colonial regimes have themselves been profoundly brutal, corrupt and incompetent. A recent book on the history of independence in Africa concisely captures this immensely discouraging historical development: "From the Hopes of Freedom to the Heart of Despair." One should also note that at least some of the news out of Africa today provides a glimmer of hope. By some measures African economic growth is keeping pace with that of other parts of the developing world. The continent still has vast mineral and fuel-related assets, for example, and should benefit from elevated global demand. Africa has benefited from an expanding global economy, more foreign investment, and debt forgiveness programs reluctantly agreed to by international financial institutions. Certainly there are now more cases of enterprising and democratic leadership. Nevertheless, there is much cause for concern for the future of Africa. Elite classes benefit disproportionately from economic growth in this continent. The policies and practices of the world's wealthiest nations continue to impact negatively on Africa, from huge subsidies for agricultural producers to diminished international aid. Many political constraints on authentic and constructive humanitarian intervention by Western nations in on-going genocides and other human rights catastrophes exist. And the internal problems afflicting the continent, indicated above, are formidable.

Genocide is often identified as the ultimate, or quintessential, crime of the state, although it also involves various non-state actors. The first significant genocide of the twentieth century is generally taken to be the massacre of some 70,000 Herero tribal people by the Germans of colonial Southwest Africa in 1904, and of course in the final decade of the century we have the Rwanda genocide of up to 800,000 people. This tragic legacy now continues in the first decade of the twenty-first century with the on-going genocidal circumstances in Darfur.

Crimes of states—including genocides, human rights violations, and corruption—have not been much attended to by criminology as a disciplinary enterprise, but have been principally addressed by historians, political scientists, sociologists and anthropologists, international law scholars, and journalists, among others. In recent years this situation has begun to change, and we at long last have the emergence of an evolving criminology of crimes of the state.

When I accepted the invitation of David Nelken to edit a volume on state crime for Ashgate's International Library of Criminology, Criminal Justice and Penology–ultimately resulting in State Crime I & II (1998)–I had the hope that the inclusion of this topic in such a series might contribute to its legitimation as a criminological concern. Penny Green and Tony Ward's State Crime (2002) is arguably the most comprehensive survey of this topic by self-identified criminologists to be published to date. Christopher Mullins and Dawn Rothe are certainly among the most enterprising and productive members of a new generation of criminologists who have responded to the call for a criminology of crimes of the state. Their first book–The International Criminal Court:Symbolic Gestures and the Generation of Global Social Control (2006)–provides a detailed description and analysis of an immensely significant new international institution, with a criminological framework as one noteworthy dimension of their approach to the topic. In the present book, through the use of detailed case studies coming out of Africa, they make a fundamental contribution to the on-going evolution of a criminology of crimes of the state, and other political actors. They explore in some depth both the large-scale violence that is so readily associated with crimes of state, as well as large-scale economic crimes, such as the theft of the mineral wealth of African countries. They explore as well the formidable challenges in establishing international institutions and policies that might at least contain if not eradicate crimes of states.

Early in their book Mullins and Rothe state both what they hope to accomplish, as well as the limitations of their analysis. They are fully mindful of the endless complexities of the forms of state crime and its control that they address. Certainly their application of an integrated theory of crime, incorporating a range of factors from the micro-to the macro-level, is responsive to this complexity. They also productively seek to demonstrate how many forms of crime in contemporary, post-colonial Africa are best understood in relation to the colonial experience. The policies and actions of colonial regimes contributed to the conditions leading to the genocide in Rwanda in 1994. An understanding of crimes of states is inherently interdisciplinary and requires systematic attention to the socio-historical context within which such crimes occur, as well as political, economic, anthropological and psychological dimensions. These authors also recognize that the Rwanda genocide can only be understood properly in relation to the global and international context of that time. A range of institutions, from the United Nations to the International Monetary Fund to the Roman Catholic Church, as well as Western powers such as the United States, all adopted policies and actions (or failures to act) that facilitated the massive genocide in Rwanda carried out during a relatively brief period of time.

This book is appearing during a time when the "American Empire"–as it is increasingly characterized–is widely viewed as engaged in a range of violations of international law. The scope and reach of crimes of the state is by some measures being amplified in this context. The term "crime" itself is an especially potent term, and has been applied in quite different ways. Some of the crimes addressed in this book, including genocide, slavery, and the employment of child soldiers, are quite distinctive to states and political entities. But other crimes–such as genocidal rape–are parallel to offenses committed in a conventional context. Of course a formidable literature now exists on conventional forms of rape, but rape in the context of war has been far less fully studied. The authors of this book recount testimony–which makes for extraordinarily painful reading–of the utter brutality associated with genocidal rape. Most cases of conventional rape do not incorporate gratuitous forms of violence. The systematic exploration of such topics as genocidal rape, it seems to me, is one important dimension of a fully developed criminology of crimes of the state, insofar as such a criminology compares both parallels and differences between genocidal rape and conventional rape, and the justice system response to them. Altogether, this book makes a valuable contribution to the understanding of crimes of states, and provides an important basis for the next stage in the realization of a fully developed comparative criminology of the whole range of crimes, and their control.

David O. Friedrichs,
Professor & Distinguished University Fellow
University of Scranton (Pennsylvania)

SERIES PREFACE

Over the past two decades, the problems of the modern state have garnered considerable media and academic attention. Issues such as poverty, homelessness, welfare, and education are no longer talked about in hushed tones. Yet the more insidious atrocities and wrongdoings of states—such as human rights violations, corruption and genocide—are typically buried in the back pages of our daily newspapers and occasionally, news magazines. These are both complicated and unpleasant acts that few people are willing to take the time to notice or even comprehend, for that matter. Acts of state crime seem remote to the average citizen, particularly when they involve countries in lesser developed continents and states such as those in Africa that, over centuries, have suffered at the whims of colonizers, dictators, puppet governments, and rulers from afar.

Nevertheless, information about these countries and of the state crimes that occur within is becoming more readily accessible. But this information and knowledge alone is not sufficient; it must be contextualized, analyzed, and put into some kind of theoretical framework if we are to understand its import.

Collecting accurate and reliable information on state crime and interpreting it in a meaningful fashion is not a simple task. We cannot be sure that the material we collect is legitimate, nor can we count on typical models in the social sciences to explain all types of state crime.

As the editor of Peter Lang's series "New Perspectives in Criminology and Criminal Justice," I'm proud to introduce you to Christopher Mullins and Dawn Rothe's groundbreaking, well-researched and documented book, *Power, Bedlam and Bloodshed: War Crimes and Crimes Against Humanity in Post-Colonial Africa*. This is the second book in the Lang series and it is a formidable piece of cutting-edge scholarship that pushes the boundaries of the disciplines of criminology and criminal justice.

Mullins and Rothe analyze a number of important state crimes that have occurred in the likes of Rwanda, Uganda, the Democratic Republic of Congo, and Sudan. The authors look at the "political, economic, social, and criminological" causes of the prominent state crimes in these countries, and at the devastating effects of these cases, and then they place them into both a macro- and micro-level framework. Moreover, they do this in a comparative fashion that moves beyond simple case-study analysis that is prevalent in the so-called "social-science comparative research."

I'm sure that scholars, instructors, practitioners, and students in many fields—not only those of criminology, criminal justice, anthropology, and sociology—will be intrigued by Mullin and Rothe's book.

Jeffrey Ian Ross, Ph.D.
Revised December 7, 2007

PREFACE

This is a book about mass criminal atrocity—the worst crimes that humans can commit against each other. It examines the causes, nature and dynamics of genocides, war crimes and crimes against humanity occurring in Africa during the late 20th and early 21st century. The genocides in Rwanda and Darfur have claimed hundreds of thousands of lives, destroying the lives of hundreds of thousands of others. As the truth about what happened throughout the cities and hinterlands of Rwanda in 1994 became apparent, the international political society dusted off its cries of "never again," seemingly placed in storage after the atrocities of the World War Two. But it happened again, a decade later and just to the north east in the Darfur region of Sudan. Between these events, many states in east and central Africa collapsed, descending into chaos and violence. While the mass killings and other abuses of soldiers and citizens in Uganda and the Democratic Republic of Congo were never quite genocidal (in some ways they are much more nuanced and complex than the simple drive to exterminate an entire category of people), the body counts and casualty lists are just as long. The effects are just as horrifying.

This is not the first book written about such wide-spread criminal atrocities and it undoubtedly it will not be the last. However, it is the first attempt to examine and explain violations of international criminal law from a genuinely criminological approach. Most of the writing on events like those discussed here has been done by historians, lawyers and political scientists. While this work has contributed greatly to our understanding of such wide-spread violence and destruction, we feel that criminology has something to say about these events as well.

ACKNOWLEDGMENTS

Christopher would like to thank his wife, Robin, for her constant support, encouragement and love. Thank you for your patience, companionship, and for reading every word of the manuscript. You're the best. Thanks also go to Jerry and Arwen for their love and their very existence. I would also like to thank my co-author Dawn for drinking the Kool-Aid on this one and for our years of friendship and collaboration.

Dawn would like to thank her children, Christopher, Nathan, and Hahnna, for their love, pride and support. I also wish to thank my brother Danny whose pride in me fills me with awe. Of course, I cannot forget to mention the importance of my two newest editions to my life, Danny and Briahnna, who let me know I have done some things right in life. Thanks also to Chris—I am grateful for your friendship and all that we have shared.

We would both like to thank our wonderfully supportive colleagues who have encouraged us along the way. We are grateful for you, your work, and your support. We also want to specifically thank David Friedrichs for his insightful comments, suggestions, and review of our manuscript and for the wonderful foreword he has provided for this book. We would also both like to thank Jeff Ross for his support in this project and insightful comments.

· 1 ·

A CRIMINOLOGY OF VIOLATIONS OF INTERNATIONAL CRIMINAL LAW

Since their independence, many African states have collapsed and public life has devolved into violence, fear, thuggery, and mass murder. This book examines the nature, causes, and consequences of pervasive war crimes and crimes against humanity within selected central African societies. The past half-century has produced a number of failed, weakened, and/or contested régimes within the continent; over half of the United Nations' peacekeeping operations authorized by the Security Council have occurred within Africa. Although not globally unique, Africa has experienced a disproportionate number of failed states and has produced a seemingly overabundant number of atrocities related to the heavy hand of military-led totalitarian governments and internecine conflicts. Millions of people have been killed, wounded, and displaced; unstable social structures have bent (and occasionally broken) under the added strain of unregulated military activity in institutional environments weakened by colonialism and colonial withdrawal.

The problems and social conditions behind and resulting from these conflicts are often not limited to a single state, but spill over unsecured borders into neighboring countries. This has led to additional conflicts within the region. For example, the civil war in the Congo twice became a location for a major conflict involving most central and eastern African countries, as Uganda, Rwanda, Burundi, Chad, and others sent troops to support various factions and to loot local natural resources (including its human population). The conflict between the Ugandan government and the Lord's Resistance Army (LRA) has long carried into Chad and the Sudan, and the Central African Republic has been destabilized by the warfare in Sudan, the Democratic Republic of Congo (DRC), and Uganda.

This book provides an understanding of the social conditions that produce these events. Through a close analysis of key cases, we hope to expand extant criminological theory and bring it to bear on such crimes. To do so, we draw upon the existing criminological literature and an integrated theory of violations of international criminal law to provide a lens for understanding: (1) how states disintegrate into wanton violence, (2) how military and paramilitary organizations become motivated to engage in widespread war crimes against each other and to use violence against noncombatant citizenry, and (3) how these crimes are enacted and structured.

Over the past few years, criminology has begun to build a body of theory and data focused on understanding not only the crimes of the powerful—a well-represented area of criminology since Sutherland's 1939 presidential address to the American Sociological Society—but the crimes of states (see Friedrichs 1998; Kauzlarich and Kramer 1998; Kauzlarich, Mullins, and Matthews 2001; Kramer 1995; Kramer and Michalowski 2005; Mullins and Kauzlarich 2000; Ross et al. 1999; Rothe 2006; Rothe and Friedrichs 2006). Although none of these works have addressed either war crimes or crimes against humanity specifically, or moved beyond the context of US violations, they have created a framework for studying crimes committed by organizations that is applicable to these events (for a few exceptions see Hagan and Green 2002; Hagan, Rymond-Richmond, and Parker 2003; Mullins and Rothe 2007; Rothe and Mullins 2006, 2007a, 2007b).

Also of importance to this work is the nature of international social control. With the newly created International Criminal Court (ICC) undertaking investigations and producing criminal indictments of war criminals (see Rothe and Mullins 2006a; Sadat 2000), an exploration of the worst crimes that states commit is not only generally relevant to expanding the contours of criminology but to help the field understand the potential nature and effectiveness of the ICC. In fact, all but one of our cases were chosen specifically because the ICC is investigating war crimes and crimes against humanity allegations; further, the court is producing indictments of these charges (e.g., Sudan, Uganda, and the DRC). The ICC is not the first example of international social control in the form of formal adjudication to be applied to cases in this area. One of the four United Nations Security Council's (UNSC) authorized war crimes tribunals was established in the wake of the 1994 Hutu genocide of the Tutsi in Rwanda. In response to the civil war in Sierra Leone, the UNSC also established a hybrid Tribunal system run jointly by local courts and judges and the international community. In fact, it is these two international interventions which gave additional energy to the ratification of the Rome Statute of the ICC (for a more detailed description of the Rome Statute, see Mullins, Kauzlarich, and Rothe 2004; Rothe and Mullins 2006a; Sadat 2000).

Before we begin a general discussion of war crimes and crimes against humanity within the African context, we must survey the general social and historical conditions that produced these atrocities. In the case of all these African states, that contextual examination begins with the nineteenth-century colonization of Africa by European powers. Colonial endeavors and environments produced a radical restructuring of social and cultural organization. This set the stage for additional massive transformations in the cases we examine. In a matter of years, most African territories were transformed from utterly subjugated regions into sovereign, independent states that had to figure out how to maintain themselves and their peoples in a globally inter-structured economic environment. Such social transformations produced the greatest atrocities. Some of these we will explore here (e.g., the Rwandan genocide, the Ugandan government's campaign against the LRA, the massive crimes against humanity in the DRC, and the genocide in Darfur). They are by no means the only instances of the pathology of social disorder (e.g., Sierra Leone's civil war with widespread murder, rape, and mutilation of its citizens; the ethnic struggles in Burundi that were a mirror image of the Rwandan conflict; the collapse of the state in Cote d'Ivoire). From there, we proceed to examine the nature and structure of nonstate militia groups. Such paramilitary (or in many cases, formerly military) groups are responsible for the vast portion of atrocities witnessed in these internecine conflicts. Being more organized than ad hoc village defense groups but not as formally organized as a state military apparatus, they represent a unique form of social organization and warrant specific examination.

Plan of the Study

Much of the work in this area has been done in the context of economics and political science. Although some criminologists have addressed issues of genocide (see Friedrichs 1998, 2006; Hagan and Green 2002; Hagan, Rymond-Richmond, and Parker 2003; Woolford 2006), as a whole the field has shown little interest in these types of crimes and have specifically ignored issues within Africa (for the rare exceptions, see Hagan, Rymond-Richmond, and Parker 2003; Mullins and Rothe 2007; Rothe, Muzzatti, and Mullins 2006; Rothe and Mullins 2006, 2007; Rothe, Mullins, and Sandstrom 2008). Some would then question the validity of criminological inquiry into the topic. However, the field has been primarily focused on street offending behaviors predominantly in the Western context. Nonetheless, criminology has produced a great deal of work focused on explaining both violence and crimes committed by and within complex organizations. Our work is a logical theoretical and empirical extension of these threads of research. If criminology is capable of producing a real understanding of violence at any level, it needs to look to such events as we do in this book. A criminology that cannot explain the sorts of widespread violence, destruction, and chaos examined here is not much of a criminology at all.

Following Mills (1959), we acknowledge that our focus upon a criminological approach to these issues stems from the simple fact that we are, for better or worse, criminologists. As Mills says, every cobbler thinks leather is the thing and we are true to our discipline. However, as the cases examined here are the worst variety of violations of international humanitarian law, we feel they fall firmly under the purview of a criminological point of view. Indeed, just as Sutherland (1940) pointed out in regards to white-collar crime, the primary reason to examine such events as criminologists is that they are against the law. We echo Sutherland's call for a more holistic criminology by also drawing a relatively unexamined set of events into our analytical light.

Case Study Methodology

Case studies are a relatively common form of analysis in both the critical criminology of state crime as well as historical sociology. Through the careful and detailed examination of a singular case, we can clarify both empirical and theoretical issues of interest. Our goal here is to not merely catalogue the details of a series of crimes against humanity within African nations in the late twentieth century. We hope the event narratives are informative and insightful, but we intend to build beyond the extant exemplar-style tradition of case studies within state crime studies. The field has matured past the point of a need to keep generating case studies; we aim to explore these cases as further extensions of the project and test the broader generalizibility of the integrated theory of crime we present later in the chapter (see Goldstone 2004, for a discussion of case studies as exemplars versus extensions of theory). Further, we seek to use these narrative case studies to not only ferret out the multiple causes of such deeply embedded criminality, but also to see how these causal forces operate differentially within variant contexts (see Ragin 1987).

Our approach for each case here is inherently inductive, though not utterly so. Through the examination of the conditions, crimes, and outcomes within each selected state, we hope to build complex understandings of crimes against humanity in general. Yet, by no means is our approach "pure" induction—we have a number of initial assumptions and precepts that guide us through the inquiry. We build strongly upon, and use as a starting point, the extant state crime studies literature (see Rothe and Friedrichs 2006 for an overview). Nevertheless, we do not assume that the cases here will fit neatly into the preestablished theoretical and typological categories. State crime studies evolved primarily in the analysis of crimes of superpowers (e.g., the United States, UK, USSR, etc. See Ross 2000). The structural, cultural, and enactment dynamics of the atrocities examined here are qualitatively and quantitatively different. We also utilize a preexisting integrated theory of international criminal law violations (see Rothe and Mullins 2008).

Our selection of cases for this study was purposeful over random. We wanted to capture both convergences and divergences contained by elements within and behind these crimes. A globally focused selection of cases may have enhanced the generalizibility of our thesis. Indeed, the problems of postcolonial social disorganization have manifested in Latin America and Southern Asia as well as Africa. We selected Africa as our focus because the ICC has begun its first investigations on specifically African cases. Within the cases we could select in Africa, an underlying logic guided our selection of cases. Rwanda was chosen for a number of reasons. The genocide that occurred there has captured the imagination of the world (both academic and public) and sits as an ideal type case for violations of international criminal law in the contemporary world. The International Criminal Tribunal for Rwanda, as well as Nongovernment Organizations (NGOs) such as Amnesty International and Human Rights Watch, has produced a wealth of information on the case. More significantly for our purposes, the disorder in Rwanda was not contained in its borders; it spilled over into Burundi, Uganda, and the DRC. The nature and outcome of the conflicts directly impacted existing conditions and tensions in these states.

Simply, our chapters on both Uganda and the DRC require a full understanding of Rwanda.

Uganda was chosen, first, for its intimate connections with both Rwanda and the DRC. The disorder and widespread appearance of crimes against humanity have not been limited to one state in eastern sub-Saharan Africa, but has particularly plagued nearly the entirety of the Great Lakes Region (e.g., Rwanda, Uganda, Burundi, Zimbabwe, and the DRC). Moreover, due to the cross-border movements of the LRA, Sudan and Chad have also been drawn into the conflict. Second, Uganda is under investigation by the ICC, which is looking into the criminal actions of both the LRA and the Ugandan People's Defense Forces (UPF) in the northern segment of the country. The court has issued indictments of Joseph Kony, head of the LRA, and his chief captains. At this point, however, the LRA has insisted that the ICC drop its charges in exchange for their participation within the peace process. Third, Uganda was a colony of the UK, whose approach to colonial rule was significantly different from the French in Rwanda or the Belgians in the DRC. We fully expect different colonial experiences to have variant impacts on the postcolonial situation.

The DRC stands as a fulcrum of postcolonial tensions and disorder. In an earlier work (Rothe and Mullins 2006), we examined the DRC in the context of the ICC's investigation of crimes in the Ituri region. The DRC conflict produced the ICC's first official charges and suspect detainment. Thomas Dyilo is currently in the court's custody and indicted with the recruitment and use of child soldiers. The DRC's colonial period was one of the most horrible cases in the history of empire—producing the phrase the "crimes against humanity." Leopold II's Congo Free State, and the later Belgian parliamentary rule, is legendary for its sheer senseless violence and destruction.

The final case we chose, the Darfur genocide, was included not only because it ties to the other cases in this volume (e.g., the events in the Sudan were strongly influenced by those in Rwanda and Uganda), but also because it too has now become a case under examination by the ICC. It has recently received the greatest amount of international media attention and generated the largest amount of global discourse. It experienced colonial domination much later in its history than the other places discussed in this volume—once utterly defined and constrained by the League of Nation's Mandate System.

Our goal is to provide a broad understanding of the political, economic, social, and criminological processes at work within these cases. Our approach has clear limitations. First, as we are drawing from a handful of cases in the same geographic region, we cannot fully generalize from our findings here to all atrocities, or even other postcolonial atrocities in Latin America or Asia. As we have noted, each case is unique with variant histories, cultures, postindependence paths, and issues of agency and as such offer inimitable factors along with those that can be generalized beyond their borders. Nevertheless, we do build a solid model of criminal atrocities as they emerged in east and central Africa at the close of the twentieth and start of the twenty-first centuries. Due to the currently limited state of criminological inquiry into this topic, our work here can serve as a starting point for further comparative inquiries.

The other major limitation of our work is the secondary nature of the data. We rely upon materials collected by others not necessarily for the purposes we put them to here. Thus, important information may be limited or absent. To counteract this general tendency in such studies, we strove to both broadly and deeply collect whatever information was useful to our explorations. We have drawn strongly on historical sources (primary and secondary), NGO reports and data where available, data of international organizations (e.g., the UN, the IMF), and international courts (e.g., the ICTR), as well as relying upon less-reliable but still valuable sources of information (e.g., media wire accounts, journalistic documentary accounts, and official information made public by various state parties). Through depth and triangulation, we believe we have put together a solid collection of data to accurately depict and analyze our cases.

A Criminology of Violations of International Criminal Law

State Crime and Crimes of Globalization Studies

Most scholars trace the origins of state crime studies to Chambliss' 1989 ASC presidential address on State-Organized crime. Exploring crimes such as piracy and smuggling, Chambliss shows how states can be crucial in the organization and support of activities that violate their own laws and international laws, and when doing so they fulfill their broader political and economic objectives (see Chambliss 1989, 1995). Criminologists, particularly critical criminologists, quickly seized upon the concept, broadening, and enriching the field (see Barak 1991; Green and Ward 2000; Kauzlarich and Kramer 1993; Kramer 1995; Ross 1995; Tunnell 1993). This early work focused not only on crimes tacitly supported or organized by a sovereign polity, but also actions committed by nation-states themselves.

Chambliss (1995: 9) again called for resolving the key question at the foundation of the discipline, the definition of crime, so that the discipline could remain viable and vital. He stated,

> State organized crimes, environmental crimes, crimes against humanity, human rights crimes, and the violations of international treaties increasingly must take center state in criminology ... Criminologists must define crime as behavior that violates international agreements and principles established in the courts and treaties of international bodies. (Chambliss 1995: 9)

As more case studies and theoretical papers were published, the subfield began to look at state criminality as actions committed by states that violated domestic, international, or human rights laws (see Barak 1991; Kauzlarich and Kramer 1998; Kauzlarich, Matthews, and Miller 2001; Mullins and Kauzlarich 2000; Ross et al. 1999; Ross 2000) as well as incidents of states or state agencies failing to take actions which they were obligated to address. Although definitional debates continue (see Rothe and Friedrichs 2006), the idea of state criminality is firmly entrenched in the field. Following Chambliss, we contend that the use of international law—Customary Law, Treaties, Charters, International Humanitarian Law, and International Human Rights Law—constitutes the strongest foundation for defining state crime as this framework includes standards such as human rights, social and economic harms, as well as providing a solid legalistic foundation (see Mullins and Rothe 2006; Rothe and Friedrichs 2006; Rothe and Mullins 2006). International criminal law covers individuals as well as states, thus resolving any ongoing reservations of state as actors versus individuals; Jorgensen (2000: 139) suggests, "all acts which constitute international crimes may in principle entail individual or state responsibility, or both." Consequently, we draw upon existing international law in the definition of an act as criminal. Having said this, although we use the standards of international law, we broaden our foci to include organizations that are not considered a state or government (e.g., paramilitaries and/or militia organizations) thereby simultaneously narrowing the standard used to define criminality for our cases to violations of international criminal law. This not only draws attention to the types of crimes that state crime scholars have focused on for the past decade and a half but also to the more widespread incidents that emerge in the context of failed and failing states, specifically the role of militias in commission of crimes against humanity, genocide, and war crimes.

An Integrated Theory of Violations of International Criminal Law

Although many mainstream and critically orientated theories of crime and criminality have relevance to the explanation of state crime, standing alone each contains serious shortcomings. Building upon the early works of Kramer and Michalowski (1990) and Kauzlarich and Kramer (1998), Rothe and Mullins (2006, 2007) present an integrated theory of violations of international criminal law that encompasses state offending as well as that of active paramilitaries and/or militias while recognizing the inherent complexity of these phenomena. Any given instance of organizational crime is a product of multiple catalysts and forces. To fully elucidate a singular occurrence, one must examine a number of factors at multiple levels of analysis. This model identifies four levels of analysis: the international, the macro level of the state, the meso-organizational level, and the micro-individual level. Such analytical acuity allows a precise pinpointing of key forces and how they interact within a specific criminal event or context.

Save for recent work on crimes of globalization (see Friedrichs and Friedrichs 2002; Rothe, Muzzatti, and Mullins 2006), most organizational criminology has ignored the social forces and incipient social structures occurring within the international realm in favor of focusing on a state itself. Moreover, when the international arena is taken into account it is done so in a rather simplistic manner resting upon a highly idealized and reified account of globalization (Whyte 2003). State policies are viewed as inevitably market driven as such, the focused is limited to the dynamics of a global and capitalistic economy, most notably, U.S. centered. However, the institutional elements and context of a state, its economic, political, cultural, and historical environment, is distinct from and often exhibiting forces in contradiction with those elements at the international level. These forces may influence the nature of social forces within a state's macro-level structure, but can also exert their own unique influences. For example, recently, there has been an increasing trend within the international society pushing for the creation and legitimation of international criminal law. Especially since the foundation of the United Nations, and seen most strongly with the codification of the Rome Statute and the creation of the ICC, the majority of countries are increasingly submitting themselves to a higher legal authority giving up absolute sovereignty. As the process of globalization continues to expand, imperialistic agendas resurface and are reshaped (e.g., the US and UK's invasion of Iraq) as drives for liberation and democratization and transnational corporations are becoming the norm in global economic relations, examining the international level is essential.

Nevertheless, these forces do not act upon homogeneous social forms. Any given state, and the social structure it represents, will be the product of long-term historical contingencies and forces that necessitate an examination of factors more traditionally referred to as macro-level forces. Broader cultural, political, and economic factors in play at a given time and space can to a greater or lesser extent produce a given crime. For example, the cases currently under investigation at the ICC share a similar history of colonial rule. However, such historical conditions did not result in consistent postindependence outcomes. Issues of states' specific religions, resources, and geographic and/or ethnic divisions were also factors leading up to the events under investigation at the court. Consequently, ignoring these state-level differences fails to holistically address the etiological and structural factors of the given crimes.

Similarly, since these are crimes committed by organizations (states, state agencies, militaries, corporations, etc.) one must explore factors at play within the organization itself—a meso-level analytical focus. As corporate crime researchers have shown, some organizations are much more criminogenic than others. As such, the social processes and organizational cultures are essential in understanding state crimes. For example, the LRA's long-standing opposition to the Ugandan government is the product of postcolonial political forces and the end result of series of coups and countercoups. Furthermore, the operative ideology of the LRA is religious in nature, replicating the discourse of Alice/Laweka of the Holy Spirit Movement Army. Moreover, there is an ethic basis to the LRA, as it is mostly composed of Acholi from the Ankula region. Within the same conflicts, the Ugandan armed forces (the Ugandan People's Defense Forces, UPDF) have also committed vast atrocities; however, many of these are the result of a lack of authority and accountability within the military command hierarchy: most of these crimes represent a form of general thuggery and banditry. In contrast, the Sudanese regime has actively created the *Janjaweed* militia to carry out massive crimes against humanity. Moreover, governmental forces aid in the militias atrocities as well as abide by a systematic state policy focusing on continuing the violence and crimes at hand. Thus, although superficially similar, each of these cases exhibits a complexity of meso-level forces.

A separate body of criminological theory emphasizes the influence of social disorder within immediate residential environments as having powerful criminogenic effects. Typically referred to as social disorganization theory (see Bursik and Grasmick 1993; Shaw and McKay 1942), this line of theorizing suggests that when communities possess a diminished capacity to create and enact informal mechanisms of social control (also referred to as collective efficacy), crime rates increase due to the lack of community self-organization. Essentially a control theory of crime, this work points out that indicators of concentrated disadvantage are largely responsible for the reduction of a community's ability to act collectively. In addition, European and American criminologists have established that these disorganized social environments also have a pronounced tendency to produce criminal enterprises of varying levels of organizations—be they street gangs, mafia groups, crime syndicates, or drug cartels. In the absence of legitimate forms of social organization, illegal organizations—or at least groups who engage in persistent criminal behavior—proliferate to provide social structures and opportunities absent due to broader conditions of institutional failures. Here, widespread social disorganization is most readily apparent in producing militias, which we will discuss later in this chapter.

There are also important elements at work on the micro- or individual level that require explanation to fully understand a given case. Perpetrators and the decision-makers in these cases possess agency. They are not automatons blindly responding to sociopolitical forces, but rather lively social actors who often wield large amounts of social power and institutional authority that can be brought to bear in the commission of a crime. Such a focus is not to deny the context in which the decisions are made, but to acknowledge the role individuals play. Moreover, an acknowledgment of agency of actors reinforces the notion of accountability for decisions and actions as well in a legal context. In addition to separating out four levels of analysis, the integrated theory identifies four specific factors that structure a given organizational crime at each level of analysis: motivation, opportunity, constraint, and control.

Motivation is the constellation of the general and specific drives that lure and entice a given organization and/or organizational actor toward offending. Specific motivating forces can include the enhancement and/or maintenance of political power (e.g., the National Resistance Army's (NRA) criminal endeavors before and after the 1986 coup and the LRA's focused attempts to overthrow the Yoweri Museveni regime), personal or organizational economic gain (e.g., the *Janjaweed*), access to resources (e.g., multiple forces within the DRC), religious factors (e.g., the LRA), or can be as simple as revenge (e.g., the Hutu). As an example, the primary motivation of LRA fighters is their belief that their struggle against the National Resistance Movement (NRM) is a divine calling that is being directed and guided by God through the prophet Joseph Kony. General motivations, although often linked to specifics, can include factors such as political marginalization of a specific group or party (e.g., colonial powers often marginalized a portion of the population, giving specific preferential treatment to one group). In turn, this can result in specific motivating factors including political or economic gain. Moreover, ethnic divisions that were created by either colonial or postcolonial authorities can lead to specific motivation including revenge and/or the destruction of a reifieddehumanized other. Furthermore, it must be acknowledged that although we identify general (or modal) motivation factors, there can also be a wide variety of motivations individually within a criminal group (see Smeulers 2008).

Opportunities are those social interactions where the possibility for a crime to be committed emerges and presents itself to a potential offender (see Felson 1998). For example at the macro level, being a state strongly enhances the ability to create and capitalize upon criminal opportunity. Even the poorest countries have tremendous amounts of human and financial capital to draw upon for crime commission. Illegal means are often available; the desirability of drawing upon these means will be even more tempting when legal means of accomplishing the goals are absent, blocked, or constrained. Moreover, the inaction of local or international bystanders will also facilitate the generation of opportunity (see Grunfeld 2007). Although this is not to say that legitimate means may also be present, due to the concept of instrumental rationality, it is often the "by any means necessary" and the least costly in terms of consequences, thus resulting in the choice of illegitimate over legitimate means (Rothe and Mullins 2006, 2008). On the meso level, opportunity for specific actors is affected by the larger organizational culture and/or state structure. As we noted with previous examples, the opportunities for the *Janjaweed* to commit the crimes against humanity thus far have been provided by the el-Bashir regime's collusion. The opportunity for the LRA to commit atrocities and continue in a 20-year-long conflict has largely been created by the direct economic and social support of the Sudanese government as well as their de facto control of the northern hinterlands.

Constraints are those social control elements that stand to make a potential crime either riskier or less profitable; offenders must navigate around them to neutralize their influence. States are often in unique positions to both navigate around extant constraints and/or to neutralize their actions. For example, Sudan was able to navigate around the constraints of NGOs by curtailing their ability to effectively monitor the regime's activities or have access to civilians that provide testimony of the abuses. In addition, states can neutralize international pressures by placing the events in question as insurgent activity and/or cases of general banditry by militias. When organizations are sponsored by the government, they are effectively freed from potential constraints of the population or foreign involvement.

Controls are a stronger form of constraint that has the ability to stave off or prevent entirely the criminal action or to address such violations as an after-the-fact control. With any type of organizational offending this typically is in the form of formal controls such as international laws or sanctions by international institutions. The most relevant examples of controls with the cases at hand would be the ICC's current cases and arrest warrants issued at this time. Although such controls have historically been highly problematic, we contend that this is indeed changing, and in the future such controls may prove to be the only form of deterrence for such state and organizational offending (see Rothe and Mullins 2006). For example, the ICC claims that their indictments have simultaneously reduced the violence within northern Uganda and compelled the LRA back into peace talks (Agirre 2007). Moreover, such controls can also be locally generated and implemented (e.g., the Gacaca's in Rwanda, see Havemen 2007). Thus, our integrated theory examines how each of the four factors work at each of the levels of analysis within the case at hand (see Table 1).

Militias

One of the hallmarks of all of the cases we explore here is the existence of nongovernmental militia groups. These loosely coupled groups of armed men and women play central roles not only in the social (dis)organization of postcolonial environments but also are central within the war crimes and crimes against humanity that we examine in this book. Most of the atrocities are committed either by the militias themselves or by government troops in response to militia threats. Not limited to this geopolitical context, militias frequently emerge in highly anomic societies during periods of transition. As social orders shift, certain populations will feel excluded or threatened—in many cases these perceptions are justified by the real conditions on the ground. Militia groups emerge in response to these real and perceived threats.

Nature and Distribution

In the wake of postcolonial social and economic disruption, many young men find themselves faced with little in the way to establish an adulthood identity.

Table 1. A Multi-level Integrated Theory

International Level	Motivation	Opportunity	Constraints	Controls
	Political Interests	International Relations	International Reaction	International Law
	Economic Interests	Economic Supremacy	Political Pressure	International Sanctions
	Resources	Military Supremacy	Public Opinion	Economic Institutions
	Ideological Interests	Complementary Legal Systems	NGOs/Social Movements Oversight	
Macro Level	Structural Transformations	Availability of Illegal Means	Political Pressure	Legal Sanctions
	Economic Pressure	Control of Information	Media Scrutiny	Domestic Law
	Political Goals	Propaganda	Public Opinion	Rebellion
	Ethnogenses		Social Movements	
	Anomie			
Meso Level	Organizational Culture and Goals	Communication Structures	Internal Oversight	Codes of Conduct
	Managerial Pressures	Means Availability	Communication Structures	
	Reward Structures	Role Specialization	Traditional Authority Structures	
			Reward Structures	
Micro Level	Socialization	Group Think	Socialization	Legitimacy of Law
	Individual Goals and Ideologies	Diffusion of Responsibility	Obedience to Authority	Perception of Reality of Law Application
	Normalization of Deviance	Perceived Illegal Means		Personal Morality
	Definition of the Situation			

Having little economic prospects, and having typically been raised in a period where ethnic ideological tensions were strong, militias are a place to achieve group membership, economic opportunities, and to actualize an ethnic and adult identity. In terms of individuals joining militias, meso-level conditions of community disorder provide strong micro-level motivations. Young men who find themselves without other social and economic opportunities will gravitate to joining the only real social organization present in their social environment. The criminological literature on street gangs has long established the draw of gangs in the absence of other empowered institutions (see Jankowski 1991; Shelden et al. 2004). Militias are merely another form of this phenomenon. With few viable institutional paths to success and survival, and no external social controls, militias can be seen by community members as the only stable and empowered social grouping within a community. They strengthen individual identity and social membership; the ethnic composition also carries identity meanings and validation for members.

Many of the militias—both organizationally and individually—are holdovers from earlier military organizations. Civil wars and coups d'etat are not uncommon in the region; when a standing government (and its loyal army elements) are deposed by insurgencies, such soldiers rarely return to the civilian population; they are even less likely to enlist in the new army. Often, they retreat into the country side (or cross into a neighboring state), regroup and resurface as a militia group (e.g., when Obote fled Uganda to return years later for a second term as head of state—see Chapter Five). Such instances produce a cohesive social group already bonded by prior military service and the underlying ideologies well established in individuals and groups when they were in power. Moreover, their "underground" status and the fact that returning to pre-conflict community life might expose them to legal prosecution or informal retaliation for past behavior, serves to produce strong bonds of solidarity amongst members.

Due to recruitment processes, militias exhibit a strong level of social homogeneity that intensifies the social bonds of members fueling a collective motivational force. As much criminology within the social learning school (Akers 1977; Sutherland 1939) has suggested, this will strongly facilitate the transmission of criminogenic values and provide a social context whereby even members less inclined toward such excessively brutal behavior will be egged on by cohorts. As seen in analyses of earlier war crimes (e.g., the socialization of Japanese soldiers to commit atrocities in the Chinese theatre of World War II, see Chang 1997), once attached to a unit engaged in these behaviors, recruits eventually begin to see the actions as normal; they experience the processes of the normalization of deviance.

As new recruits are exposed to the typical militia modus operandi, they become more comfortable and more inured to the commission of atrocities. For example, many of the child soldiers interviewed by Human Rights Watch who were abducted by the LRA in Uganda reported that early during their confinement, they were forced to enact discipline upon their fellow abductees. Forced to march over long distances, children who fell, developed blisters on their feet, or otherwise voluntarily or involuntarily delayed the march were beaten, often severely. As often as not, the LRA soldiers forced other abducted children to carry out the beatings (Human Rights Watch 2003a, 2003b). These experiences begin the process of desensitization and the normalization of deviance. Once they have had to beat their fellows, often kin or age-grade cohorts, their ability and willingness to use violence against the citizens they encounter on later raids is increased, or at least their resistance to such actions are reduced (as those who refuse to violently discipline their peers are beaten themselves).

Opportunities for militia members to engage in criminal actions are nigh omnipresent. With little formal law enforcement active within militia-dominated regions and many territories uncontested by government troops, paramilitaries are allowed to operate with impunity. Through their organizational and military technologies, there is no realistic on-the-ground opposition to their depredations on the locals. For all intents and purposes they are the law and have the ability to back up their will with force, which is used routinely to quell resistance in the hinterlands.

Likewise, state-supported militias (i.e., the *Janjaweed* in the Sudan or *Interhwame* of Rwanda) who cooperate with, if they are not directly commanded by, state forces find themselves in a unique position of power. Due to the overt or covert assistance of the state in which they operate, such groups can act with total impunity and with financial and tactical supports. In a state of economic crisis, resources are crucial. Consequently, militias under these conditions serve their own self-interests while fulfilling state political goals. In the case of the *Janjaweed*, they were rewarded with tangibles beyond weapons and money. They received countless herds of livestock that provided them with the ability to gain economic status by selling the livestock as well as secured the level of subsistence by having livestock on hand for products and food. Personal gain and empowerment is clearly a strong motivation for those in power (e.g., government officials) or in strategic positions (e.g., members of a militia). Military leaders, both regular and irregular, stand to personally profit politically and economically from their positions. With no formal social control mechanisms to dissuade them, they become the embodiment of law and order in the lands their militias control.

Terror and Thuggery

Militias have come to the international attention fo[r] wanton murder in their carrying out of military-rela[ted] militias' destruction of the Tutsi population in Rw[anda]. Reports from the hinterlands that militias control indicate that frequent crimes the militias perpetrate is simply general thuggery. From petty theft and robbery to assault (sexual and physical), as militias move through villages and the countryside they harass and victimize the civilians they come across. Other conditions can result in the militias' use of thuggery, theft, and/or robbery. For example, in Darfur the Sudanese Liberation Army (SLA) has been responsible for attacks on civilians, abductions, and endangering humanitarian access. The insurgents, like all civilians that are left in Darfur, were running out of basic necessities including food, medicine, and the fuel required for their continued mobility and military survival. It would be naive to think it likely that under such conditions the insurgents would not resort to illegal activities to feed themselves and to secure what was needed to sustain their campaign against Khartoum's genocidal actions.

Moreover, as we noted, governmental agents including the military and police often partake in general banditry, violence, and/or terror for their own self-gain. Such has been the case in Uganda, where such agents of the state have been accused of raping civilians for their own entertainment to general petty theft of property left behind by the growing Ugandan refugees. The Ugandan People's Defense Forces (UPDF), the government's army, has also been accused by NGOs of pillaging in regions traditionally opposed to President Museveni.

Both militia groups and regimes often explicitly draw upon terror tactics to generate fear and compliance among the civilians. In Sierra Leone and Uganda, militias have become infamous for cutting off civilians' arms, hands, lips, and tongues as a way to spread fear. For example, victims of the LRA have stated that they have been held down while other militia members "picked up an axe. First he chopped my left hand, then my right. Then he chopped my nose, my ears and my mouth with a knife" (Ross 2004: 1). As locals resisted or tried to call for standing governments (or NGOs) to intervene, they became targets for torture and mutilation. Moreover, NGOs were often targeted for torture and/or death for intervening in the situation. For example, NGO workers were considered to be legitimate military targets by the LRA because of their for what they called Museveni's "concentration camps." Consequently, [they] attacked humanitarian food convoys from the World Food Programme (WFP) and threatened the lives of the workers. As is often the case when humanitarian workers are not afforded security, NGOs often withdraw leaving the remaining victims to fend for themselves.

Slavery

Once settled in an occupied territory, militias often organize forced labor programs. Some of the most extensive have been those designed to revitalize a mineral extraction industry that collapsed in the more general political and social disorder of state collapse. The blood diamonds industry of Sierra Leone and the gold and colton industries in the Itrui region of the DRC are excellent cases-in-point. In both cases, militias first moved in and violently established military control of the geography that contained mineral production sites. Once they solidified their control, they turned to pressing the local population into forced servitude to engage in dangerous and low-technology mineral extraction activities. However, the simple possession of raw ores does little to enhance the economic or military positions of the militias. To capitalize on these enterprises, they must find foreign markets willing to purchase the illicit commodities. Such buyers are not difficult to find. Neighboring states and local companies make deals with both standing governments and militias to gain access to natural resources. Once access to the region has been obtained, it is a not too difficult a task to remove the minerals or other valued commodities over a nearby border and ship the goods into one of the many free ports—markets where no records concerning the origins of items or accounting of amounts sold are made—such as Sweden's, where they find major transnationals eager to purchase the materials (e.g., Metalor, De Beers). Many of these larger jewelry dealers or mineral processing companies can easily hide illegally expropriated minerals in their larger stocks.

Child Soldiers

The first set of criminal charges issued by the ICC were allegations of the recruitment of child soldiers by Thomas Dyilo, the leader of one of the DRC's strongest militia groups. The DRC is not the only place in Central Africa where the abduction and pressing into service of children has become a central feature of militia life. Sierra Leone, Central African Republic, and Uganda have also experienced widespread use of underage troops. International law, specifically the Rome Statute, makes it illegal to use anyone under the age of 15 as a combat solider, not to mention the use of abducted or coerced soldiers. In these locales, both boys and girls have been kidnapped and forced into service. Although mainly assigned to the menial labor required of an armed group, for example, fetching water, carrying supplies, digging latrines, both males and females receive military training in the basic use of firearms. In addition, the children are used as the frontline of military engagements (e.g., the UPDF and LRA practice of using child soldiers). For example, children may be used for direct combat to compensate for the weakened forces of a militia or a regime; they may be forced to walk across a field believed to be mined, to ensure that the adult men do not set one off. In firefights, the children are often used as a screen to protect the adults from gun fire. By placing the children in the front of a charge (or a defensive line), they will absorb much of the incoming fire.

These troops are viewed by the militia commanders as expendable. This is further seen in the generally brutal treatment the children receive at the hands of their new masters. When on a march, children who slow down, stumble, or fall are often beaten until they either get back up and resume the march at the speed desired by the commanders or collapse into unconsciousness (and death). Escaped children who have talked to Amnesty International, Human Rights Watch, and representatives of UNICEF have also indicated that they were deprived of food and water. Girls, although initially used as burden-bearers and frontline combatants, are given to soldiers, typically commanders, as "wives" once they hit puberty.

The use of child soldiers seems especially prevalent in long-term conflicts. Lengthier struggles will reduce the functional size of militias as troops are killed, wounded, and deserted. In the decades long conflicts seen in Uganda and the DRC, the militia have developed difficulties recruiting new members, especially if they make a habit of victimizing and terrorizing civilian populations. To fill out the ranks, paramilitaries use abduction and forced service to maintain their strength. Children are desirable for a number of reasons. They are much easier to control than adults. Physically smaller and much easier to intimidate, they pose little threat to adult soldiers. Furthermore, due to the plasticity of youth, children present the potential to be indoctrinated into the prevailing ideologies within the militia. It is much more likely that a child who hears the officer's propaganda will believe and internalize it as their own worldview, thereby creating a loyal solider to the cause. In the DRC, this constant threat of abduction has created a population of "night commuters"—children who travel into central urban areas every night to sleep to avoid roaming militia groups. Train stations and other public venues become filled with children every evening, who then return to their villages outside the cities each morning (Human Rights Watch 1997, 2003a, 2003b, 2004, 2006).

Rape

The sexual assault of women within combat zones and occupied territories is one of the not-so-secret dirty elements pervasive within the history of warfare. Historically deep in origin, anthropologists and historians have long noted its occurrence—it has been recorded in essentially every war in human history. Treatment of women in this matter boils down to issues of property rights and the "proper" disposition of property after a military episode. When women are property, women are plunder. The benefits of defeating an enemy in combat are the spoils of the battlefield. Before the rise of professional armies, loot was the way in which men were paid for their services and motivated into hostilities. The possibility of a single sexual release was a minor reward, though the taking of a foreign woman as a "wife" due to military victory was common—this is *rapine* in the, literally, classical sense of the term. Abduction of women into sexual and domestic servitude was part and parcel of the rights of plunder.

Brownmiller (1975) suggests that all wars produce rape because war becomes a fulcrum for masculinity enactment. Such a hostile enactment of gender is the focus of solider-solider hostilities; once a given engagement is finished, the women in the occupied territories then become the site for a similar process. Nevertheless, this does not adequately explain the widespread nature of the events or the systematic use of rape as a weapon of warfare within genocide or crimes against humanity events.

In the postcolonial African context, rape has been as pervasive as in any conflict. Militia and regular army routinely rape women and girls once a village is taken; some of them are forced into marriages or held in sexual slavery for months or years at a time. In addition, due to the high rate of HIV/AIDS in many of these countries, the rape serves as a transmission episode and the inevitable death sentence that the disease brings. When looking at the manifestation of rape in association with recent atrocities, we see an intensification of the nature and scope of sexual assaults on female civilian populations. In the former Yugoslavia, Rwanda, Cote d'Ivoire, Central African Republic, Uganda, the DRC, and the Darfur region of Somalia domestic conflict has produced widespread rape scenarios that go beyond the individualistic scenario of men satisfying their immediate sexual desires in a forceful demonstration of hypermasculinity. In such cases, rape has been used as a tool of terror and of population elimination—a phenomena termed genocidal rape. We define genocidal rape as a systemically organized military tactic of terror and genocide, used to (1) generate fear in subdued population, (2) humiliate the population (both men and women), (3) derogation of women (spoilage of identity), and (4) create a cohort of mixed-ethnic children to maintain the humiliation/spoilage/domination. Such a use of sexual assault is an orchestrated tactic of warfare. As has been reported both in Bosnia and in Rwanda, certain military units were tasked by their commanding officers with the task of moving systematically through an occupied village and raping all the females they could find.

Fear of rape is a common emotion that all women near or within a combat zone experience; the widespread existence of this type of assault clearly enhances the stresses and anxieties already experienced by civilians. Genocidal rape capitalizes upon this and elevates assaults to a tactic of terrorism. Another primary motivation for mass rape is the humiliation of male community members. Often men were made to watch as their wives and daughters were assaulted; isolated reports of soldiers forcing men to rape their own daughters have also emerged. Such actions are vivid demonstrations of the new found powerlessness of men in the combat zone. Having to either actively or passively participate in this process is an assault on the masculinity of husbands and fathers; due to long-standing patriarchal value systems, these men and women simultaneously are reduced to nothing via the destruction of their ability to enact enforced gender norms.

Derogation and identity spoilage of the rape victims are another set of key motivators behind genocidal rape events. Again due to strong strains of patriarchy within the cultures, unmarried women who have been raped are typically no longer looked upon as potential wives—the rape has destroyed their marital desirability. Moreover, they can also in turn be shunned by family members and have no where to turn for survival. Such women will either starve or live the rest of their lives in highly marginal social positions (e.g., begging, prostitution, etc.). Such conditions are genocidal as they increase the overall death toll related to the genocidal event, even if indirect and down the line. In raw terms, this is the removal of women from the breeding population and prevents a population from recovering from a genocidal event.

Finally, as seen in the former Yugoslavia, such widespread rape often produced a birth cohort of mixed-ethnic children. The effects of this are twofold.

First, it provides a long-lasting reminder of the humiliation and derogation of the people as a whole. The children that survive to birth and into youth are a constant symbol of the genocide experience. Second, as the children and their mothers are often outcasts from their kin groups because of the assaults themselves, this enhances the social disorganization of villages and cities that now bear the burden of either caring for or ignoring this new underclass of community members.

Summary

In this chapter we have provided an overview of the plan of the book. We endeavor to expand the purview of criminology through the exploration and examination of four cases of genocide, war crimes, and crimes against humanity in central and eastern Africa. Although this is only a sample of such crimes that have occurred globally, or even on the African continent, they provide enough information to allow a basic understanding of the etiology and enactment dynamics of these phenomena. To date, the criminological literature on crimes of the state and of other widespread violations of international law has yet to fully engage these acts, their origins, and consequences. This book aims to fill that gap in understanding. From here, we proceed to a sociohistorical discussion of the development and implementation of international criminal law as both a body of proscriptive law and of social control.

· 2 ·

WHITHER JUSTICE? INTERNATIONAL LAW

Although International Law as a framework of social control has existed for centuries, it is only in the past few decades that it has evolved to become an established legal framework for the control of individual and organizational actions. The modern era of the state has seen a slow creation and implementation of an international criminal legal code, originally emerging from bilateral and multilateral agreements, to an encompassing and overarching structure of legal regulations consisting of both substantive and procedural law. As the twenty-first century begins, there are numerous bodies of international law in effect; from the laws of war, to the laws of the air and seas, and human rights law. However, all of these do not hold the same justiciability status; they are enforceable in various modalities. Moreover, there are two established international courts for the hearing of cases that violate these laws—the International Court of Justice and the International Criminal Court (ICC). The United Nations Security Council (UNSC) also has the ability to establish special tribunals for trying violations of international humanitarian law (e.g., the Nuremburg and Tokyo tribunals, the International Criminal Tribunal for Yugoslavia (ICTY), the International Criminal Tribunal for Rwanda (ICTR), and the special joint international-local court in Sierra Leone). Nevertheless, many jurisdictional gaps remain and these international legal codes do not possess the enforcement power of most domestic legal codes.

The development and codification of international law as *law*, over international relations, is a product of the evolution of an international society. As the world's peoples and states have recognized the necessity of cooperation and as the linkages among countries have become more multitudinous and intricate, law as a system of social control has been increasingly seen as one way to regulate the behaviors of international actors. Although slow, and still in process, the trend over the twentieth and into the twenty-first century has been an increase in the number of legal codes, an increase in the number of venues to hear cases, and increased jurisdictional authority.

Generally, scholars recognize that international law arises from four different sources. The one most generally recognized by legal and nonlegal scholars alike are international conventions, or treaties, that specifically create rules acknowledged by states. Whether these are bilateral or multilateral agreements or domestically ratified conventions of the United Nations (UN), they bear the most resemblance to traditional state legal codes. These agreements are neither as legally solid nor as adjudicatable (be it from vagueness, lack of will, or the common practice of signing/ratifications with reservations) as traditional state law, but they do hold international force.

The second source of international law is international customs, the acknowledgment of historical past practice and belief by states. This was the original source of the laws of war, which have since been codified into probably the most solid example of extant treaty law. Moreover, they are considered general legal principles recognized by all countries. Customary laws are based on common and constant practices of states out of a sense of *opinio juris*—an ideal of natural law based upon legal obligation and principles. Simply stated, the fundamental principles behind customary laws are founded on willing state participation and a historical recognition of consistent state practices. Customary laws are viewed as *jus cogens*—in that they are internationally accepted principles, norms, and are binding without exception. Unlike treaties, charters, and resolutions (which are codified laws and compelling only for the signatory states), customary or *jus cogens* laws may or may not be *erga omnes*—or law which flows to all. Many times customary law becomes codified into treaties or statutes between states; however, the compulsory nature of customary law and general principles remain as the scaffold of international law to date. Moreover, the principles of *jus cogens* and *erga omnes* can often be conflicting (Bassiouni 1999; Danilenko 1991). If a law is *jus cogens*, it should follow that it is *erga omnes* (Bassiouni 1999). When something is compelling to and for everyone, it would stand to reason that it should be applicable for all. However, this is not always the case. For example, International Human Rights Laws are compelling but not necessarily flowing to all. This is, in part, due to preexisting agreements that can cover specific situations. In the case of Human Rights Law, they are not applicable during a time of war, as these legal conditions are addressed by the Geneva Conventions, which articulate similar principles, as they are to play out within a theatre of combat. As stated, customary laws, *jus cogens*, often find their way into multilateral treaties and as such are not only universal in nature but justicable as well.

The third source of international law are judicial decisions; however, precedent decisions do not hold the same level of influence in international law that it does in common law legal systems. Nevertheless, they are significant in guiding the behavior of courts and legal processes. For example, as we explore later, the precedent decisions made in the ICTY have had a strong influence on the conduct of the ICTR and the functioning of the ICC—especially within the realm of defining as illegal and prosecuting sexual violences. The fourth source includes some of the writings of influential legal scholars whose ideas have been brought into adjudication processes over the decades (e.g., Grotius, von Glabn, and Taulbee 2007).

The Structural Contradiction of Sovereignty

The core tension within the establishment and adjudication of international law has long been the issue of sovereignty—the innate and unalienable right of a state to self-determination. Such a right to self-rule has often been the defining criteria of a state itself. For example, the 1933 Montevideo Convention on Rights and Duties of State used a rather simplistic means for defining statehood. A the state has (1) a defined territory and population, (2) said territory and population are under the control of its own governmental apparatus, and (3) the entity engages in or has the capacity to engage in formal relations with other states. International relations and law have also long held that any given state has the right to determine the nature and course of its own affairs without interference from others. However, Article 4(1) of the UN Charter explicitly mentions the ability and willingness "in the judgment of the Organization" to carry out international obligations as a criterion for admission of new member states to the UN, and consequently, as recognition of statehood. All other requirements for statehood according to international law, in particular the existence of effective power of control over a territory and its inhabitants, are derived from this one criterion: the necessary ability and readiness to act in accordance with international law. Thus, contemporary statehood becomes defined by international recognition, self-determination (UN Charter 1: 2), and willingness to fulfill international obligations and relations. Statehood becomes defined internationally using either the constitutive approach—recognition by other states—or the declarative approach—which sees states as having a legal personality de facto regardless of international recognition or UN membership. Moreover, states can voluntarily limit the extent of their sovereignty through domestic legislation, bilateral and multilateral treaties, and the willful adoption of international conventions (e.g., the Rome Statute of the ICC). Doing so, though, must be voluntary and in line with domestic law procedures.

The entirety of international law seemingly defines the core principle of statehood and self-determination. However, there is another side to the sovereignty coin. To wit: one state's sovereignty ends where another's begins. Although a given country has the right to determine its own direction of affairs and actions, it does not have the right to lawfully interfere in the affairs of another. Herein lays the contradiction. What is to be done in a situation where states conflict with each other in the exercise of their inalienable right of self-determination? Historically, governments could resort to diplomacy and warfare. However, in the modern climate, the realization of the innate destructiveness of warfare and its ultimately dysfunctional approach to international relations and interactions has produced a body of law that limits a state's autonomy insofar as other states are concerned. In addition, the basic need for international law to limit self-rule on factors that impact other states is essential when one considers the stratified nature of international society. When certain states are allowed to act with impunity due to the fact that they control vastly more resources than their neighbors, the idea of sovereignty-as-right is meaningless without some broader social force or organization to protect those states less able to protect themselves: hence, the obligation to international law as predicated by the UN.

At its core, international law is a limitation on autonomy, yet one that only has its maximal force when other states are willing to act in its name. The twentieth and twenty-first centuries have shown that when states elect to act "in the name" of international law (especially when acting to enforce UNSC resolutions) they often do so (or refuse to do so) out of an expression of their own political and economic interests rather than within the interests of an international social order. Within our current milieu, this contradiction has made international law and its enforcement piecemeal, problematic, and unsure—three conditions that law cannot hold if it is to be seen as legitimate. There is no incipient solution to these contradictory forces and conditions at the current juncture in history; international law and justice is still a work in progress. However, that does not make it unimportant or unworthy of examination and discussion. In fact, we believe the opposite is true. This chapter presents an overview and examination of extant international law, especially those relevant to crimes of postcolonial disorder in the African states under examination in this volume. We focus our discussion on International Criminal Law: War Crimes, Crimes Against Humanity, and Genocide. We discuss the extant body of substantive law as well as the mechanisms in place to provide international jurisprudence and adjudication.

Overview of International Law

There is no single collected body or jurisdiction that constitutes international law. It is a culmination of bilateral and multilateral treaties, conventions, resolutions, customs, and precedents. States have varying levels of adoption and commitment to these bodies of law; the ability to adjudicate violations of the law are similarly dispersed and varied. International criminal law is composed of substantive law and procedural law. For the purposes of our case studies, it is the substantive law that is relevant. This is the body of rules indicating what acts amount to international crimes, elements required for them to be considered prohibited, and under what conditions states must prosecute or bring to trial those accused of violating such laws (Cassesse 2002a). Despite the current state of enactment, there are a number of widely agreed upon and strongly defined areas of international law which warrant our attention. The most established and widely accepted areas of international criminal law that we will explore are: International Humanitarian Law (the laws of war); Genocide; Crimes Against Humanity.

International Humanitarian Law

International Humanitarian Law is a product of the long-term evolution of the laws of war. Apart from the laws of the seas, this is one of the oldest areas of international agreements, with early treaties in Europe dating from the 1800s. They are by definition *jus in bello*, meaning the law governing how war may be fought once under way. Even before express treaties were signed and ratified, the laws of war held force as customary international law (Glueck 1944) and held justicable characteristics (see von Glabn and Taulbee 2007). The twentieth century saw refinement and extension of the basic principles here, first within the older Geneva Accords, and then later within the UN's establishment of the Four Geneva Conventions and its attendant protocols. Finally, the Rome Statute of the ICC restated these laws and centralized them. We now turn to a brief overview of the history and key provision of these legal codes.

The *International Declaration concerning the Law and Customs of War* signed in Brussels on 27 August 1874 was the first international codification of the rules of war as they evolved during the eighteenth and nineteenth centuries. Within European-based cultures, the development and refinement of the notion of war crimes, behavior defined as legal (as opposed to simply unacceptable) actions that occur on the field of battle, has been steadily ongoing since the 1700s. As technologies of warfare became increasingly lethal and civilians progressively more affected by combat, Western countries moved to limit the types of weapons and tactics used. This landmark treaty outlined prohibitions on the behavior of armies in occupied territories intended to limit the general destructiveness of military action upon civilian populations, and to reduce the amount of harm an occupying army causes on that populace. It constrains actions during combat by limiting weapons, killing soldiers who are injured or have surrendered, and prohibits the issuing of "no quarter" orders (e.g., when troops are ordered to permit no survivors). It also details rules for the treatment of spies, prisoners of war, and the enemy, sick, and injured. Although rarely followed in the wars that ripped apart Europe after its signing, the main tenants of this treaty resurfaced in the later Geneva Conventions of the 1920s.

Although a historical and legal landmark treaty, the late 1800s and early 1900s saw these principles repeatedly violated in subsequent conflicts. It would not be until the wake of World War II that the creation and implementation of a set of laws of war would be coupled with enforcement mechanisms. The demand for trying Axis war criminals was in part a response to the abject, and at the time often unbelievable, horror of the crimes committed by allied troops. In addition, there was lingering international tension and dissatisfaction with how German war criminals escaped prosecution and justice after World War I (see Gleuck 1944). The Nuremberg and Tokyo tribunals set the international standard for the convening of special courts to try cases of war crimes (and crimes against humanity). These tribunals were initiated and governed under the Nuremberg principles, whose primary purpose was to establish a set of guidelines for defining and identifying war crimes. Principle VI, section b, defines War crimes as

> [v]iolations of the laws or customs of war which include but are not limited to, murder, ill-treatment or deportation of slave labor or for any other purpose the civilian population of or in occupied territory; murder or ill-treatment of prisoners of war or person on the Seas, killing of hostages, plunder of private or public property, wanton destruction of cities, towns or villages or devastation not justified by military necessity. While these principles were designed *post hoc* to try German Nazi and Japanese Imperial leaders, and the legitimacy and fairness of the ensuing tribunals have been questioned, these principles form the bedrock of later UN definitions.

Following the Nuremberg principles, a complex set of definitions and rules of warfare were codified. Today, the term "war crime" typically refers directly to a violation of *The United Nations Convention for the Amelioration of the Condition of the Wounded and Sick in Armed Forces in the Field*—hereafter referred to as the Geneva Convention of 1949 (entry into force: 21 October 1950) and its attendant protocols. These laws are applicable to every extant and recognized nation as recognition by the UN requires not only ratification of the UN Charter but also the ratification by the applicant state of these conventions. Geneva governs the ways in which armed forces are allowed to operate within theatres of battle and occupied territories. Specific laws govern weapons and tactics, perfidery (false use of army uniforms or symbols), allowable selection of targets for hostility, treatment of medical and religious personnel, the treatment of prisoners, and how the armed force is to interact with noncombatant citizens, the local environment, and natural resources. The reduction of harm to all is the main goal, with the protection of noncombatants (be they civilians or soldiers no longer able to participate as combatants) as paramount within the treaty. In general, the provisions within Geneva are based on the core principle that has underwritten every treaty on the conduct of warfare: not all means of waging war are legal. There are limits to what can be done in the name of war. Excessive harm to enemies is to be avoided, as is any intentional and unnecessary harm to civilians.

In addition to governing the behavior of uniformed troops, the Protocol Additions to Geneva extend the rules to essentially any and all people operating within a combat zone (e.g., militias, nonstate party belligerents, mercenaries, etc.). In addition, specific procedures for governing occupied territories during and after hostilities are outlined. Simply, if you are within a combat zone or an occupied territory, you are subject to both the rules and protections of Geneva. Geneva does distinguish between uniformed regular army troops, militias, nonstate belligerents, and civilians but expressly extends its jurisdiction to all. The only difference between a combatant attached to a state and one not attached to a regular army is that a nonstate belligerent does not have to be repatriated to their home country with the cessation of hostilities. They may be detained and tried by the capturing party.

Essentially every state has regulations and procedures for the definition and prosecution of war crimes within their own domestic law. Most of these are essentially mirrors of the Geneva Conventions. The precise nature of the rules and procedures will vary from state to state, but the overall ability of a given nation to police itself in these regards is well established in both domestic and international law. The primary responsibility for both identifying and prosecuting war crimes rests with the state of which a given accused war criminal is a citizen.

International measures have historically been taken when the crimes have been a general policy of a state itself and/or if it has been established that the domestic powers that have jurisdictional control over their military have no interest in legal accountability. The UNSC can establish military tribunals to identify and prosecute war crimes. Most recently it has done so for the civil wars in the former Yugoslavia and Rwanda and created a hybrid court for the war crimes in Sierra Leone. In these cases, the appointed prosecutor is completely responsible for investigating allegations, determining and filing charges, and carrying out the actual prosecution. Typically, these courts focus on identifying those responsible for crafting policies of war crime commission, or as in Rwanda, local political officials complicit with the policies. The International Military Tribunals do not solely investigate or prosecute the singular soldiers responsible for atrocities.

With the entry into force of the Rome Statute for the ICC, a new venue and procedural laws were developed for defining and identifying war crimes. In terms of definition, the Rome Statute essentially replicated the extant Geneva agreements, identifying problematic tactics, weapons, and protecting the treatment of civilians and enemy combatants. In fact, Article 8(a) explicitly identifies the 1949 Geneva Conventions as the source of prosecutable war crimes. The rest of Article 8 restates the basic principles of Geneva (though not every principle within the four conventions and all of its protocols), thereby bringing the most serious breeches of the laws under the court's jurisdiction.

One of the most controversial yet most important aspects of the Rome Statute involves the jurisdiction of the court itself (see Broomhall 2003; Rothe and Mullins 2006a, 2006b; Sadat and Carden 2000). In order for the court to have jurisdiction over a crime, it must have occurred within the territory of a state party, have been committed by the troops or foreign diplomats of a state party, on the territory of a state party or referred by the UNSC. Moreover, due to the court's complementary nature, it will not move forward with a prosecution unless the state of the accused is unwilling or unable to prosecute the alleged crimes. With these requirements satisfied, cases can be brought before the court by a State Party to the Rome Statute, referred to the court by UNSC, independently investigated by the court's Prosecutor, who receives open inquiries and recommendations from the global community. For example, the ICC undertook its investigation of crimes in northern Uganda at the request of the sitting government who claimed they could not prosecute the Lord's Resistance Army (LRA) leaders responsible for widespread atrocities. When the ICC's prosecutor filed charges related to the Darfur genocide in February 2007, it provided the justification that the standing government of the Sudan was unwilling to prosecute parties responsible.

In order to be considered an illegal behavior under the Rome Statute, a war crime must not be a singular instance, or even a series of potentially isolated incidents. For the court to intervene and try a case, it must be established that the crimes are "committed as a part of a plan or policy or as part of a large scale commission of such crimes" (Rome Statute, Art. 8(1)). In part this requirement was a response to an understanding of the realities of war and also a response to countries that feared future political prosecutions; the court leaves prosecution of isolated or individualized incidents to domestic courts and parties. This is exactly what the court ruled in terms of U.S. and UK behavior in the Iraqi war. Although there were clear incidents of war crimes committed, the office of the chief prosecutor claimed that (1) they were not evident as part of a widespread plan and (2) home governments were engaged in (at least symbolic) prosecutions of responsible parties. However, it is positioned to be central in the adjudication of widespread atrocities. The Rome Statute is not limited to war crimes, but includes the authority to try cases of genocide and crimes against humanity. It is to the former category of law that we now turn.

Genocide

The term genocide was originally coined by Ralph Lemkin in 1933. Lemkin suggested a treaty should be created to make attacks on religious, ethnic, or national groups an international crime. He called this genocide: from the Greek word *genos*, meaning race or tribe, and *cide*, the Latin term for killing. Lemkin (1944: 88) states,

> By "genocide" we mean the destruction of an ethnic group ... not necessarily ... the immediate destruction of a nation, except when accomplished by mass killings of all [group] members ... It is intended ... to signify a coordinated plan ... [for] the destruction of essential foundations of the life ... with the aim of annihilating the groups themselves.

Four years passed before genocide was recognized as an international crime by treaty. However, the legal foundation was first put in place during the 1945 Nuremberg Trials and subsequent Nuremberg Charter. Genocide was used in the indictment against the Nazi war criminals that stated that those accused "conducted deliberate and systematic genocide ... the extermination of racial and national groups, against the civilian populations of certain occupied territories in order to destroy particular races and classes of people and national, racial or religious groups" (Orentlicher 2006: 2). Nuremberg prosecutors also invoked the term in their closing arguments. Although the Nuremberg Charter did not use the term genocide per se, its definition of crimes against humanity was very close to the idea of genocide Lemkin proposed. The difference was the requirement of specific intent in the case of genocide, which is lacking in the definition of crimes against humanity.

In 1946, the UN General Assembly adopted a resolution establishing genocide as an international crime. The resolution defined genocide as "a denial of the right of existence of entire human groups, as homicide is the denial of the right to live of individual human beings" (Resolution 95(1)). In 1948, *The Convention on the Prevention and Punishment of the Crime of Genocide* was adopted by the UN. Article 1 states that "the Contracting Parties confirm that genocide, whether committed in time of peace or in time of war, is a crime under international law which they undertake to prevent and to punish" (General Assembly Resolution 260 A (III)). Thus genocide may be committed by an individual, group, or government, against one's own people or another, in peacetime or in wartime. This last point distinguishes genocide from "crimes against humanity," whose legal definition specifies wartime. In addition, the Convention obligates state party members to "prevent and punish" genocide. Although more restrictive than Lemkin's definition, genocide is defined in Article 2 as any of the following acts committed with intent to destroy, in whole or in part, a national, ethnical, racial or religious group, as such:

(a) Killing members of the group
(b) Causing serious bodily or mental harm to members of the group
(c) Deliberately inflicting on the group conditions of life calculated to bring about its physical destruction in whole or in part
(d) Imposing measures intended to prevent births within the group
(e) Forcibly transferring children of the group to another group.

As with any Western criminal law, the establishment of an action as genocide not only involves *actus reas*, or the act itself, but also *mens rea*—intent. Establishing that a series of actions not only had the effect of near eradication of a category of persons is not enough to constitute genocide. Prosecutors must also establish that the intent of the actions was the entire or the partial annihilation of an entire or partial given group. This creates a legal space for denial, equivocation, and obfuscation where the accused party denies genocide not by denying a series of systematic actions, but rather, denies intent. As intent is extremely difficult to prove, this definition included a restrictive component that has allowed state and political leaders to deny and/or raise doubt about whether genocide has occurred.

At the same time, the 1948 Convention Article 3 does include the following acts to be punishable by law:

(a) Genocide
(b) Conspiracy to commit genocide
(c) Direct and public incitement to commit genocide
(d) Attempt to commit genocide
(e) Complicity in genocide.

Since its development in 1948 there has been a dearth of precedents that enforced the Convention. Specifically, it was not until the 1990s that the international arena recognized and prosecuted acts defined as genocide: the establishment of the 1993 ICTY and 1994 ICTR. Then in 1998, with the development of the Rome Statute for the ICC, the crime of genocide was again reaffirmed as an international crime; the requirements of both a physical element (comprising certain enumerated acts) and a mental element (intent) are central to Rome's definition. Case law developed especially through the

ICTY has emphasized that this later element be present for a genocide label to be applied. Specifically, Article 5 of the ICC lists genocide (and crimes against humanity) as a crime of "most serious crimes of concern to the international community as a whole." Genocide is then defined in Article 6. Both the physical and mental requirements of the 1948 Convention were carried over and included in the Rome Statute.

International criminal laws are also hierarchically organized. Specifically, genocide is considered a graver offense than crimes against humanity. The ICTY Trial Chamber developed such a distinction when it produced the following rank order among crimes against humanity: (1) genocide; (2) crimes against humanity of a persecution type; and (3) crimes against humanity of a murder type. This is significant when considering not just the gravity of actions but also the subsequent punishment and charges of those who partook in such atrocities. Although, to date, an international equivalent to sentencing guidelines has not yet emerged, the ICTR and ICTY judges focused on the gravity of the offence, the level of involvement of the accused in the crimes, and other aggravating and mitigating factors to determine sentences. The determination of the relative gravity has concrete implications for the application of punishment (Frulli 2001). As such, it would stand to reason that charges of genocide would merit a harsher sentence than one based on crimes against humanity.

Defining acts as genocide have been heavily debated based on two components: a legal definition that satisfies the requirement of intent and one based on the political interests of a given state be they economic, political, or military. Together these have led to a bleak perspective on the international society's seriousness of ending genocides. The verbal manipulation of the term has led to a plethora of instances wherein interest groups claimed genocide under circumstances far from intentional mass killings of a protected group (e.g., oppression, famines, and widespread malnutrition). In addition, political leaders have manipulated the use of the term to ignore acts as genocide when it is not in their state's political, economic, or military interests (e.g., the former Yugoslavia, Rwanda, and Darfur).

As is typical within any legal system, the laws governing genocide have been modified and extended through the processes of case law precedent. For genocide jurisprudence both the ICTY and the ICTR have made major decisions that have refined and reinforced extant laws concerning the willful slaughter of an entire category of peoples. In the Akayesu Trial held before the ICTR in 1998, paragraph 497 of the ruling states that "genocide does not imply the actual extermination of [a] group in its entirety, but is understood as such once any one of the acts mentioned in Article 2(2)(a) through 2(2)(e) is committed with the specific intent to destroy 'in whole or in part' a national, ethnical, racial, or religious group" (see also Rutaganda 6 December 1999, para. 48–49). Such a reconfiguration places the prosecutorial emphasis on intent, which has two simultaneous effects. First, it can make prosecution more difficult in that establishing the existence of a mental state—notoriously difficult to factually establish—becomes primary. Second, it allows for the prosecution of "interrupted" genocides, allowing justice after an international intervention before widespread death, though such international interventions often occur well after the genocide is well under way.

Recent case law developed by the ICTY and ICTR have further refined the legal category of genocide within international law. The primary precedents include, most significantly, the recognition of rape as a form of genocide, protections applying to specific groups within the domestic populations, and the requirement for intent of a group in whole or in part.

In the Akayesu case, the ICTR found Jean-Paul Akayesu guilty of rape as a form of genocide (2 September 1998). This was a landmark decision in that it was the first time that rape was legally found to be both a form of genocide and a crime against humanity. The tribunal's decision was based on evidence that he, as a community leader, had witnessed and encouraged the rape of women in the course of a genocidal campaign against the Tutsis. In this decision, the ICTR described a situation in which a rapist might deliberately impregnate his victim with the intent to force her to give birth to a child who would, because of patrilineal social conventions, not belong to its mother's group. The tribunal noted that such an act might be a constitutive element of genocide. The Rwanda tribunal statute enumerates "outrages upon personal dignity, in particular humiliating and degrading treatment, rape, enforced prostitution and any form of indecent assault" as war crimes, following the formulation of Common Article 3 of the Geneva Conventions and Article 4(2)(e) of Protocol II.

The Akayesu Trial Chamber (2 September 1998, para. 731) also stated that "these rapes resulted in physical and psychological destruction of Tutsi women, their families and their communities. Sexual violence was an integral part of the process of destruction, specifically targeting Tutsi women and specifically contributing to their destruction and to the destruction of the Tutsi group as a whole" (see also Kayishema and Ruzindana, Trial Chamber,

21 May 1999, para. 95). The Chambers held that acts of sexual violence can form an integral part of the process of destruction of a group. As a result of these landmark findings, the law on sexual violence as an international humanitarian crime has developed at a startling pace (see below for a full discussion). By virtue of a combination of statutory law and case law, massive and systematic rape is now considered a type of genocide, a war crime, and a crime against humanity.

Protection of Specific Populations

Case law was established during the ICTY and the ICTR, establishing that tribal groupings do qualify for the status of a "group as a protected category of persons." Under international humanitarian law, to qualify as genocide, the targeted group must represent a distinct national, racial, ethnic, or religious category of person. This can be established objectively, as in the case of Nazi war crimes against the Jewish peoples, the Turkish attempted genocide of the Armenian peoples, or in the former Yugoslavia. In all of these cases the victimized population was clearly ethnically and religiously different from the victimizers. The distinction can also be established subjectively when a population is considered a group either through their own perspective or through the perspective of those engaged in the attempted destruction.

For example, the ICTR was confronted with the fact that there were few externally objective differences between the Hutu and Tutsi populations (e.g., based upon racial makeup, languages spoken, and religion practiced). Nevertheless, due to the colonial experiences in Rwanda, the French clearly made distinctions between the populations. The Tutsi were singled out to become an allied, administrative class of persons while the Hutu were constructed as a laboring class. Consequently, the people themselves internalized these colonially constructed differences. This created intense and long-standing friction between the groups, which, in part, produced the genocide of 1994. Since the Hutu and Tutsi perceived themselves as separate groups and the drive behind the Hutu violence was the elimination of all Tutsi peoples, the ICTR ruled that, on subjective grounds, the Tutsi were a protected population. A victim's category membership is then critical to defining genocide events. The precedence set by the ICTR on protected groups played a significant factor in the ICC prosecutor's decision to bringing charges against the genocide of the Darfurians by the hands of the Sudanese government and sponsored *Janjaweed* militia.

Genocidal Intent to Eliminate in Whole or in Part a Protected Group of Persons

Intent is indeed a crucial component of any legal case. As discussed above, to be prosecutable, a potential genocide must possess the appropriate *mens rea* component of intending to destroy, in whole or in part, a group. Again, precedent was set in the Akayesu Trial held before the ICTR in 1998. Paragraph 497 of the ruling states that "genocide does not imply the actual extermination of [a] group in its entirety, but is understood as such once any one of the acts mentioned in Article 2(2)(a) through 2(2)(e) is committed with the specific intent to destroy 'in whole or in part' a national, ethnical, racial or religious group" (see also Rutaganda, 6 December 1999, para. 48–49).

There has never been genocide without survivors. No such episode has produced total slaughter. Even the Nazi's kept some Jews alive to be used as forced labor (e.g., in Volkswagen and Ford auto plants, see Matthews 2006). The Japanese did not kill every Chinese prisoner of war and civilian during their infamous Nanking campaign (Chang 1997). Although the rhetoric of genocide suggests the complete destruction of a population, in reality this never happens. Primarily, the necessary organizational apparatus rarely exists to do so. Even for a supremely centralized state (i.e., Stalin's USSR), the organizational capacity necessary to fully genocide a population is nigh unattainable. In this finding of fact, the UNSC Investigatory Commission is producing a narrow definition of genocide based almost solely upon the intent of the Nazi Holocaust and uses the death camp as its model for enactment. Moreover, there is no case law precedent for complete eradication as the definitional norm. In the *Jelsic* case tried before the ICTY, testimony was presented that there was intent to kill 70% of the Muslims detained in the Luka camp. No legal (or other) push emerged to deny the genocidal intent of the Serbs at Luka. In fact, that testimony was entered to establish *Jelsic's* genocidal intent. Moreover, the ICTY's appellate ruling in the *Jelsic* case has become precedent in genocide trials, especially in terms of the definition of intent. The court established that intent could be established via direct evidence or indirectly inferred from the body of facts and circumstances within the case, including issues of scale, systematic targeting of a group, or repetition of similar actions.

In the Akayesu trial, the ICTR ruled that "methods of destruction by which the perpetrator does not immediately kill the members of the group, but which, ultimately, seek their physical destruction" can be included to prove intent.

This includes, "subjecting a group of people to a subsistence diet, systematic expulsion from homes, and the reduction of essential medical services below minimum requirement" (2 September 1998, para. 505–506; see also Rutaganda, Trial Chamber, 6 December 1999, para. 52; Musema, Trial Chamber, 27 January 2000, para. 157).

The requirement of classification is not *in whole*; group(s) *in part* may also be classified as genocide. In addition, intent does not need to be overt for every action that occurred during genocide. In the proceedings of the tribunal for Yugoslavia, *Kayishema and Ruzindana*, the ICTY agreed with *Akayesu* ruling that intent might be difficult to determine. As such, it stated that the accused's "actions, including circumstantial evidence ... may provide sufficient evidence of intent," and that "intent can be inferred either from words or deeds and may be demonstrated by a pattern of purposeful action." The Chamber stated that indicators could be inferred from "the number of group members affected ... the physical targeting of the group or their property ... the use of derogatory language toward members of the targeted group ... the methodical way of planning ... the systematic manner of killing" (1999, para. 93, 527). In addition, in the Kayishema and Ruzindana Trial, the Chamber ruled that "the *mens rea* must be formed prior to the commission of the genocidal acts ... [T]he individual acts themselves, however, do not require premeditation; the only consideration is that the act should be done in furtherance of the genocidal intent" (21 May 1999, para. 91).

Genocide laws, albeit mass genocide or genocidal rape, attempting to control them garner serious international public and media attention, for good reason. Yet, a genocidal event is not the only form that widespread atrocities may take. For those events where the express intent is not the complete destruction of an entire category of people, the legal frame for Crimes Against Humanity apply.

Genocidal Rape

One crime emerging with disturbing frequency within the cases under examination in this volume is that of genocidal rape: the use of widespread sexual violence within a broader genocidal event. Although we have already provided an overview of the motivation, opportunity, and enactment of such events, here we turn to an analysis of the extant law regulating these crimes. Within international law, the extant prohibition of such behaviors are drawn from both International Humanitarian Law and International Human Rights Law, yet codified into a justicable body by judicial decisions in the ICTR and ICTY. As we noted, the earliest codification of principles governing the behavior of soldiers within combat zones rest in the Hague conventions, more properly titled the *International Declaration concerning the Law and Customs of War* signed in Brussels on 27 August 1874. Although the treaty does not mention rape specifically, drawing upon the above framing of rape as a right of plunder, two articles within the agreement are relevant. First, Article 38 establishes that "family honor and rights, and the lives and property of persons ... must be respected. Private property cannot be confiscated." The sexual assault of a civilian women would distinctly impinge upon the family honor of her husband or father, as with the extant sexual double standard, her victim status would stigmatize her and her family as a "fallen woman" and her potential value (socially and economically) as a wife would be minimized. In addition, Article 39 states: "Pillage is formally forbidden." The prior rights to take sexual liberty with a conquered population's women as a form of plunder are denied by this article.

One key portion of the Nuremberg charter is directed toward these behaviors. Article 6, section c reads:

> CRIMES AGAINST HUMANITY: namely, murder, extermination, enslavement, deportation, and other inhumane acts committed against any civilian population, before or during the war; or persecutions on political, racial or religious grounds in execution of or in connection with any crime within the jurisdiction of the Tribunal, whether or not in violation of the domestic law of the country where perpetrated.

This treaty would classify rape and sexual slavery (e.g., Korean Comfort Women) as both "enslavement" and "inhumane acts." Although this article was not used in the war's aftermath to prosecute sex crimes by Axis soldiers (or, Allied soldiers for that matter), it is significant for our purposes here as the language will appear in later documents and international law agreements which will be brought to bear on sexual violence in theatres of war. Specifically in reference to what was earlier defined as genocidal rape, post World War II treaties further developed a legal framework for the prosecution of mass sexual assault as a crime of war. The *Convention on the Prevention and Punishment of the Crime of Genocide*, ratified on 9 December 1948, was a clear product of the Western response to the Nazi Holocaust.

Two aspects of Article 2 are relevant here. Section (b) prohibits "causing serious bodily or mental harm" to others. This firmly established the literature on Rape Trauma Syndrome, sexual assaults be they individualized actions or systematic genocidal in direction, fulfill this criteria. More directly, section (d) prohibits military victors from "imposing measures intended to prevent births." Although typically interpreted as a ban on forced sterilization or abortion of a conquered population, as has become apparent in the aftermath of Rwanda, Bosnia, and Kosovo, brutal mass rapes often leave a woman sterile, especially when excessive force is used by the perpetrators, or, worse and all too frequent in reportage, foreign objects are used in the attack. For example, the Human Rights Watch Report (1996) on the mass rapes in Rwanda frequently cited victims with heavy genital bleeding and mutilation post-rape. Those who survived were often sterile afterwards.

Article 48 of the 1948 Geneva Conventions articulates the basic rule of combatant/noncombatant interaction, demanding that armed forces "distinguish between the civilian population and combatants ... [and they] shall direct their operations only against military objectives." Those actions that we have defined as genocidal rape above clearly violate this basic principle. The purpose of mass rapes, be it in Nanking or Rwanada, are military in nature and distinctly directed against civilian populations as a form of terrorism and as a form of ethnic cleansing. Such behavior is a direct violation of Article 51, section 2 that states: "civilian populations shall not be the object of attack. Acts or threats of violence the primary purpose of which is to spread terror among the civilian population are prohibited."

Specifically in the realm of directing sexual (or other) violence against women, Protocol I establishes a special legal status for women in combat zones. Article 76, section 1 unequivocally states that "[w]omen shall be the object of special respect and shall be protected in particular against rape, forced prostitution and any other forms of indecent assault." This article represents the culmination of thought enshrined in a legal principle that denounces military rape, be it individualized or systematic, as a "rule of war." As with many other aspects of Geneva, here a time immemorial practice is condemned and criminalized.

Another body of international law applies to military inspired sexual violences that occur when social order breaks down. The landmark treaty of broadest importance for Human Rights Law is the *Universal Declaration of Human Rights*, ratified by the UN General Assembly resolution 217 A (III) on 10 December 1948. For example, when investigating and preparing reports on the sorts of crimes explored here many legal bodies and NGOs fall back on these treaties and agreements in framing the criminal nature of the widespread sexual assault and abuse opposed to relying upon Geneva or other relevant militarily focused legal codes.

Article 3 promises all people the right to "life, liberty, [and] security of person." Clearly sexual assault victimization is a violation of personal security and, all too often, can result in the loss of life due to victims not seeking or being unable to obtain appropriate medical treatment. Article 4 states that "no one shall be held in slavery or servitude." Although not applicable to a single episode of sexual assault, in many war zones, especially those that we have characterized above as genocidal rape situations, reports indicate that women are frequently held for days or weeks at a time, are forced into marriage to a militia member or forced into prostitution. Such actions constitute slavery and servitude. Further, Article 16.2 promises "free and full consent of intending spouses on entry to marriage." As with Article 4, this article becomes relevant in relation to forced marriage; reports from Rwanda, Uganda, and the former Yugoslavia establish that women were forced into relationships defined as marriage by their abductors and communities. For example, as we will explore in detail in Chapter, the LRA in Uganda has long abducted children to act as porters, laborers, and soldiers. Some of the female children were chosen as "wives" by military commanders, with Joseph Kony, the leader of the LRA, reportedly having multiple wives who originated as abductees (Human Rights Watch 2005).

Although many of the victims of genocidal rape within the Rwandan conflict referred to their captors and rapists as their "husbands," once freed from servitude, they were clearly conflicted about the situation. As one interviewee explained, "When my family was killed and I was taken like this, I thought that I would have to live with this man forever because I had no where else to go" (Human Rights Watch, 1996: 20). Similar situations and responses have been reported in the Democratic Republic of Congo, Angloa, Cote d'Ivoire, Uganda, the Sudan, and Chad.

Another relevant international law is the *Convention on the Elimination of all Forms of Discrimination Against Women*, adopted on 18 December 1979. Firmly a part of the broader movement toward solidifying women's rights in the Western world and around the globe, this treaty codifies basic principles of gender equity into human rights law. Although it is not a piece of International Criminal Law, it has influenced the creation of precedents within international war crimes tribunals. Article 6 states that "States Parties shall take all appropriate measures, including legislation, to suppress all forms of traffic in women and exploitation of prostitution of women." This is an all too typical fate of many victims after the initial round of sexual assaults—forced prostitution and/or forced marriage to their assaulters.

Further, since the 1990 International Tribunals for Rwanda and the former Yugoslavia, there is a strong case, based on precedent law that genocidal rape constitutes a grave category in its own right. For example, in the Akayesu case, the ICTR found Jean-Paul Akayesu guilty of rape in the form of genocide (2 September 1998). This was a landmark decision in that it was the first time that rape was legally found to be both a form of genocide and a crime against humanity. The tribunal's decision was based in part on evidence that he had witnessed and encouraged rapes and sexual abuse of women in the course of a genocidal campaign against the Tutsi population while he was a communal leader. The Rwanda tribunal statute enumerates "outrages upon personal dignity, in particular humiliating and degrading treatment, rape, enforced prostitution and any form of indecent assault" as war crimes, following the formulation of Common Article 3 of the Geneva Conventions and Article 4(2)(e) of Protocol II. The Akayesu Trial Chamber (2 September 1998, para. 731) also stated that "these rapes resulted in physical and psychological destruction of Tutsi women, their families and their communities. Sexual violence was an integral part of the process of destruction, specifically targeting Tutsi women and specifically contributing to their destruction and to the destruction of the Tutsi group as a whole" (see also Kayishema and Ruzindana, Trial Chamber, 21 May 1999, para. 95). The Chambers held that acts of sexual violence can form an integral part of the process of destruction of a group.

Moreover, the ICC has made it clear that sexual violence against women will be one of its major loci of prosecution. As the international criminal tribunals took both the mass rapes and genocidal rapes of women in the former Yugoslavia and Rwanda seriously, the ICC has included sex crimes within its mandate. Article 7, section 1, subsection (g) of the Rome Statute, delineating Crimes against Humanity criminalizes "rape, sexual slavery, forced prostitution, enforced sterilization, or any other comparable form of sexual violence of comparable gravity." Similarly Article 8, section 2(b) subsection 22 identifies these violations as war crimes in international hostilities; Article 8, section 2(c) subsection 7 criminalizes these acts within internecine conflicts. Ocampa, the chief prosecutor for the court, has repeatedly promised to take sexual violence seriously and his earliest indictments reflect this: the court's indictments of key leaders of the LRA. Of 33 counts listed within the indictments of 5 people, 3 of those counts are for sex crimes, 1 for sexual exploitation classified as a crime against humanity, 1 for rape as a war crime, and 1 for rape as a crime against humanity.

Crimes Against Humanity

The international arena's early attempts to develop humanitarian law during the nineteenth and early twentieth centuries focused wholly on war crimes—violations of the four Geneva Conventions—and crimes against humanity during war. The term, crimes against humanity however, originated in the 1907 Hague Convention preamble that codified extant customary law of armed conflict. This was based on existing state practices derived from the values and principles deemed to constitute the "laws of humanity" (Bassiouni, 2006). After World War I, in connection with the 1919 Treaty of Versailles, a commission to investigate war crimes was created. They relied on the 1907 Hague Convention as the applicable law. In addition to war crimes committed by the Germans, the commission also found that Turkish officials committed "crimes against the laws of humanity" for killing Armenian nationals and residents during the period of the war (Bassiouni 2006: 2).

In 1945 the United States and Allies developed the Agreement for the Prosecution and Punishment of the Major War Criminals of the European Axis and Charter of the International Military Tribunal (IMT), which contained crimes against humanity in Article 6(c). The Nuremberg Charter was the first document wherein crimes against humanity were established in positive international law. The concept originated in order to prosecute Nazis and Japanese warlords for the atrocities of World War II that were outside of the existing 1907 Hague Conventions. Acts like the Nazi Holocaust cried out for international legal action, but there was no international law to draw upon. As many of these actions were not committed by uniformed armed forces on the field of battle, existing war crimes laws did not hold jurisdiction.

Crimes against humanity have been included in the statutes of the ICTY and ICTR—a key expansion of international law and jurisprudence. In addition, the ICC has included it within the Rome Statute. Specifically, Article 7 states that "crime against humanity" means any of the following acts when committed as part of a widespread or systematic attack directed against any civilian population, with knowledge of the attack:

(a) Murder;
(b) Extermination;
(c) Enslavement;
(d) Deportation or forcible transfer of population;

(e) Imprisonment or other severe deprivation of physical liberty in violation of fundamental rules of international law;
(f) Torture;
(g) Rape, sexual slavery, enforced prostitution, forced pregnancy, enforced sterilization, or any other form of sexual violence of comparable gravity;
(h) Persecution against any identifiable group or collectivity on political, racial, national, ethnic, cultural, religious, gender;
(i) Enforced disappearance of persons;
(j) The crime of apartheid;
(k) Other inhumane acts of a similar character intentionally causing great suffering, or serious injury to body or to mental or physical health.

The term, crimes against humanity, is far more expansive than genocide. In many ways it has come to "mean anything atrocious committed on a large scale" (Bassiouni 2006: 1). To some extent, crimes against humanity overlap with genocide and war crimes. But crimes against humanity are distinguishable from genocide in that they do not require an "intent" to "destroy in whole or in part," as cited in the 1948 Genocide Convention, but only target a given group and carry out a policy of "widespread or systematic" violations (Bassiouni 2006: 2). This body of law governs the behaviors not only of one state on another's citizens, but also a state's treatment of its own peoples.

Child Soldiers

The recruitment (whether voluntary or involuntary) of children to serve in armed forces is forbidden under the Geneva Conventions and reinforced within the Rome Statute. The primary legal authority for these indictments comes under Article 8 of the Rome Statute. Article 8, section 2(b) subsection 26 criminalizes "conscripting or enlisting children under the age of fifteen years into the national armed forces or using them to participate actively in hostiles," within an international conflict, while Article 8, section 2(c) subsection 7 provides the same classification within an internecine conflict. General enslavement of people, including children, is a crime against humanity under Article 7, section 1 subsection c. Within the LRA indictments issued, 2 of the 33 counts are specifically on the enlistment of child soldiers as war crimes.

Whether in general legal codes and principles expressed within Geneva or the Rome Statute, within the legal arguments made during indictments or prosecutions, or case law precedents established during trials and appeals, international criminal law is central to our endeavor here.

Institutions of International Adjudication

As mentioned above, one of the core problems that the adjudication of internal law violations has faced is the general lack of venues to try such cases. These violations can be tried by any willing state party under their own domestic law (e.g., the Pinochet and Charles Taylor cases). Yet, such actions are far from certain and inter alia do not remove the widespread impunity perceived by genocidiers and other violators of international law. In an international context, there are currently four venues for the hearing of cases that involve the violation of international criminal law: domestic courts, the International Court of Justice (ICJ), International Military Tribunals (e.g., Nuremburg, Tokyo, Yugoslavia, Rwanda, and Sierra Leone), and the ICC.

Domestic Courts

Under internationally accepted principles of jurisprudence any country that has ratified certain international treaties can try individuals for the violations of those laws with their own courts under the rules of those courts. For example, any state that has ratified either the Geneva Conventions or the Genocide Convention could, if they apprehended him, try Radovan Karadzic, the so-called Butcher of Belgrade for crimes in the former Yugoslavia. Although he has been indicted by the ICTY, and one would suspect any foreign power who takes him into custody to turn him over to the tribunal, they are not expressly obligated to do so. This was also the justification for the arrest and indictment of Augusto Pinochet in the UK on a Spanish arrest warrant. Although his trial was suspended for health reasons before his death in 2006, the UK intended to try him for massive human rights violations while he was the head of the Chilean state. Their authority to do so rested on the *erga omens* nature of this branch of international law. Such provisions are essential in providing a *potential* control on the worst of offenders; they are far from certain in their application.

The International Court of Justice

Article 14 of the League of Nations provided the authority for the creation of a permanent court of justice with the hope that there would finally be a court to try international legal disputes and violations of the then incipient international criminal law (e.g., the Hague Convention of 1907). This was not the first attempt to create an international court, nor did the envisioned authoritative court come into being on the basis of Article 14 (see Rothe and Mullins, 2006a, Chapter Three, for the history of the drive to create an international criminal court). However, it did create the Permanent World Court of Justice that heard cases from 1921 to 1940. Most of the cases were more in line with what contemporaries would think of as civil law, with trade disputes, the laws of the seas, and other bilateral treaty violations being the frequent source of cases. The court did not meet during the Second World War, and was replaced in the wake of the war when the UN created the International Court of Justice (ICJ).

The ICJ, still extant despite the creation of the ICC (see below) possesses no criminal jurisdiction (unlike the ICC). The ICJ is a court for state arbitration, not for addressing individual criminality. Similar to the ICC, ICJ jurisdiction is only applicable if the states involved have accepted its jurisdiction. Exceptions to the court's mandate for consensual jurisdiction can occur by "virtue of a jurisdictional clause, i.e., typically, when they are parties to a treaty containing a provision whereby, in the event of a disagreement over its interpretation or application, one of them may refer the dispute to the Court" (ICJ 2005: 1).

Although, essentially, any dispute can be brought before the court, for either a contentious case hearing (the equivalent of a trial in Western proceedings) or parties can simply ask the court to issue an advisory opinion. Neither produces truly binding rulings that can be externally enforced. However, if parties do not comply with the court's decision, they can be taken before the Security Council for enforcement action. If the judgment were against one of the permanent five members of the Security Council or its allies, any resolution on enforcement would be vetoed (e.g., this was case in *Nicaragua v. the United States*). The court is simultaneously a court of original jurisdiction—meaning that it is the first stage of a litigation event—and a court of final resort, as there is no appeals court superior to the ICJ. In addition, only states can bring cases in front of the court; individuals and NGOs are excluded from the processes unless they can find a state-sponsor to take the case to the court for them.

Ad Hoc Military Tribunals

During the twentieth and twenty-first centuries, there have been seven military tribunals established to try cases of war crimes and crimes against humanity committed during major conflicts. World War I produced the Leipzig trials created for German war criminals and another to prosecute Turkish atrocities related to their genocide of the Armenians during the war. After World War II, tribunals were established in Nuremburg to try Nazi war criminals and in Tokyo to try Japanese offenders. The recent decades have seen the creation of the ICTY, dealing with the crimes of the Serbian-led genocides in the wake of the disintegration of the former Yugoslavia and the ICTR, created to prosecute the perpetrators of the Hutu-led genocide of the Tutsis. Finally, a tribunal is operating in Sierra Leone that is a blended tribunal, partially international in nature and partially domestic.

Such tribunals have been strongly criticized as violating some of the basic recognized principles of law. First, they are typically post hoc prosecutions—laws that are the core of the prosecutions are often written after the events in question have occurred. For example, the Nuremberg principles that guided the prosecution of Nazi war criminal were written not only after the atrocities had been committed, but also after the defeat of Germany and her European allies were assured. The second criticism of IMTs is that they represent "victor's justice" in so far as the tribunals are organized by the winners of a conflict and those put on trial are from the power that was defeated. Some critics see this as inter alia problematic. Law becomes a tool used in the endgame of resolving a conflict to provide further punishment and humiliation to a foe. Other critics note that war crimes committed by the victorious power are not prosecuted in these trials. For example, the allied powers during World War II did commit atrocities and war crimes violations while prosecuting hostilities against the Nazis. The most well-known example is the allied bombing campaign marshaled against Dresden, where the entirety of the city was leveled without regard for the welfare of citizens (and Allied prisoners of war held in the city). If nothing else, these approaches to the prosecution of war crimes undermine the legitimacy of international law itself. To be seen as fully just and empowered, all violators must be brought to justice.

Furthermore, due to their ad hoc nature, Tribunal procedurals have proved to be more than challenging (e.g., the Tribunals for Yugoslavia and Rwanda). In part, this was due to the costs associated with IMTs, the complexities of reaching consensus on the procedures or desires for an IMT, and because of the veto power of the Security Council that allows for a selectivity of cases that would be eligible for IMT prosecutions (Bassiouni 1999). Because of the aforementioned problems associated with these types of ad hoc tribunals, the

Security Council has become less willing to continue the processes of ad hoc Tribunals. Further, with the creation of the ICC, the necessity of other tribunals is now questionable, especially for those powers who have signed onto the Rome Statute. Time will tell if the UNSC authorizes new tribunals as situations arise, or simply rely on the ICC.

The International Criminal Court

With the ratification of the Rome Statute for the ICC 1998, the landscape of international criminality now has the potential to be significantly altered. The intention of the ICC is to provide an international system of justice that can address the most heinous crimes against humanity when a state is unable or unwilling to investigate or prosecute an individual accused of the crimes specified in the Rome Statute (Rothe and Mullins 2006). A key distinction between the ICC and other institutions of social control at the international level is that it addresses crimes of individuals versus states. The ICC is a permanent court able to prosecute war crimes, genocide, and crimes against humanity. The court is a complementary court, meaning that its jurisdiction only triggers when a signatory state is unable or unwilling to prosecute a crime. If a state is willing to try its own accused citizens, then the court has no ability to prosecute (even if the prosecutions are merely symbolic). Furthermore, the court's jurisdiction operates on an opt-in principle. Countries must submit themselves to the court's authority. This can occur through the state ratifying the Rome Statute in accordance with their local legal systems or through a country voluntarily submitting to the court's authority for a single case.

Cases can be brought before the court in a number of ways. First, a state party itself can request that the court intervene (this is what occurred in the situation within Uganda). Second, a case can be referred to the court by the UN Security Council (this is what occurred in the situation in Darfur). Third, any NGO or individual can submit a case for consideration. Regardless of the course, the prosecutor then examines the presented evidence and decides if a greater investigation is warranted. If so, then the prosecutor can begin their own fact-finding investigations to build a case to issue indictments. If indictments are issued, the court then relies upon members of the international community to apprehend the indicted and turn them over to the court (see Rothe and Mullins 2006a for a full exploration and critique of the court).

Summary

The twentieth century saw a major evolution in the nature and extent of international criminal law, that which governs genocide, war crimes, and crimes against humanity. Especially in the wake of World War II, the incipient international political community began to seriously pursue the criminalization and adjudication of atrocities. Although the earliest attempts as such law enforcement, the Leipzeig tribunals, were pure failures, over the course of the century, international actors continued to build a consensus for, and a legal code governing, real criminal justice systems for the prosecution of the worst crimes. The cases we examine in this volume are all under the purview of international adjudication and jurisprudence. The ICCt has active investigation in Darfur, the DRC, and Uganda, having produced indictments in all three cases.

· 3 ·

THE PATHOLOGY OF DISORDER: POSTCOLONIAL SOCIAL (DIS)ORGANIZATION

The dividing of the continent among European colonial powers occurred late in the colonial period. The so-called scramble for Africa divided most of the continent between European powers in a short period between the 1884–5 Berlin–West Africa Conference and a host of bilateral treaties between major European powers in 1890–1 that finalized borders (Chamberlain 1999). By the time Europe seriously began to engage in the domination of Africa, most of the colonial countries had extensive experience in North and South America, South Asia, and the Pacific. The UK held massive holdings worldwide; France had won and lost an empire in the New World and in Africa saw the chance to regain those losses. Other countries, such as Belgium and Germany, had largely missed out on the colonization of Asia and the New World. For them, Africa was an opportunity to join the ranks of Imperial Powers. The African colonial experience stands as one of the starkest examples in global history of the utter and complete domination of hundreds of cultures and millions of peoples.

Primary Motivations

The search for economic resources was a leading factor in Europe's drive to colonize Africa. To European powers in the process of industrialization, Africa offered a wealth of natural and mineral resources, as well as seemingly ample land for the creation of cash crop plantations. As European markets and economics continued to grow, the demand for cheap goods and natural resources rapidly increased. With a seemingly full colonial penetration of the world, and with many of those former colonies moving toward—or having gained—independence (e.g., the United States, Australia, and Canada) new territories were needed to maintain Europe's current path. Eyes turned to Africa. Although some portions of Africa had been subjugated by non-Africans at the start of the nineteenth century (e.g., South Africa by Europeans and, centuries before, North Africa by South Asian and Middle Eastern populations), the bulk of the continent south of the Sahara was seen as "open" by the Europeans.

That doesn't mean the Europeans had no knowledge of the region nor that it existed in a "pristine" historical social and cultural configuration unaffected by external forces. Both Eastern and some Western African peoples had longstanding contact (trade and otherwise) with Arabic populations from the east. West Africa particularly had been devastated by the trans-Atlantic slave markets, which were still active until the 1920s when slavery was finally abolished by the last of the New World nations. Ironically, as the Middle Passage slave trade diminished in profitability, European powers began to use the remaining Arab-based slave networks as rationale for colonial domination. As part of the broader discourse on "civilizing" Africans, procolonial groups also emphasized the Christian duty not only to convert natives, but the need to "save" people from Arabic slave traders who still moved people eastward.

Central Africa had been largely ignored by European colonial invaders due to the presence of tropical diseases for which the Europeans had no natural immunity. Whereas disease had been the "point-man" for the European colonization of North, Central and South America (e.g., small pox), in Africa it worked in the opposite direction. Malaria, trypsanomosis (African Sleeping Sickness), and other virulent illnesses devastated Europeans who tried to settle in the region. Even with a desire to dominate the area, maintaining a large-scale European population through the eighteenth century was not practical. However, owing to European medicine's discovery of quinine and other antimalarial treatments, these diseases could be brought under enough control to make habitation possible.

International politics also drove colonial enterprises. Long-standing dynamics of competition—militarily and economically—fueled the desire for greater and greater colonial holdings. Nations measured their international prestige in a large extent by their imperial ambitions and successes. As the modern European nation-state system began to develop, colonial domination and competition was a central aspect of this power struggle. Acquisition of military advantage further drove colonial domination. Colonial holdings provided key tactical advantages for the dominating power. As countries jockeyed for a position in a global race for superiority, a colony's geographic location was highly valuable. Naval powers sought bases for resupplying their vessels as well as locations that would allow them to exploit and to dominate major trade routes. Locations for land bases were also essential in protecting and expanding empires. Thus, some strategically key locations—such as the modern state of Somalia on the horn of Africa—were frequently contested and disputed locations.

Colonial holdings also provided much needed human capital to bulk out an imperial army. Both France and the UK utilized native conscription to fill out the regiments to establish and maintain control over the colonial holdings. While many of these regiments would be composed of native troops under the command of European officers. Even when populations with a cultural history of warfare were recruited (which was often), Europeans didn't trust the skills of experienced native commanders. These processes were not limited to colonial expansion; both world wars saw successful deployment of indigenous African units whose participation was key to a number of military victories, even if they were more likely to be fielded as fodder and therefore seen as expendable.

Part of the broader military competition between European powers was an arms race propelled by increasing industrialization of military technology and production. Conflicts in Africa and elsewhere often served as "testing" grounds for new equipment, weapons, and tactics. For example, the South African war between the British and the native Zulus saw the introduction of several new weaponry technologies, especially early machine guns. Such experiences were crucial to continental military development as they allowed for the identification and refinement of military technologies and the development of tactical shifts to take full advantage of them.

Variant Colonial Approaches

Each colonial power adopted different approaches to their overseas territories, many developed different strategies of domination and control in different holdings as well. Although there are commonalities in the effect of colonialism across the continent, to fully understand the situations and contexts in each society, we need to briefly overview the approaches of three colonial powers: the United Kingdom, France, and Belgium. These were the powers responsible for the establishment of colonial and postcolonial environs for the cases we explore later in the book.

The United Kingdom

The UK approached the main body of Africa with a long history of expansionist colonial experiences. The New World, Australia, Hong Kong, India, and southern Africa had already been exploited and dominated. It had mastered a variety of colonial approaches and had learned to draw upon a variety of strategies depending upon the immediate context. For example, in North America, the British had relied upon corporations to fund settlement enterprises and then colonists to found and maintain new agriculturally based export-focused holdings. At the time, there were strong economic and population pressures within the UK operating as push factors for settlement. For middle-class and aristocratic citizens, new territories provided opportunities for commerce, land acquisition, and political power. For working-class populations, the New World provided the possibility for social mobility previously unavailable due to the rigid class system of the UK. When faced with a life of competition for low wage jobs in the burgeoning industrial urban landscape, life as a colonist at least held potential for a future, even if it would be a hard-won future born out of hostile environments. In addition, as colonies such as Georgia and Australia were founded, they became the primary repository for convicts—an increasingly large population due to the combined forces of urbanization and increasing centralization of state criminal justice authority. For the social elites, the colonies were the prime repository of this growing "surplus population" and took an edge off of growing class-based conflict and tensions.

India presented a different set of problems and possibilities. Rather than lead the enterprise with settlers and the founding of colonies, the early entrée into the continent was made by export companies—particularly the East India company. Through deals with local elites, the company established profitable and extensive economic holdings. Later, they began to arm and fund one set of local elites against others, using existing political and military tensions to divide and conquer the region. This strategy was highly successful for the East India Company; as it continued to grow its private army that began to rival the power of the Queen's forces in the region.

Thus, when the UK turned its attention toward Africa, it had numerous successful colonial experiences with a number of different strategies. In Eastern Africa, the British relied heavily upon white settlers and colonial agents in the development of its colonies. As an export plantation economy developed, a large ex-patriot British population settled in. They inserted themselves into the major social institutions, controlling political, military, economic, religious, and education organizations. Land was divided up into privately held plantations and mining grants; indigenous peoples were assigned to these geographies and their labor expropriated.

In Western Africa, the UK relied much less on settlement to colonize, but rather seemed content to establish political and economic dominance with a small white population. The UK relied upon 8,000 whites to control about 26 million indigenous peoples. In Nigeria, the UK fielded only 85 police officers (Hargreaves 1988). This was facilitated by the existence of hierarchical, quasi-imperial societies within the region. Well before European contact, indigenous African kingdoms had developed and dominated large swathes of territory. Such conditions were exacerbated by the middle-passage slave trade networks, where people would enslave their neighbors and sell them into the European and Arabic slave networks. Here, the UK had to acquire the compliance of the existing ruling elite, or provide resources to allow the ascension of a rival group.

The UK worked more than the other powers to educate the elite population, drawing heavily upon its experiences in India, and to create an indigenous administrative class that could implement a colonial apparatus. Both through exporting the children of elites back to England for formal education and through the establishment of schools and colleges in Africa, a generation of individuals loyal to a Western worldview, if not the west itself, was cultivated.

France

France focused her desires to recreate her empire on Africa. While earlier in the colonial epoch, France controlled holdings in North America (e.g., Canada and the vast Louisiana territories) and elsewhere. At the height of its holdings, France controlled about one-third of the entire continent. By the late nineteenth century its holdings were limited to small outposts like the West Indies. In Africa and to a lesser degree in Indochina that empire could be remade. France took a different overall approach to it colonial holdings and their administration. Like the UK, they too attempted to identify collaborator groups to administer the colonies for them. Yet, while the UK tended to identify existing local elites, France looked to previously subjugated populations and elevated them into positions and power over their former dominators. This had the result of creating a population that owned cultural, economic, and political debt to the

French, thereby potentially creating a sense of loyalty. Yet, it further exasperated existing ethnic tensions and conflicts. Where there was little-to-no existing tension the situation created cultural identities directly tied to the colonial order. While the newly elevated population may have developed a sense of obligation to France, the newly subjugated population had even more reason to resist domination. In several cases we explore in this volume, these tensions explode in the postcolonial period and provide motive and socioemotional fuel for genocidal programs and other crimes against humanity.

As the twentieth century wore on, France looked upon its colonial holdings as not just a source of economic and political capital, but as sister states to France herself. In fact, French officials avoided the term empire or colony, but preferred the appellation "*La France d'outer-mer*—France overseas" (Chamberlain 1999: 70). As is still the predominant ideology in the country today, outsiders were welcomed into the French Empire as long as they assimilated into mainstream Gallic society. They did not desire task masters and petty bureaucrats, they sought nothing less than an extension of Franco-Gallic culture into the African realm. For example, during the post–World War II period of colonial upheavals, French President de Gaulle did not move toward liberation of France's African holdings, but rather stated that the official French position was one of pure fraternity with their African brothers. Instead of independence, the new Republic would move toward "gradually eliminating unjust differences in the condition of its peoples" either at home or abroad (Hargreaves 1988: 64).

Belgium

The horror and infamy of the Belgian conquest of the Congo River basin remains in many ways *the* object lesson of colonial harm. Leopold II, King of Belgium, yearning for greater importance and power, chaffed against both the fact that his nation was small and almost insignificant in the European power hierarchy and that his monarchial powers were limited by a Constitutional parliament. Almost immediately upon his assumption of the throne, Leopold II saw colonial holdings as the solution to both of his problems. The more territory Belgium could control outside of Europe, the stronger economically it would be. While it could not compete militarily on the continent, Leopold hoped it could overseas. Further, if he managed to acquire a colony, he hoped to establish himself as the sole sovereign over the region, allowing him to rule without parliamentary oversight (Hoschild 1998).

Failing to find powers willing to sell off holdings, his eyes turned toward sub-Saharan Africa—specifically the unexplored wilds around the great Congo river. He hired the famous explorer Stanley to establish a base on the Congo River and to negotiate international recognition of the territory as Belgian. Most countries simply ignored Leopold; as industrialization increased the demand for raw materials in Europe many powers were beginning to see Africa as a potential source for items other than slaves. Due to essentially a diplomatic accident, the US officially recognized Leopold's claim, a claim that he cemented control over through the many diplomatic conferences held on Africa at the end of the nineteenth century (Hoschild 1998; Nzongola-Ntalaja 2002).

The mass atrocities and horrors of Belgium dominance of the Congo was aptly described in Joseph Conrad's novel *Heart of Darkness*, a barely fictionalized account of his travels along the Congo river during Leopold's reign. From the start of European interactions in the Congo river basin, the focus has been on facilitating private corporations' extractions of the natural resources of the region—especially mineral wealth and later rubber. Even with independence, this situation would not change. Hargreaves suggests that conditions in what would become the Democratic Republic of the Congo were different as "Belgian rule [of the Congo] … was … intensive; in relation to population there were more white officials, more paramilitary forces, more agricultural officer enforcing more drastic programmes of compulsory cultivation, than elsewhere in tropical Africa" (1988: 176). The sole goal of the Belgian Congo was profit generation, with a brutal eye to the bottom line. The levels of sheer brutality and raw violence created an international outcry, which eventually led to the Belgian Parliament taking control of the Congo Free State. This, however, did little to change conditions on the ground in the Congo.

Colonial Consequences

Whichever government was in charge, the colonial experience left African peoples in a state of civil, social, and economic disorder. Overall, the primary goals of the colonial endeavor were to create export economies in the subjugated territories. The creation of plantation and mineral extraction industries required massive amounts of labor. Not only was Africa attractive to European powers because of an abundance of untapped natural resources that could be exported to aid the continued industrialization of the home countries, but it was also the source of a huge amount of human capital. Locals were immediately pressed into service—either via direct force and slavery-like relationships or indirectly through the manipulation of local markets, cultural practices, and political systems. The Belgians used forced conscript labor, while the UK in Eastern Africa imposed taxes on all households that could only be paid in English Pound Sterling. To bring labor to the fields and mines, the British colonial authorities ensured that the only way for natives to gain pounds was to work in some segment of the colonial economy. These practices necessarily reduced the labor available for subsistence endeavors. Men left their villages, drastically altering the existing division of labor within the indigenous social systems; women, the young, and the aged were left to handle both productive and reproductive labor in the communities.

Indigenous economies were subordinated by the new colonial markets; relationships of ownership and production were fractured. This disrupted existing kinship systems that had previously organized economic production and distribution. Traditional subsistence knowledge was lost. Food procuring and tending practices that had evolved over millennia were quickly replaced with activities focused on the production of crops that the Europeans valued. Local peoples had to accommodate their economic behavior to the newly formed and reorganized markets. This often involved the introduction of alien ideas of privately held property, over communally or kin-group held property. Social structures were refocused on more atomistic family units; adopting more individualized Western notions of economic responsibility undermined reciprocity networks in place that had emphasized more equitable distribution of resources within groups and creating bonds of solidarity amongst the peoples. Such economic reorganization also altered existing political networks, which were also typically based upon the kinship structures increasingly weakened by shifts in ownership and production. Due to intense levels of social integration between social institutions, this further weakened forces of social control.

At the time of colonization, Africa exhibited a huge array of political organization. From the loosely organized Mbuti food foragers (see Turnbull 1965) to the United Kingdoms of the Ashante (see Hoebel 1974), almost every form of political structure defined by anthropologists existed in some shape or form. In the creation of overarching political structures, at best the preexisting institutions were subordinated and delegitimated; at worst they were utterly destroyed. Due to the intricate integration of institutional structures within the precolonial environments, this would have far-reaching influences and effects ultimately undermining kinship, economic and religious institutions and practices. Where colonial powers elevated certain groups to rulership positions over their formerly equal peers, this created (or exacerbated existing) tensions. Local systems of community decision making, dispute resolution, and intergroup relations were replaced with colonial power structures and entities.

Foreign educational programs further eroded the traditional culture's basis and power. With selected leaders chosen to receive a European education, assimilation of Africa's elite into a Western worldview was amplified. Being offered Western university educational curriculum—whether it was at universities in the colonial power or those developed in Africa itself—not only created a technically competent bureaucratic class, but also created a generation and more of individuals (primarily men) who not only understood the technical aspects of managing a colonial apparatus but had begun to think and perceive the world and their positions in it in a more Western fashion.

Education also produced other immediate impacts. For example, in some of the cases, most educational institutions were located in the urbanizing areas, "schools emptied the villages and filled the cities ... thousands of young able-bodied people left the sparsely populated regions where labor was short and move to urban centers where jobs are scarce" [sic] (Reader 1997: 626). This further exacerbated the undermining of subsistence economies taking place due to pressures of men to work in wage economies to, for example, meet the new tax polices often implemented. In other examples, education was used to give preferential treatment to a specific group within the occupied lands as they were viewed as "natural born leaders" and as such in the interest of colonial powers to use them for a form of indirect rule. This was the case in Rwanda wherein the Tutsis were given educational preference. This had a direct impact on economic abilities of the remaining Hutu within the localized economy.

The Mandate System

In the early twentieth century, European powers rearranged, at least symbolically, their relationships with colonial holdings. In the wake of World War I—a war that was a world war due to the fighting in the colonies—the League of Nations was established as a clearing house for the peaceful resolution of international disputes. Part of a broader development of international cooperation and the early signs of an incipient international community (see Rothe and Mullins 2006), an early task for the League was to approach the issue of colonies. In the wake of war, the allied powers had fought "in the name of Democracy" there was a growing sense in the international discourse that colonialism was nothing more than a form of mass slavery. Instead of dismantling the whole system, something that no colonial power was in favor of, the League developed the Mandate System which would establish rules for operations in colonial societies and provide oversight of how states treated their colonial holdings. The express goal was a consideration of the human rights of colonized populations, yet, there was often little change in the on-the-ground conditions experienced.

According to the League Covenant—the foundation document that created the League setting out its basic structures and responsibilities—the primary concern of colonial powers was to be "the well being and development" of indigenous peoples in the controlled territories (Article 22). Although it demanded independence for elements of the former Turkish Empire, it specifically identified Central Africa as less ready for self-rule, stating:

> the Mandatory must be responsible for the administration of the territory under conditions which guarantee freedom of conscience and religion, subject only to the maintain of public order and morals, the prohibition of uses of the slave trade, the arms traffic and liquor traffic, and the prevention of the establishment of fortification or military and navel bases and of military training of the natives for other than police purposes and the defense of territory. (Article 22)

Further, the League required that Mandatorys provide an annual report to the League concerning their progress in the region.

Rajagopal (2003) suggests that the League was primarily responsible for creating a technocratic infrastructure to administer colonial holdings that was cloaked in humanitarian discourses. It was significant in its extension of international law itself, but did not achieve the desired outcomes on the ground in colonies themselves. Although oversight systems were established, they really were never implemented; the new principles were never enforced. Yet, an important culturally symbolic stance had been reached: the innate right of a nation to be a colonial power with absolute sovereign rule over foreign territories had been challenged. A limited, though nonetheless real, conceptualization of human rights and human dignity had been fully extended to non-Western peoples; this fundamental principle had been enshrined in international law. The Mandate System would also provide a location for political, legal, and moral anticolonial rhetoric (for both the colonized and those in Europe discontent with colonialism) during the decolonial period.

The Move Toward Postcolonialism

The political, economic, and cultural structures of the colonial world in Africa changed massively during the middle and later decades of the twentieth century. The Mandate System was seen as no longer functional, never having lived up to either its promise or its state purpose. Due to political and economic reasons, over a period of decades, European colonial powers turned over sovereign political authority to indigenous governments. Thus began the postcolonial era: the nature and ramifications of this period are central to understanding the cases we explore throughout this book.

World War II and Its Aftermath

Both allied and axis powers in Europe found their peoples and infrastructure utterly devastated by the war. France, Germany, Italy, the UK, and other locations of intense fighting during the war faced massive reconstruction efforts. Roads, bridges, electrical grids, factories, and other elements of basic infrastructure had been destroyed during the course of the war. Local currencies were stressed, or downright worthless; huge portions of the local populations were displaced. To regain political stability in the wake of the war, major reconstruction projects would be needed. As one of the few allied powers that did not suffer major destruction of its infrastructure, the United States established the basic parameters for postwar reconstruction. The Marshall Plan created a set of financial policies to fund these processes. Two major financial institutions were created at this time to facilitate the fiduciary arrangements: the World Bank and the International Monetary Fund (IMF).

World Bank

The World Bank is not a "bank" in the common sense. It is a specialized agency currently composed of 184 member countries. The World Bank, conceived during World War II at Bretton Woods, New Hampshire, United States, initially helped rebuild Europe after the war. For example, in the early days of the World Bank, Europe, Japan, and Australia were the primary loanees, all in serious need for reconstruction funds. Its first loan of $250 million was to France in 1947 for postwar reconstruction. It once had a homogeneous staff of engineers and financial analysts, based solely in Washington, DC (WB 2004). More recently the Bank became a group of five closely associated development institutions: the International Bank for Reconstruction and Development (IBRD), the International Development Association (IDA), the International Finance Corporation (IFC), the Multilateral Investment Guarantee Agency (MIGA), and the International Centre for Settlement of Investment Disputes (ICSID). The World Bank is a closed system. Votes allocated to member countries regarding specific programs are linked to the size of its shareholding. Initial membership in the Bank gives equal voting rights but additional votes are given based upon financial contributions. Aid recipients also hold voting power, but only at a fraction of the number of votes lenders have.

During the 1980s, the Bank went through an extensive period focused on macroeconomic, especially debt rescheduling, issues. The World Bank's activities include providing loans to member countries experiencing economic developmental crisis. The Bank requires that political measures be taken, for example, to foster "democracy." In addition to financing, the World Bank Group provides advice and assistance to developing countries on almost every aspect of economic development. Since the mid-to late 1990s the Bank utilizes the Private Sector Development (PSD) as its strategy to promote privatization in developing countries. All other strategies must be coordinated with the push toward privatization. Though repeatedly relied upon by impoverished governments around the world as a contributor of development finance, the World Bank is often criticized for undermining the national sovereignty of recipient countries through its pursuit of economic liberalization (see Friedrichs and Friedrichs 2002; Rothe, Mullins, and Sandstrom 2008; Rothe, Muzzatti, and Mullins 2006). The Bank also operates under the marked political influence of certain countries (notably, the US) that would profit from advancing their interests for attaining further capitalistic markets as well as specific resources available in less developed states such as cheap labor, gold and diamond mining, peanuts, and electric industries. Moreover, having a notable political influence on the World Bank's policies of restructuring, the G8 states' priorities are directed toward private ownership policies (in the form of export). Consequently, economic enterprises funded by the World Bank are often a detriment to the people of which it was alleged to help and in contradiction to the needs of specific states (keeping in mind each state's historical, cultural, economic, and political structures). As stated by Rothe and Friedrichs (2006: 154):

> It may well not be the intention of these institutions to do harm—indeed they claim as a central mission the alleviation of economic and other forms of suffering. But the privileging of transnational corporate interests and the interests of the most powerful

states, and a certain arrogance with which these institutions implement a top down form of globalization, does demonstratably have immensely harmful consequences.

Some scholars and critics of globalization suggest that the nature of the World Bank's relationship with its contemporary borrowers mirrors the older colonial system, where if local populations wanted to benefit from the extant system they had to ideologically adopt the worldview of the Western powers. The difference here is that the industries and economics established are not fully and totally under foreign control. Yet, the World Bank's use of structural adjustment policies and the way in which it determined eligibility for debt relief and additionally development funding requires that a state implement political and economic practices demanded by the bank.

International Monetary Fund

The International Monetary Fund (IMF) is also composed of 184 member countries and is headquartered in Washington, DC. The IMF was established in 1945 to promote international monetary cooperation, to foster economic growth and to provide temporary financial assistance to needy countries. It "is the central institution of the international monetary system—the system of international payments and exchange rates among national currencies" (IMF 2006). Since the IMF was established, its purposes have remained unchanged, but its operations such as surveillance, dialogue among its members on the national and international consequences of their economic and financial policies, financial assistance, loans, and structural adjustment policies have changed throughout its history.

The IMF demands that countries adopt what it believes to be "sound economic policies," what most commentators refer to as neoliberal economics. The approval or voices that are represented in these "sound policies" are not equally distributed. Voting power is distributed in the same fashion as in the World Bank. Many international observers have been questioning the effectiveness of the remedies embodied in IMF-supported adjustment programs—especially those backed by the ESAF, the facility established in 1987 through which the IMF provides low-interest loans to poor countries with specific demands that must be followed. These policies are accompanied by specific requirements for the "borrowing" country, for example, currency devaluations and peggings, cuts in social programs, spending on civil works, and opening state-run industries to private, international investment. As noted by the IMF (1999: 1), "some even described these remedies as part of the problem rather than the solution." As the IMF's remedies are framed in a capitalistic vacuum that ignores the primacy of citizens' human rights and the overall social, political, and economic health of a nation.

Economic Pressures

Even with the assistance of the Marshall Plan and the new institutions of global financing, European powers were economically crippled by the war. In the postwar era, most European powers were too focused on rebuilding their own cities than attempting to develop their colonies. In 1946 and 1947, the UK Pound Sterling had essentially no value in the global economy. While the US underwrote loans to support the UK's currency, when the loan conditions demanding that the pound float freely were implemented, the lack of public and market confidence completely eroded the currency reserves. Everyone who could was selling pounds; the program was suspended after 40 days (Hargreaves 1988). In the early negotiations about the nature and structure of rebuilding programs, the issue of the colonies was raised. At this point in history, states exercised colonial authority under the auspices of the Mandate System established by the League of Nations. One central mandate was the administration of the colonies in the interests of the local populations. North Africa was a theatre of military operations and, as with World War I, colonial powers drew heavily upon their African subjects for military conscription. Again, as before, these regiments served with distinction and deserved high praise for their service—much more than they received. Initially, the US and other donor nations assumed that the colonial holdings would be the site of reconstruction efforts as well; many colonial powers felt differently. The UK insisted that their colonies not be a part of the Marshall plan; they wanted the money for the motherland (Hargreaves 1988). The UK still needed her African holdings. Not only did they need the cheap raw materials to reestablish industrial production, they required a market for those produced goods. The other European powers were in the same situation. This economic demand would strongly shape the nature of the decolonization process. Whereas politically independent states would be created, economically the ties of dependence would remain. Ownership of industry and land would remain significantly in the hands of Europeans; economic survival depended on maintaining export relations with the former colonial power. As we explore later in this chapter, such exploitative relations placed the new societies in awkward positions of maintained dependence.

Political Pressures

The allied nations prosecuted World War II under the banner of liberation of a conquered France, and the spread of freedom and democracy. During the course of the war they joined together to create the UN whose primary purpose was, and remains, the maintaining of peace on global scale, but also served to create an international area for political and economic issues. The UN was founded on the basic principles of peace, human liberty, dignity, and respectful egalitarian cooperation. This discourse did not sit well with the raw facts of colonial domination. Even the Mandate System was unsuitable in this new intellectual and ideologically environment.

As the century unfolded, many imperialistic countries found their own citizenries less and less supportive of the colonial project. What was a point of nationalistic pride half a century prior was increasingly seen by European citizens as an economic liability to the motherland and as economic competition for the working classes back home. Growing union movements saw colonial sources of production as direct competition; their ability to extract better wages, benefits, and working conditions from European capitalists was severely weakened by the potential for industrialists to seek labor in the colonies. Increasingly influential Marxist political groups, both domestic and international, took a strong anticolonial position. They called stringently for decampment. Much of this European anti-imperialism was not based on principles of human rights and a shared sense of human dignity. Rather, French and British Marxists were primarily anti-imperial due to the economic situations the colonies created. European workers could not compete with lower wages and horrendous working conditions that existed in the colonies; dominated Africans were competition, not brothers-in-arms. Although some of the labor rhetoric identified a need to decolonize regions to allow for the socialist revolutionary transformation of Africa, the bulk of the political push was to simply abandon the region thus providing the European working class with a stronger basis to negotiate wages, working conditions, and political-economic power in the industrial economy (Hargreaves 1988).

The new shape of international politics, especially as embodied within the UN served to build major external political pressures for colonial decampment. The strongest pressures to do so had developed earlier in the century during the tenure of the League of Nations and the creation of the Mandate System of colonial administration. The Mandate System sought to place restrictions on how dominating states could treat their holdings; within the very logic of the system, was the argument for the end of colonialism itself. If basic principles of human dignity called for a foreign government to rule a people in their own best interests, then the step toward granting self-determination and even sovereignty was not a radical new direction but merely the next extension of the idea. This was part of a growing drive toward universal inalienable human rights—a condition that could not coexist with colonialism.

The Postcolonial Turn

Independence

Leading up to, and continuing throughout the initiation of the postcolonial turn, many African countries produced homegrown liberation movements, often led by the European-educated and favored elites. Having been socialized into the ideology of democracy and citizen-led governance that predominated in the colonial motherlands, this newly educated elite turned the discourse of human liberty and democracy acquired within European Universities back upon the colonizers—in essence calling their ideological bluff. Enhanced by general international forces pushing for human rights, the recognition of universal human dignity and the stark economic realities of postwar Europe, the discourse of self-government, and later full independence found support within the colonies as well as in the colonizer.

In other cases, the educated elite saw a potential to replace the colonizers and become the complete ruling authorities, with access to all resources. Having benefited from colonial authorities' preferential treatment including economic security, the elite foresaw an opportunity to gain additional political and economic powers. This was the case with the Tutsis in Rwanda. In response colonial authorities and the Catholic Church supported and promoted the Hutu 1959 revolution. Quite simply, these early agitators for independence had learned their Western lessons too well; by establishing themselves as capable of acquiring Western culture and practices, they undermined the racist ideologies of colonialism that justified empire on the ground of the innate inferiority of the African peoples and their supposed inability to engage in civilized behaviors.

Applying the tools of elected governance, which they had been taught by their colonizers, some of the earliest freedom movements took the forms of establishing regional or ethnic congresses to represent the interests of a given population. Such endeavors were often attended and run by European-educated Africans, some of whom had their earliest political experiences as bureaucratic administrators and then later as African representatives to European parliaments.

Decampment

All of the forces discussed above led to European nation-states withdrawing from their colonial holdings. Just as each had taken a different path through the processes of colonization and of administering those colonies, they also took divergent paths to removing themselves from Africa. As the UK's style of colonial administration had been bifurcated in Africa, their approaches to decampment were also varied. In regions where an elite, educated African class existed, the main drive was to slowly but steadily transfer the remainder of governmental duties and authorities to the indigenous administrators. In areas where there was not a largely indigenous administrative class, the development of local governmental infrastructure was much more difficult and tended to be dominated by European expatriates.

Whereas the UK was devising ways to divest herself of African holdings, France tried to hold on to her empire either formally or informally. In the early period of decolonization she abjectly refused to withdraw from North African holdings, leading to one of the more well-known campaigns of resistance of domination in the later twentieth century: Algeria. She was also resistant to withdraw from French Indochina, ultimately leading to the prolonged Vietnamese civil war. At the same time, France did help develop indigenous parliamentary government, especially in regions where she felt she could maintain economic domination while allowing political independence (e.g., West African countries such as Senegal and Cote d'Ivoire).

Although the Belgian government followed her European peers in attempting to establish an independence process for her colonies after World War II, it was more reluctant to pull out completely; her economy depended too much on colonial revenues. Belgium initially established a 15-year plan for extracting itself from the Congo region. This changed in response to widespread riots in Leopoldville in January of 1959 and a dawning realization on behalf of Belgian ministers that the colonies might be an economic burden rather than an asset, especially when the global copper market collapsed diminishing the value of key exports (Chamberlain 1999; Hargreaves 1988). Even though colonial forces brutally suppressed the riots, the King announced that Congo would be given her independence. Talks began in January of 1960; 30 June 1960 saw the official transfer of sovereign power from the Belgians to an indigenous government. In a week's time the infant nation tore itself asunder. On 5 July, rebels attacked remnant Belgian officers; on 11 July, Katanga province succeeded from the state followed on 8 August by South Kasai. This widespread disorder led to one of the UNSC's first peacekeeping missions, which didn't keep the peace so much as it attempted to nation-build by establishing a pro-Western government (Chamberlain 1999; Hargreaves 1988; Hochschild 1998; Nzongola-Ntalaja 2002). Alongside the UNSC's intervention in Angola, this mission is widely perceived as one of the earliest and most severe failures of peacekeeping operations and would lead to decades of UN hesitancy to intervene (see Adebajo and Sriram 2001). Many of the conditions we examine later are a direct result of these early failures.

New Economics

The drive for peace and order, especially in central Africa was made even more difficult by the fact that local, indigenous economies had long been destroyed. In many of these cases, the major sources of capital were still controlled by foreign nationals and investors, providing little in the way to create a local economy to support the newly founded states. Attempts to restore indigenous economies were futile; the peoples of new African countries essentially had one economic option: continue their relations of exploitation with the developed world by maintaining their export economies.

Due to their colonial experiences of exploitation and domination, many postindependent states began to reorganize their economic institutions; they found themselves dependent upon obtaining and maintaining foreign investment. Without an indigenous ownership class or the resources to create state-run enterprises, these states required an infusion of foreign capital. While in the short term, such non-African ownership provided much needed monies for initial development, in the medium- and long-term situations such dominance by foreign investors created more economic insecurity and native resentment. As the bulk of profits from the economies were still being expropriated, there was neither the growth of wealth among the locals nor the building of state tax-base resources needed to further develop needed infrastructure (Chamberlain 1999; Hargreaves 1988; Nzongola-Ntalaja 2002).

Underdeveloped and overly controlled by foreign investment, local peoples and institutions had difficultly reaping the rewards of even a functional economy. Even where certain economic sectors (be they agrarian, mineral, or industrial) were healthy, the ability of these revenues to be spread through the entire population was highly problematic. Local areas benefited strongly, but their economic health often stood in contrast to other provinces or regions without such a resource base. Such cases typically could be traced back to colonial authorities' preferential treatment of one geographic area wherein monies and a strong economic foundation were seeded in a regionalized area at the expense of other regions within the country (e.g., Uganda). In other cases, economic collapse can be precipitated by ecological factors including desertification and long periods of drought bringing additional hardships and tensions to bear on an already tumultuous economic situation (e.g., Darfur).

In some cases, former colonies did not have the power to control their own currency values. This was especially true in former French holdings, where "France kept control of the national currency, by means of banking operations and the so-called 'colonial franc' tied to the French franc" (Davidson 1994: 226). As independence grew, these colonial economic polices were reinforced by the IMF, which continued to "peg" African currencies to European currencies as a way, in their eyes, to stabilize the value of the money. Yet, this made the overall values of a given state's economy a byproduct of a European economy. Political sovereignty had been provided in the decampment periods, but economic independence was withheld. For example, in Senegal, this prevented the formation of a robust indigenous economy, especially when the debt repayment demands of the World Bank and IMF became more severe (see Rothe, Muzzatti, and Mullins 2006).

What was necessary within Africa was the development of favorable terms of trade between former colonies and the West. Specifically, import prices needed to be low and export prices high to rectify trade imbalances and develop economic institutions. This has yet to happen. "Africa's economic product is only 1% of world product and its share of the later has been in decline for some time" (Herbst and Mills 2003: 29). Rather, most countries have turned to international institutions of finance to build infrastructure and/or for short-term aid in the face of economic crisis. Although such arrangements do provide essential capital infusions, they often come at a high price. "In 1985, Africa's total foreign debt exceeded double the value of all of its export earnings; in 1987 it exceeded three times the value of its export earnings" (Davidson 1994: 241). The IMF insists on governments tightening their belts, demanding that they devalue their currency, spend less on social welfare, abandon development projects, remove trade barriers (namely import tariffs), and open state holdings to foreign investors.

Rothe, Muzzatti, and Mullins (2006) showed how the IMF's and WB's economic policies led to state crime in Senegal surrounding the sinking of the ferry *Le Joola*. Under the imposed structural adjustment policies, the government was forced to reduce expenditures on social and other infrastructure aspects. This included a reduction of maintenance expenditures for its navy. Due to imposed spending mandates, the Sudanese government kept *Le Joola* in service despite its outdated nature and its inability to provide proper maintenance on the vessel. The engines did not work at full power and there were not ample life-saving technologies on board (e.g., life boats). Further, since the number of ferries that the navy could afford to keep running was limited, the ship often took to the seas with far more than the maximum passenger and cargo load. Due to low pay of the crew, all safety and cargo regulations were not followed, leading to the ship's cargo not being properly secured. Although the Senegalese government took full responsibility for the negligence that led to the sinking of the ferry, the lack of appropriate funds was a result of the structural adjustment policies, not any innate corruption or ill will on behalf of the government.

This is not the only example of negative consequences arising out of the operational status quo of the IMF and WB (see Friedrichs and Friedrichs 2002, for a similar case in Thailand). These exploitative conditions of debt repayment play a role in encouraging militias to engage in illegal mineral expropriation and exportation. For example, Liberia, Sierra Leone, and the Democratic Republic of Congo (DRC) have all experienced civil wars that intensified and were prolonged as various factions continued to fight over control of mineral deposits. The mineral-rich northeast of DRC was a strong factor in the international involvement of Rwanda, Uganda, and others in Congolese wars. According to Le Billion (2005: 45) "the ability of belligerents to draw on private financial flows decreases the potential level of multilateral agencies ... exercised through grants and loans." As local states gain more economic power, through legal or illegal export industries, they not only gain economic growth that can alleviate financial pressures within their own society, but such revenues can also lead international institutions of finance to reassess the overall economic health of a state, providing greater access to development funds or to qualify for debt relief programs. As we explore in Chapter Five, this is precisely how Uganda achieved its preferred-lender status in the eyes of the IMF and WB, via the illegal exportation of Congolese gold.

Political Orders

As European powers loosened and cut their ties with their former colonies, the ideal of democratization was pushed by a number of stakeholding populations. Being democratic themselves, most former colonial powers pushed for the creation of parliamentary systems. The international community, especially as embodied by the UN, held the same view. Since the early political leaders in most of the new nation-states were locals who had obtained European-style university education, they too pushed for pluralistic political structures. In the countries we examine in this volume (as well as many others throughout the continent), these early governments failed. Most often, they fell victim to a military-led insurgency.

Military coups d'etat are all too common features of central Africa during the later portion of the twentieth century. Whether instigated as a response to a corrupt régime, ethnic hostility and disenfranchisement, or driven by a powerful charismatic leader, these movements typically produced a one-party state under the control of a single, populist leader and his coquetry of kin and allies. The dictators and their group of social elite allies often see the state as a personal source of wealth and comfort. "During periods of relative calm, conflict has tended to mutate back into more institutionalized forms of corruption" (Keen 2001: 4). Often, these coups were initially welcomed by citizenry as they brought stability and socioeconomic order. Yet, in most cases, these regimes became thoroughly corrupt and violent toward resistance in the population. For example, the reigns of Mobutu Sese Seko in the Congo (which he renamed Zaire), Milton Obote and Idi Amin in Uganda, and Charles Taylor in Liberia were all characterized by the use of the nation's resource reserves as personal enrichment enterprises for the sociopolitical elites. Harsh programs of disappearances, extralegal executions, and other crimes against humanity were par for the course in these administrations. The violence and corruption of such regimes ultimately led to their own deposal by subsequent coups that typically then set up their own one-party state. These policies heightened the pervasive social disorder and chaos, often in the form of militia movements and civil wars.

Such internecine wars too frequently become international affairs as opposition groups that initially fled the coup, found safe haven in neighboring countries where they may have ethnic, linguistic, or political ties. Given aid, training, arms, and frequently supported by the harboring state's army, the refugee military forces reorganize, plan, and eventually execute an invasion (e.g., Rwandan Tutsi refugees; Museveni and the NRA). Foreign powers often assist these groups directly or indirectly for several reasons (e.g., Sudan's support of the LRA). First, they may be just as apprehensive of the dictator as the refugee army is. If a leader uses systemic violence against his/her own citizens, what promise can be made to satisfy a neighbor that the sovereignty of a shared border will be honored? Second, due to the arbitrary nature of colonial territorial lines, and their reinforcement in the postcolonial period, the neighboring power may have strong ethnic or other cultural ties to the refuge population. Such connections often provide encouragement to get involved with a neighbor's internecine struggles. Third, backing an insurgent group if successful can bring territorial or other natural resources or trade access for the abetting party. For example, Rwanda and Uganda both invaded the DRC, in part to obtain control over mineral-rich areas of the DRC's northeastern territories.

In many of the situations, even though the new nation-states were nominally independent, the former colonizers played large roles in establishing the structure of the new governments. In East Africa, specifically Uganda and Tanganyika, for example, reluctant to simply walk away, the UK molded the governmental forms as they took shape. Unlike the other states, there was a history of colonial de-evolution in certain segments of the British Empire. It had lost holdings to revolutions and, for some territories, had created the idea of a commonwealth that would provide self-rule for certain territories yet still keep the peoples "in the fold" as UK citizens. When faced with African decolonization in the eastern part of the continent, the UK took steps to structure the transition but in doing so sought to make the process very conservative. Their goal was not full liberation but an attempt to protect the status quo of extant socioeconomic interests:

> Constitutional draftsman applie[d] their principles of partnership through a political arithmetic which gave … [more] weight to … subjective assessment of what the 3 main racial groups would offer infant nations. Europeans would bring scientific and technological expertise and mature political wisdom, Asian commercial entrepreneurs and lesser technical skills; Africans had … their labor. (Hargreaves 1988: 73)

Thus the "new" order would look like the old both socially and economically. The indigenous peoples would receive no real benefit under the plans.

Ethnic Identity Formation and Crystallization

During the precolonial period, Africa was highly ethnically diverse. There was also a huge variety among intergroup interactions, running the gambit from general suspicion and tension through warfare and enslavement, avoidance, peaceful trade, to interethnic interpersonal relationships. In many colonial environments, dominating powers were either indifferent to this difference or manufactured identities. Africans were Africans and variant cultural and social patterns were unimportant. What mattered was that all of the peoples in an area adhered to the new colonial pattern. However, in many regions, the imperial power implemented its new social order by selecting, if not outright creating, "favored" groups. Whether because they were conveniently located, submissive to the new régime, or viewed as racially and intellectually superior than their counterparts, members received real benefits compared to their neighbors. Their new positions provided them with better jobs, living conditions, educational opportunities, and access to a wealth of social resources. By elevating certain ethnic groups over others, lines that were previously nonexistent or blurred were brought into sharp relief and given solidity. Political and economic competition and resentment began to simmer; even previously peaceful relations could easily deteriorate into open or latent hostility due to the new resource distributions. In the postcolonial environment, while the overarching rule that had created the divisions (or at least intensified them) was gone, the on-the-ground differences in life chances and experiences remained. Resentments and outright hostilities often came to the surface as subordinate peoples demanded position in the new social order, and those who had been privileged under colonial rule sought to maintain and extend their positions of advantage.

Following the principles internalized during their European educations, many of the new African leaders attempted to develop state-specific nationalisms. Often, leaders or would-be leaders needed to crystallize a power base. Discourses that drew strong lines between insiders and outsiders are fairly common elements in this process. Initially, much of this rhetoric was focused on differentiating between colonizers and the colonized. Local populations were presented as having the essential rights to political and economic capital sources that had been stolen and co-opted by European invaders. Yet, that approach could only go so far in uniting the population. Although such a vision did generate social solidarity, it did nothing to erase the on-the-ground differences between local populations. Such differential access to a variety of social resources was often the product of a number of factors, including urban versus rural, geographic proximity to political capitals or major ports, and the nature of colonial relations with various regional and ethnic populations.

These disparities were not solved with pro-African or other specifically nationalistic discourses, and tensions between populations remained. This led some leaders to further highlight preexisting differences or attempt to construct them out of whole cloth. In the short term, these processes could garner the support of a more numerous or a more socially empowered population, but at the cost of disenfranchising other segments of the population. Often, these otherizing discourses became amplified once they had taken strong root. Continued differential treatment of subgroups became self-rationalizing; simultaneously creating more anomic tension within the targeted group and legitimating this treatment in the eyes of the empowered group. Consequently, the drive to resist increasing inequity grew stronger among less-advantaged populations while increasing the possibility that empowered groups would use social or physical violence to maintain the status quo. We are not suggesting that the internecine conflicts were purely the product of symbolic discourses of divisiveness; resource distribution, colonial tensions, and regional conflicts all play a role in the collapse of states and the associated war crimes and crimes against humanity. Yet, this cognitive divide between "true citizens" and "interlopers"—be they European or African, intensified the effects that these other macro conditions have as well as facilitating the said crimes.

Real or constructed, this ethnic hostility served to develop and intensify the internecine conflicts and undergird the crimes that are the subject of our study. Not only did it create indigenous justifications and worldviews that motivated and structured atrocities, it allowed the international community a convenient set of neutralizations for ignoring these situations. This created a space devoid of social control and this "[i]nternational confusion and pessimism in the face of 'intractable, ancient ethnic hatred' or 'irrational rebels' allow[ed] for planning and carrying out human rights abuses with minimal international repercussions" (Keen 2001: 6). Foreign powers saw these wars as "civil wars" and "internal matters" to the given state, getting involved only when it met their broader geopolitical goals (see especially Chapter Six and the relationship between the US and Mobutu Sese Seko). The 1990s in particular showed the dangerousness of such a view. Both in Rwanda (see Chapter Four) as well as the former Yugoslavia, genocidal programs were carried out as the world stood by and watched, unwilling to intervene in a complex scenario of events and conflicts until it was far too late to do anything meaningful.

The Social Context and Typical Elements of the Crimes

We now turn to a broad overview of the general social conditions that have produced widespread atrocities in the region and the most typical forms and elements these crimes take. Civil wars, genocides, and crimes against humanity do not merely appear; they are produced by a complex intersection of social, political, economic, and cultural factors in a specific time and place. To fully understand the etiology of these phenomena, we must thoroughly understand the broader structural contexts out of which they emerge and the basic forms that these events take. In this final section, we examine the structural commonalities of central African nations that developed into internecine conflicts producing the crimes of interest to this volume. We then lay out a modus operandi, if you will, of the typical elements with these widescale criminal events. This is not to say that these are the complete etiological and enactment factors, as we noted, each case is unique within a specific time-space milieu.

Social Disorder

Many of these newly formed states entered the world community with underdeveloped and ill-functioning social institutions and patterns of social organization. With indigenous lifeways either subordinated or destroyed during colonization and many aspects of the colonial order dismantled, newly independent peoples were confronted with having to rebuild a meaningful social order from the ground up, often with little to build upon. Political institutions simply have not been stable save under one-party states ruling through fear and force. Such states often strongly benefit only a portion of the population; the nature and direction of control and stability is typically in the direction desired by the ruling elite. As long as the charismatic leader can control the military and structures of political authority, there is a veneer of stability and order. Yet, by these very policies, the seeds of discontent and insurrection are often sown by the processes that bring temporary stability. As a consequence of the nature of a one-party state as well as the Western colonial model, many state actors became quickly corrupt, using the nations' resources for their personal gain and that of their kin and allies (e.g., Amin in Uganda, Habyarimana in Rwanda). The recent history of African political conflicts is filled not only with coups d'etat, but countercoups designed to remove despots from power. These wars frequently become international affairs as opposition groups that initially fled the coup found safe haven in neighboring counties where they may have ethnic or linguistic ties. Given aid, training, arms, and frequently supported by the harboring state's army, the refugee military forces reorganize, plan, and eventually execute an invasion—continuing the violence and disorder, often with the deposed power then reforming as a militia or rebel force to continue to plague their usurpers (e.g., Uganda and the DRC).

Domestic economies and markets have been profoundly unstable in the postcolonial environment, an instability amplified by the instability of international commodity markets. As postcolonial African economies are dependent upon export economies, fluctuations or collapses in specific commodity markets can have drastic effects. For example, Rwanda suffered substantially due to the collapse of coffee markets. Compared to Western, and many Asian, economies, central African economies are less diversified, which amplifies the influence of the drop in value of a given product on the economy as a whole. Further, transnational corporations are often directly involved in black-market and/or illegal export and importing of state resources. As Human Rights Watch and the UN have reported, numerous transnational corporations have traveled to the Ituri region of the DRC to directly negotiate with warlords controlling the mines. From there, agreements are reached to transport the minerals across the border into Uganda, which then exports the minerals typically in the European markets and exchanges. Particularly, these strategies take advantage of the Swiss freeport system, which allows for the open and anonymous importation and sale of commodities from around the globe. Such activities exasperate the already tumultuous economic conditions of states.

Ethnic Tensions and Divisiveness

A central element within these atrocity-producing environments are a set of intense ethnic rivalries and tensions often—at least in the contemporary postcolonial environment—focused on resource access, be it political, social, or economic. Despite the way in which these issues are typically covered in the media as long-standing, precolonial disputes (e.g., media coverage of Rwanda and Darfur), many of these countries did *not* begin their postcolonial experiences with deep divisions built along tribal or ethnic lines. Although colonizers in many cases (e.g., Rwanda and Burundi) drew arbitrary divisions among peoples and reinforced those splits via their political and economic policies, at the moment of liberation these tensions were rarely forefront in the society.

In the period leading up to the civil wars, and the associated crimes, political parties often played up these tensions in order to create a power base both within the governments and within the citizenry. Due to long periods of colonial domination, there were few natural lines along which political parties could be formed and fewer preexisting bases of political power for a party to mobilize. In fact, the most "natural" divisions leading to party formation in newly democratic states was geographic in nature and rooted in the existing resource base (be those resources mineral, agricultural, or human capitals). Although there was some general correspondence between peoples and territories, these early geographic divisions often cut across ethnic lines. The result was a political scene with dozens of parties possessing unarticulated goals, visions, and motives. While all wanted a share of the new political power, a lack of general political drives, positions, and ideologies produced hosts of parties indistinguishable from each other save by name. Such political hyperplurality produced more disorganization than organization; many of these new governments were dissolved in coup d'etat that established one-party states, that often began to exacerbate the increasingly important ethnic divides. To maintain power, leaders often began to generate public discourses of racial and ethnic differences and exclusion. Ethnicity became a political tool to stabilize a government and as these states weakened under their own weight of corruption, ignorance, and inefficiency, ethnicity became a polarizing force dividing the societies as they moved toward violent civil wars.

Overpowering ethnic identity is central in our analyses in this volume. Scholars of genocides and other war crimes have long pointed toward the "otherizing" effects of ethnic polarization and dehumanization as facilitating violence in general and widespread lethal violence in particular. Just as colonial powers dehumanized the peoples of Africa to legitimate colonial domination, ethnic groups dehumanized each other facilitating political and economic subordination as well as wanton violence and destruction (e.g., Rwandan Hutus). Such divisions operate on the micro level to facilitate the widespread abuse and slaughter of targeted peoples. In ethnic-otherizing processes the humanity is removed from the targeted group that in turn facilitates and legitimates violence against them. At the meso level, ethnic polarization serves as a bond of solidarity for militia formation and continuation. Simply, it is a symbolic identity that draws recruits and rallies members around a common cause that is inter alia violent. At the international level the discourse serves to negate the responsibility of political and social authorities for creating, stimulating, and continuing the conflict. Once framed as a tension existing from deep in history or tied to the colonial period of a country, the standing government, which often encourages such tension for its own purposes, can reduce its perceived responsibility and professed ability to control the violence.

Summary

This chapter provided a historical, social, political, and economic context with which to understand the nature, distribution, and social forces behind war crimes, crimes against humanity and other state crime within postcolonial Africa. The countries we analyze in this book have experienced a scale of social disorganization, reorganization, and failure the likes of which the world rarely sees. From the utter domination of the colonial period to the international market's attempts to resubordinate them in the postcolonial era, it has been centuries since African peoples and their societies have possessed anything near self-determination. Yet, in and of itself, this is not a necessary condition for widespread state criminality and collapse. Essentially every African territory experienced colonialism and postcolonial reorganization; not all degenerated into single party states and vicious civil wars. Even fewer have produced the war crimes and crimes against humanity that are our core focus here. Thus, our individual case studies, as well as broader examination of macro-level forces across states in the region will have to identify and distinguish causal and influential aspects that allow us to better understand the nature of our topic. From here, we now turn to our first case, 1994 Genocide in Rwanda.

· 4 ·

CUTTING THE TALL TREES

For months during the spring and summer of 1994, Rwandan Tutsis, and many of their Hutu friends and family, lived in abject terror as the *Interhawme* and regular citizens slaughtered hundreds of thousands of their fellow citizens. Beginning on the night of 6 April, gangs of armed men went from door to door raping and killing those they referred to as *Inyenzi* (cockroaches). Calls to slaughter aired on national radio stations, barely coded in phrases like, "It is time to cut the tall trees," a reference to the Tutsi's being generally taller than their Hutu counterparts. The world, well aware of what was happening, did nothing until June.

The genocide did not occur in a vacuum. Nor did it materialize out of whole cloth. To understand how it occurred, we must explore the structural, political, religious, and economic history of Rwanda. As such, we have divided this chapter into three main sections. We begin with situating Rwanda in a historical context, under precolonial, colonial, and postcolonial rule including the events leading up to the genocide. From there, we provide a detailed discussion of the events in the genocide. Yet the roots of the genocide began decades before the actual violence in the spring of 1994. To establish the context of these killings, we first turn toward the colonial history of Rwanda.

The Historical Context

Precolonialization

Prior to the first European expedition to the regions now called Rwanda and Burundi, the indigenous population was linguistically and culturally homogenous with no Hutuland or Tutsiland. The only differences between the populations were physical attributes and differing means of subsistence. The "Hutu," the vast majority of the population, were peasants who cultivated land and had a body type much like the Ugandans. The Mutwa, only about 1% of the population, were pygmy hunter-gatherers, and the Tutsis, who were by nature very tall and thin, were predominantly cattle herders.

Given the obsessive preoccupation with creating "scientific" racial categories of the late 1800s, these physical differences led to a lot of theorizing and romanticizing of the three groups that inevitably led to the eventual politicalization of "racial" differences and preferential treatment under colonial rule (Prunier 1995). In addition, the anthropological and exploratory writings of this time period depicting "scientific" racial categories conditioned the views and attitudes of the Europeans that would come to govern the decisions made by the Germans and Belgians toward the population of Rwanda during colonial rule. Of course, this ignored the fact that intermarriage between groups was common and any social classification that was present did not play a significant role in Rwanda. Clans (*ubwoko*), consisted of members that were Tutsi, Hutu, and Mutwa.

Prior to colonialization, Rwanda had undergone some political changes, mainly the extension of the ruling King's power, Kigelie IV Rwabugiri, though his control did not cover the entire regions of Rwanda. There were Hutu principalities in the north, northwest, and southwest of the state (Prunier 2005). However, as the King's power came to be more centralized, divisions of the population were made. Yet, they were not based on Hutu or Tutsis instead they were based on the center versus periphery.[1] As such, marginalization and abuse of power was hailed upon both Tutsi and Hutu, defined by their geographic location not pseudo scientific racial divisions. It was not until the death of Kigelie IV Rwabugiri, which created significant internal political turbulence, and the timely arrival of the first colonizers that any divisions based on physical characteristics occurred.

The Onset of Colonialization

The arrival of the Germans in Rwanda (1897–1916) had a minor impact in comparison to later Belgian rule. Having a light presence, in 1914 there were only 96 Europeans including the missionaries (Prunier 1995: 25), the Germans used indirect rule and allowed the political exploitation of their intervention by the newly formed central state as a means to advance their colonial goals. As such, they inadvertently reinforced and supported the use of the existing chiefly hierarchy and royal court which continued to undergo political turmoil following the death of Kigelie IV Rwabugiri. The German presence supported and continued the precolonial transformation towards a centralized state and the assimilation and annex of the Hutu principalities. In the wake of World War I, the responsibility for administering colonial rule in Rwanda was given to Belgium under the League of Nation's Mandate system.

The Belgian began their colonial control in 1919. Unlike the German occupation, Rwanda was seen as a significant and a valued part of the growing colonial empire. However, the early years of conquest were spent with a hands-off or indirect manner. The progressive implementation of colonial rule did not begin until 1926 (Prunier 1995). From 1926 until 1931 several measures were undertaken that altered the relations and divisions of the population. These policies were heavily influenced by Bishop Classe's advice. In a 1927 letter to the Belgian government:

> The greatest mistake this government could make would be to suppress the Mututsi caste. Such a revolution would lead the country directly to anarchy and to hateful anti-European communism. … We will have no better, more active and more intelligent chiefs than the Batutsi. They are the ones best suited to understand progress. … The government must work with them. (Quoted in Prunier 1995: 26)

Ignoring the first part of Classe's advice, the Belgians replaced Hutu chiefs with Tutsis, giving them near total domination of political structures. By the end of Belgian rule in 1959, 43 out of 45 chiefs and 549 subchiefs out of 559 were Tutsi. The system of taxes and public interest work was redesigned under colonial conquest. Previously this had been called "Corve'e." This included a forced labor system wherein individual obligation overtook the previous system of family obligation to the government. Instead of one family member fulfilling the obligation for the whole, every male, and many women and children owed service. Between 1920 and 1940 the burden of taxation and forced labor resulted in a manpower exodus for the British colonies, including Uganda, where there was plenty of work.

The Tutsi's preferential treatment allowed them, with Belgian support, to modify existing land control rights. The land, no longer recognized as undivided *usufruct* tracts by lineage groups belonging to collectivity, were considered vacant and the state took the right to dispose of them as they saw fit with little compensation. As such, the state, mainly Tutsi, gained control of the traditional landholdings including the Hutu northwest and southwest areas that had remained to some degree separate principalities. This included privatizing grazing lands leading to the altering of previous practices of *ubuhake* contracts: a new synthetic policy developed by colonial Tutsi chiefs under Belgian sponsorship. This would lead to much hostility and retaliation during the 1959 revolution. It was also reflective of the colonial policies representing forced integration into the ideology of western capitalism—individualism and privatization.

Such a move changed the socioeconomic practice of Rwanda replacing the traditional Rwandese society. The reorganization of the Rwandese society was perhaps finalized by the Belgians with the removal of then King Yuhi V Musinga and replacing him with his son Mutara III Rudahigwa in 1931 (Prunier 1995). The core drive behind the coup was Musinga's unwillingness to convert to Christianity; his son was seen as an easy convert to Catholicism and malleable for Belgian control. With the removal of King Musinga, came the consecration of ethnic segregation by the Belgian authorities. This included a system of identity cards put in place in 1933, legally forcing individuals to claim an ethnic/racial group: Hutu, Tutsi, or Twa. Cattle ownership was central to this process; if one owned 10 cattle or more they were a Tutsi. Unless clearly a member of the pygmy Twa, all others were Hutu. This constructed identity created an irreparable cleavage in Rwandan society (Berry and Berry 1999).

The King was viewed by Belgian authorities as more malleable to their policies and was forced to adapt to the colonial system and to the demands of the ever growing institutionalization of the church into every sphere of Rwandan life. In 1946 he consecrated Rwanda to Christ the King. While conversion in the general population was slow, the population saw that conversion was a prerequisite to becoming a member of the ruling elite. A wave of elite conversions took over pleasing the missionaries. As such, growing numbers of Tutsi continued to join the church and it's mission to rid Rwanda of 'pagan' policies and practices (e.g., polygamy and adultery). This strengthened the role of religion and religious interests in the Belgian reorganization of the state and a growing change in Rwandese cultural beliefs. This also ended the underlying thoughts of promoting Hutu into positions of ruling that was once considered by Classe and others when relatively few Tutsi were willing to convert to Christianity.

By 1932, the church had become Rwanda's main institution presiding over converts including the colonially chosen King. The church also had the monopoly on education. Tutsis were given priority in education—ensuring the church played a central role in developing the future elite. The goal of Christianity and Rwandese education was made clear two decades earlier by Catholic missionary, R.P. Loupias when he stated: "We will not have any scholars, but will be largely satisfied if, through schooling, we are able to train an enlightened Christian elite who will pass on the faith to those around them" (Erny 1981: 55).

For the Hutu to stand a chance at education they had to become theology students; their lack of formal education lead to a lack of employment opportunities. However, as more Hutu's were tracked to seminar schools their growing numbers increased their presence in the church ranks, eventually leading to a growing discomfort among the soon to be minority white clerics and subsequent changing church attitude from supporting the elite Tutsis to aiding the Hutu. This, along with the churches changing social approach after World War II, was a significant factor in the upcoming 1959 revolution. Perhaps as significant, the Hutu extremists' movement that mobilized the masses to violence was birthed in the Catholic Center at Kabgaye, the residence of Monsignor Perraudin a Swiss Bishop that arrived in Rwanda during the mid-1950 (Research Center on Socio-Political Information in Brussels 1960). The role that the Catholic Church and Bishop Perraudin played in the 1959 revolution, and more importantly the 1994 genocide, was recognized in a statement on April 17, 1994 by Monsignor Perraudin when he was asked about his silence and complicity during the 1994 genocide. He stated that he "condemns but understands," condemning because of his Christian beliefs, but understanding because he played a role in the process of the institutionalization of ethnic divisions and aiding the spread of Hutu propaganda during the late 1950's (Berry and Berry 1999: 37).

Administrators, priests, Belgian officials, government anthropologists, and missionaries all contributed to a changed Rwanda; one dominated by the Tutsi. This was cemented by the 1952 decree that created "elective councils" at every administrative level based on nominations, over public election. This system enhanced the power of the Tutsi elite (Prunier 1995: 38). This also led to colonial fears of a real challenge of their authority by the once 'favored' Tutsi. The racialization of consciousness affected the population as a whole, including the nonelite Tutsi whom did not benefit from the larger policies that generated favoritism. They too internalized this ideology of superiority, creating an additional rift between fellow Hutu neighbors and/or relatives. This was further reinforced by the identification card system that forced the population to self-identify with a contrived racial construct. Between the white foreigners' actions, policies and beliefs, pseudo scientific racial and culturally constructed groups, myths became reified into a reality: the real Rwanda.

In March of 1957, a group of nine Hutu published a pamphlet called the *Notes on the Social Aspect of the Racial Native Problem in Rwanda* hoping to influence the arriving United Nations trusteeship mission. This article came to be called the Hutu Manifesto and read in part:

> The problem is basically that of the political monopoly of one race, the Mututsi. In the present circumstances, this political monopoly is turned into an economic and social monopoly ... and given the de facto selection in school, the political, economic and social monopolies turn into a cultural monopoly which condemns the desperate Bahutu to be for ever subaltern workers. ... In order to monitor this race monopoly we are strongly opposed to removing the labels Mututsi, Muhutu, and Mutwa from identity papers. Their suppression would create a risk of preventing the statistical law from establishing reality of facts. (Quoted in Prunier 1995: 46)

The use of the term race is a significant key representing the product of years of European claims-making of racial identities including a superior race, the Tutsi. This statistical information would become a tool for setting guidelines and as a monitor of democratization (quota democracy) for the soon to be independent Rwanda.

Other factors would quickly lead to the 1959 revolution. This included the decree of 1958 made by the Court Notables banning fraternity between Hutu and Tutsi. This led to mass political rivalry and enhanced the growing roots of deeply seeded racism. At the same time political parties were quickly forming. They included: the Hutu Social Movement (MSM). later the Democratic Rwandese Movement/Party of the Movement and Hutu Emancipation (MDR-PARHEMUTU); the Association for the Social Promotion of the Masses (APROSOMA); and the Rwandese National Unity (UNAR a conservative Tutsi political party). The UNAR was hostile to the Belgian rule, wanting political power and control to maintain the Tutsi elite status. As such, it was supported by the growing cold war communist countries. This furthered the growing concern of the Belgian colonizers. As stated by Harroy, the Vice Governor General, in his memoirs:

> From then on, the unspoken agreement of 1920 with the Tutsi ruling caste in order to further economic development was allowed to collapse. ... The administrations was forced to toughen its attitudes when faced with such obstruction and hostility coming from chiefs and subchiefs with whom we had collaborated for so many years. (Quoted in Prunier 1995: 48)

To counter the conservative Tutsi political party the Belgians supported the creation of the Rwandese Democratic Union (RADAR). Though they were scrutinized as the political party of the colonizers and made up of more liberal and marginalized Tutsi, the party did not stand a chance in the realpolitiks of Rwandan political affairs. At this point social and political tensions were running very high and the conditions were ripe for a violent societal shift.

The 1959 Revolution and Rise of the Hutu Republic

On 1 November 1959, Dominique Mbonyumutwa, a Hutu subchief and PARMRHUTU activists, one of the few Hutu in a symbolic political position, was attacked by members of the UNAR. False reports spread that he was murdered and Hutu activists began to retaliate by attacking Tutsi chiefs and other known UNAR members. General fighting followed and many Tutsi homes were burnt without recognizing the differences that were truly created of the elite Tutsi and the rest of the population. As such, even the peasant Tutsis were targeted. The UNAR retaliated by organizing commandos to attack the Hutu, especially APROSOMA members as they were perceived as the most dangerous to the positions existing of political power (Prunier 1995).

As we discussed, by this time the Belgian authorities had shifted their support to the Hutu, as did the clergy, thereby ensuring their authority against the rising and demanding Tutsi elites. Feeling betrayed by the Tutsis, the colonial authorities explicitly supported a 'social revolution' that was advised against back in 1912 by Classe. Rather than an outright social revolution, the violence was more an ethnic transfer of power. Nonetheless, these differences were more symbolical than real. For example, in the mid 1950's a survey of incomes revealed a relative economic balance between groups: Tutsis with 287 households had an average income of 4,439; Hutus with 914 families had an average income of 4,249. Of course, with any use of statistical means, such closeness can be from a majority of the Tutsis and Hutu having a low income with a minority of elites having higher holdings, thus balancing the mean close to each other (there is no available record on the median incomes). The fight then was between the elite Tutsi and growing group of elite Hutu (Prunier 1995). Nonetheless, the poor Tutsi and Hutu stood by their elites due to their internalization of the constructed racial ideologies.

Belgium was loosing control of the situation; as such they launched the notion of self-government in November of 1959. To do so would require that they formally take sides in the ongoing civil unrest and violence. The colonial powers began replacing most of the Tutsi chiefs with Hutu. When this occurred the new Hutu chiefs organized a persecution of the Tutsis on the hills they now controlled, especially in the areas that once were Hutu principalities. This started a massive flow of refugees, nearly 130,000, to the Congo, Burundi, and Uganda. he complicit role that Belgium played in the revolution was noted by the Report of the International Commission of Inquiry (ICIR), November 1959:

> The Belgian authorities exercised a decisive impact on the evolution of the unrest. ... In certain chiefdoms in the north Rwanda, practically no Tutsi household was saved. The repression organized by the Tutsi leadership was quickly suppressed by military action undertaken by the Belgian government. (ICIR 1960: 1)

By midsummer 1960, the Belgians organized communal elections despite the ongoing violence and insecurity. With conditions as they were and the majority of the population being Hutu, the PARMEHUTU won with 2,390 out of 3,125 votes (Prunier 1995: 51). Colonel Logiest, detached to Rwanda in 1959 by General Janssens from the Congoloese Public Force, declared in October 1960, "the revolutions over." However, the reality on the ground suggested the violence was far from over. Additionally, the UN Trusteeship Commission was displeased with the situation, in part as a result of the growing incorporation of other "third" world states and the position that colonialism was starting to be questioned and delegitimized. Then Secretary General of the UN, General Dag Hammarksjold was against the Belgian rule and agreed with the UN to give its support to the Tutsi party. As such a UN Resolution was passed that directly challenged the policies carried out by the Belgians since November of 1959. In reaction to this, Logiest and Gregoire Kayibanda, originator of the PARAMEHUTU political group, arranged a legal coup to halt any further tinkering of Rwanda's political and social situation by the UN.

On 28 January 1961 the sovereign Democratic Republic of Rwanda was declared. It was seen by Logiest as the consecration of the 1959 revolution and an overall victory for Rwanda (Logiest 1988: 199). The UN had to reconcile this independence of a territory that had been at least theoretically placed under its mandate and the Belgians no longer had the authority or legal responsibility for the continuing acts of violence. However, Tutsi houses continued to be burnt and within a few more months over 22,000 more people were displaced.

In September 1961 legislative elections were held and the PARMEHUTU again kept the majority of votes; Kayibanda became the official president of Rwanda. The UN responded after the elections with:

> The development of these last eighteen months have brought about the racial dictatorship of one party ... An oppressive system has been replaced by another one. ... It is possible that some day we will witness violent reactions on the part of the Tutsi. (UN Trusteeship Commission Report March 1961)

The prophetic words of the Commission were accurate, however, it was not a matter of someday—the early stages of planning were already underway. Small groups of exiled Tutsis, referred to as *Inyenzi* (cockroaches) by the Hutu, had already begun to stage counterattacks from Uganda.

Postcolonial rule: 1962 to 1973

Rwanda formally gained its independence on 1 July 1962. The political strife was far from over. Exiled groups, while holding different ideological and political goals, continued to carry on even after independence, each faring differently dependent on their hosting country. At this point there were approximately 50,000 refugees in Burundi, the home of exiles that were attacking Rwanda, and thousands more in the Congo, who aligned themselves with the Movement National Congolese (MNC) rebels during the civil war that lasted until 1964 (Prunier 1995). Exiles in Uganda were kept under tight control as they were personally supported by King Mutesa II making them automatic opponents to and the recipients of hostility from Prime Minister Obote (Lukawgo 1982). It is this latter group that undertook a desperate insurgency attempt from Burundi, invading Bugesera, however, they were beaten back by a massive wave of repression in which 10,000 more Tutsis were slaughtered in December 1963 and January 1964.

Since independence, relations with the former colonial powers and donors became exceedingly complex. Ethnic segregation prevailed in the various 'military', 'human rights' and 'macro-economic' interventions undertaken from the outset of the civil war in 1990. Intergroup divisions were continuously reified within Rwanda under President Kayibanda including the belief in the 'intrinsic' worth of being a Hutu. As Prunier (1995: 59) notes, "An egalitarian racial ideology buttressed an elitist and secretive authoritarian government" which created a false land of virtue not far removed from those of the colonial powers wherein attendance at mass was routine and peasants worked the land while asking no questions. Censorship of the population came in from two sources, the triumphant Catholic Church and the government. Viewed as the *mwami* of the Hutu, Kayibanda ruled with an authoritarianism and secretiveness similarly to what Jean-Jacques Maquet (1961: 186–187) suggested was the old kings authority and leadership approach, "When the ruler gives an order, he must be obeyed, not because his order falls into the sphere over which he has authority, but simply because he is the ruler." Kayibanda was also responsible for all appointments and nominations throughout his administration. This along with the cultural ethos of unquestioned obedience to authority would play a key role in the 1994 genocide.

Rwanda followed a policy of ethnic quotas. While politically and ideally this was to rectify the imbalance of Tutsi rule created by the colonial powers, it instead fed into the growing ideology of Hutu supremacy and subjugation of the Tutsis. There was officially 9% of the population listed as Tutsi. Under the quota system, it followed that only 9% of the student population, clerks in civil service, or any other sector of employment could be Tutsis (Chretien 1912). During the early 1970's vigilante groups were organized to make sure the quota system was being 'respected'. This ensured the Hutu would benefit from removing 'extra' Tutsis out of their jobs, especially those of higher status or political positions. The economic effects, psychological imprint, sporadic violence, the reified Hutu supremacy ideology, and disturbances from the vigilante quota groups triggered additional immigration of Tutsis during 1972 and 1973. Estimates suggest that between 1959 and 1973, 700,000 refugees fled political persecution (Prunier 1995).

The Habyarimana Regime: 1974–93

On 5 July 1973, a coup headed by Major-General Habyarimana, resulted in a new set of political actors, though regime policies changed little. The political immobility and regionalist fighting that had escalated under the Kayibanda regime had driven the elite into complete and utter frustration. Additionally, the politically motivated move towards Tutsi persecutions brought fear to the Tutsi community and many of the general Hutu population. As such, Habyarimana's coup was met with little resistance, and perhaps some relief among the general population. No significant changes were occurring during this time—Rwanda was as stable as it would be at least for the next few years. The Habyarimana military regime was kept tightly closed with no Tutsi representatives; this exclusion went as far as creating regulations prohibiting marriage of a Tutsi woman by any [Hutu] armed service personal. The prevailing segregation rules that permeated throughout Rwanda was not just carried out by the regime. Even foreign aid workers, NGO's and businesses that employed Tutsis discreetly obeyed the ethnic and regional divisions without sending any alarms outside as to the internal conditions (Berry and Berry 1999).

Immediately after seizing the reigns of political power, Habyarimana outlawed all political parties, though the following year he created his own: The Movement Revolutionnaire National pour le Developpment (MRND). This was later enshrined in the Constitution with Article 7: a state based on a single party system (Le Monde 1982). All citizens were required to be a member not unlike all other totalitarian regimes. Additionally, recalling the use of identity cards, all citizens had a place of residence written on each card. Moving was extremely difficult, had to be applied for, and was generally not approved unless one had connections within the political elite (Prunier 1995). During 1981, the regime decided to create a parliament called the Counseil National du Developpement Rwanda (NDC). Habyarimana was reelected in December 1983 and 1988. A Hutu government was viewed as legitimate by the international community and generally democratic, despite the authoritarian one-party system that had been installed. As with other authoritarian regimes, Rwanda continued to place itself in political and economic isolation. It was one of the poorest countries in the world; Rwanda entered the ranks of internationally indebted countries by joining the International Monetary Fund (IMF) on 30 September 1963.

There is no doubt that the evolution of the postcolonial economic system played a decisive role in the development of the Rwandan genocide during 1994 (see Rothe, Mullins, and Sandstrom 2008). While some economic progress was recorded since its independence—it was viewed from the Western capitalistic perspective of diversifying the national economy. However, the colonial export economy based on coffee established under the Belgian administration was maintained, providing Rwanda with approximately 80% of its foreign exchange earnings. Poverty levels remained high during the 1970s and 80's especially for the rural economic areas.

While the Rwandan rural economy remained fragile in part due to land fragmentation and soil erosion, general food self-sufficiency did persist. Coffee remained the primary source of the economy. It has been estimated that approximately 70% of rural households cultivated the product, yet it constituted only a fraction of their total monetary income. However, the food situation started to deteriorate in the early 1980s with a marked decline in the per capita availability of food (Chossudovsky 1995).

The reliance on foreign aid had become significant by the late 1970's continuing to increase well into the late 1980's. As stated by Hanssen (1989), "Rwanda was not only the land of the 1,000 hills but also the land of 1,000 foreign aid workers." According to the OCED, in 1973 foreign aid represented only 5% of the GNP but rose to 11% in 1986 and 22% by 1991. Belgium remained the main donor of aid, however, the United States, France, Germany, Canada, and Switzerland were all lenders.

In 1987, the system of quotas established under the International Coffee Agreement (ICA) started to fall apart. World prices plummeted; *the Fonds d'egalisation*—the state coffee stabilization fund—that purchased coffee from Rwandan farmers at a fixed price began to accumulate a sizeable debt. During 1989, the Rwandan budget was reduced by 40%, offset mostly by reducing social services. Such policies proved unpopular with the peasants already overburdened with taxes and increased requirements of mandatory labor for the government. The situation was exasperated by the mini drought that caused additional famine and sent thousands of others fleeing to Tanzania in search of food. Land was also becoming a contentious issue with the increase in population. Stories of land grabbing further irritated the general peasant population. This was heightened by the regimes benefit of the Gebeka project, funded by the WB. The project included the state seizure of the last primary growth forests in Rwanda that was logged to clear the land for European cattle to graze and start a dairy business. While the lands remained public, the profits from the 'development' were shared between the "regime and WB expatriates that had invested in the scheme" (Prunier 1995: 88).

Export earnings continued to decline by nearly 50%. When coffee prices plummeted, famines erupted throughout the Rwandan countryside. According to WB, the growth of GDP per capita declined from 0.4% in 1981–6 to –5.5% in the period immediately following the fall of the coffee market from 1987 to 1991. In 1988, a World Bank mission went to Rwanda to review its public expenditure program. This led to a series of recommendations established with a view to putting Rwanda back on the track of "sustained economic growth" (Chossudovsky 1995). The WB presented a plan to the Habyarimana regime two policy options. One was entitled "No Strategy Change," essentially the option of remaining with the current system of state planning. The other option was a macroeconomic reform with "transition to the free market." The World Bank concluded that if Rwanda adopted option two, levels of consumption would increase markedly over 1989–93 alongside a recovery of investment and an improved balance of trade. To accomplish this, other factors would have to be carried out including trade liberalization, currency devaluation, lifting of all subsidies to agriculture, ending the *Fonds d'egalisation*, privatizing government held enterprises and a general reduction in civil employees. Within months of the Rwandese government adopting option two, another harmful economic blow occurred.

In June 1989, the ICA reached an agreement deadlock as a result of political pressures from Washington on behalf of the large U.S. coffee traders. At the conclusion of the now historic meeting of coffee producers held in Florida, coffee prices plunged in a matter of months by more than 50%. For Rwanda, the drop in price wreaked havoc with an already fragile economical situation. The economic foundations of the postindependent state remained tenuous. The collapse in coffee commodity prices precipitated the crisis in the state's public finances, due to the high dependency on a single crop. As the debt crisis unfolded, a larger share of coffee and tea earnings had been earmarked for debt servicing, putting further pressure on small-scale farmers.

As often occurs in heavily indebted countries that undergo additional economic stressors or near collapse, the Habyarimana regime opted for the WB's plan. The "With Strategy Change" was adopted and almost immediately a 50% devaluation of the Rwandan franc was carried out (November 1990). The devaluation was posited as the key to boost coffee exports and a means of rehabilitating a war-ravaged economy. From a situation of relative price stability, the plunge of the Rwandan franc contributed to triggering inflation and the collapse of real earnings and the outstanding external debt which had already doubled since 1985, increased by 34% between 1989 and 1992. While import prices soared, the price at which coffee was bought from local producers was frozen. As a result, hundreds of thousands of small coffee farmers were ruined (Maton 1994). Alongside the poorest sectors of the urban population, these destitute farmers became a permanent reservoir of recruits for the *Interahamwe* militia and the army.

By the end of 1990, the Rwandese economic and political scene was one of a pervasive crisis. With the political system on the verge of collapse and as outside forces were in talks at the Franco-African summit, Habyarimana was pressured to allow a multiparty system, which he did in July of 1990. Conditions were ripe for the Rwandan Patriotic Front (RPF) to make a move; a group of intellectuals released a manifesto demanding democratization and began forming opposition political parties. This further motivated RPF forces, exiled in Uganda, to prepare an invasion.

On 1 October 1990 the RPF made its first strike near the Rwandese border, opening fire on guard posts. The civil war had begun. While short lived, the fighting lasted less than four weeks, it required the Habyarimana regime to protect itself and encouraged internal opposition groups to begin their struggle for recognition. The Habyarimana regime used the border skirmishes as an excuse to begin a crack down on Tutsi within Rwanda; the so-called "Tutsi threat" was used to reestablish widespread support for the government that it hadn't seen since the onset of multiparties and the democratization movement (Prunier 2005).

Using the attacks, including the alleged attack on Kigali during 4 and 5 October as a pretext, a massive wave of arrests began. The arrests were not limited to RPF supporters, but instead targeted the educated Tutsis, Hutus in political opposition with the regime, foreign residents and anyone else that had sent levels of discomfort to the political power elite. Political leaders were being replaced. Propaganda was used to incite the population and instill loyalty to the regime. The Minister of Defense used the national radio to request the population to "track down and arrest infiltrators" (quoted in Prunier 1995: 109). This resulted in the mass killings of hundreds of defeated RPF who had taken refugee in the Mutara region. It turned out that the 350 'RPF' fighters were all regular Tutsi civilians. Additional violence ensued with over 500 houses burnt. The violence, as will be repeated again in the next few years, was organized and led by local authorities.

The invasion had also rekindled strong fears in the Hutu MRND elite. These fears were translated into a mass recruitment drive for the Rwandese army. On October 1, the army numbered 5,200 but by mid-1991 had grown to 15,000 and continued to increase to 50,000 by mid 1992. With such increased numbers, state finances had to address the significant increase with a massive military budget increase. Again, the IMF would play a role by approving an additional credit of 41 million U.S. dollars, primarily used to increase the strength of the regime and the Rwandese military (Nduhungirehe 1995).

International financial institutions were ill pleased with the large military expenditure increases and verbally demanded the regime stop using funds in this manner. Yet, they allowed the regime to account for the sums loaned by the WB and the IMF by presenting old invoices based on an antiquated accounting system for all imported goods. This allowed the regime to finance massive arms purchases that would later be used in the 1994 genocide. For example, large trucks imported for the army were put on the Transport Ministry's account and fuel used for militia and army vehicles was recorded on the Health Ministry's account (Toussaint 2004).

By 1 November 1990 the RPF headed back to Uganda to regroup in hope of a later attack on Ruhengeri—a city in the northwest, near the Ugandan and Zairian (now DRC) borders where the largest Rwanda prison was located. Most inmates in the facility we held for political reasons and were thus an opportune target for a high-profile "liberation" attack. By early 1991, the RPF grew to over 5,000 men; by the end of 1992 they numbered nearly 12,000 (Prunier 1995). On 23 January 1991, the RPF carried out their attack on Ruhengeri, causing a ripple of panic throughout Rwanda. Their attack was a ready made excuse for Habyarimana to arrest more civilians. As Felicien Gatabazi noted, "Each time there are some difficulties [in the political arena] there is a flare-up of tribal violence instigated by the regime, and threats of civil war are used to justify the status quo" (*Le Monde* 1992: 1). The opposition pushed for quick political change while the MRND hardliners began to see Habyarimana as being too soft. In response, he made a speech promising a multiparty system, a constitutional referendum would be slated for June 1991, and for the Tutsi population, a promise that ethnicity would be removed from all future identification cards and all official papers.

In March 1991 a group of over two hundred opponents published an appeal for the recreation of the *Mouvement Democratique Republician* (MDR); several other political groups formed in anticipation of the constitutional change and to change political leadership. On 10 June 1991 the new constitution was created which included the acknowledgment of a multiparty political system. However, for Habyarimana, these political parties were little more than symbolic appeasement, not real political actors. His goal was to maintain the old system regardless of the constitution. To do so he favored and supported the creation of nearly a dozen ineffectual opposition parties who took no active role in politics until 1993 when Habyarimana used them to block peace negotiations with the RPF. Rwanda remained in a near civil war situation with low intensity operations continuing even though the RPF had again withdrawn.

The RPF statement of equality for all Rwandans was not accepted by many of the population, who viewed the RPF as dangerous extremists. With every move the RPF made into new areas of Rwanda, local Hutu peasants would flee showing "no enthusiasm for their liberation" (Prunier 1995: 36). Civil violence also continued leading to sporadic massacres of Tutsi. In conjunction with these violent outbursts, media warfare began. A pamphlet attributed to the *Parti Liberal* was circulated, calling on Tutsis to rise up and massacre all Hutu. State radio carried to 'story' extensively, to 'warn' the Hutu population. More massacres of Tutsi ensued in the name of self-defense and were carried out by ordinary peasants.

The economic crisis reached its climax in 1992 when Rwandan farmers in desperation uprooted some 300,000 coffee trees. Despite soaring domestic prices, the government had frozen the price of coffee at its 1989 level, under the terms of its agreement with the Bretton Woods institutions. The government was not allowed under conditions of its the World Bank loan to transfer state resources to the *Fonds d'egalisation*. Further, a significant portion of the existing profit was appropriated to local coffee traders putting further pressure on the peasantry. In June 1992, a second devaluation was ordered by the IMF leading to additional escalations of prices for fuel and consumer essentials. The income derived from coffee had been erased; there was nothing for the majority of peasants to fall back on. With the economic liberalization of trade and the deregulation of grain markets as recommended by the structural adjustment program (SAP), cheap food imports and food aid from the other countries were destabilizing any of the local markets for food that had managed to sustain themselves. The entire agricultural system was pushed into crisis as a result of the austerity measures and sinking civil service salaries. This inevitably contributed to exacerbating the climate of insecurity.

During this upheaval, a new cabinet was sworn in nearly a year after the new constitution was implemented. For the first time the MRND had to share power. Policies were put in place attempting to circumvent many of Habyarimana's practices. This included the abolishment of the 'policy of equilibrium' that had allowed the government to choose based on ethnicity the origin of students with general entrance exams. Habyarimana resigned as the head of armed forces but the political and social conditions remained tense. By April 1992 negotiations with the RPF were in planning. The Foreign Minister, Boniface Ngulinzira, met with RPF leaders on May 24 in Kampala for a first round, announcing that direct negotiations would continue in Paris during June. Rumors that peace with the RPF would bring about large scale demobilization created additional insecurity and outbreaks of disorder. This catalyzed a meeting between key opposition political parties (MDR, PSD, and PL delegates) and RPF leaders. On 6 June the RPF announced that the armed struggle was over, their resistance was now political. On 14 July an official cease-fire was signed.

Within days the MRND ministers began boycotting cabinet meetings. President Habyarimana tried to justify the need for peace to appease the displeasure it brought to his supporters. For the hardliners, a doubt surfaced that Habyarimana was selling out to safeguard his own political position, however, the RPF made no balms about his support and in a radio station, owned by the RPF, claimed that his support for peace was not genuine and he had attempted to undermine and the cabinet's actions during the Arusha peace process, thwarting any real gain. On that same day, an agreement was reached with the RPF by government delegates for a pluralist transitional government, one that the RPF would have a place in. Within days, massacres once again started and the hardliner fractions of the MRND were starting to take on an open defiance against Habyarimana.

The *Amasau* (bullets) secret society was created within the army that consisted of extremist officers who destroy the RPF, not share power with it. The creation of "Zero Network" a death squad based on the Latin America model made up of MRND militiamen supported by the army was implemented at this time. A new brand of extremism was emerging from the ranks of the old repressive order that wanted absolute power even if that meant using absolute terror (Prunier 1995).

The MRND continued to protest the lack of consultation in the peace process; Habyarimana delayed the RPF incorporation into Rwandan politics. In a speech on 15 November, he called the July cease-fire agreement a piece of "trash" that the government was not obliged to follow or respect. Throughout the next couple of months frequent demonstrations occurred both supporting the peace process and/or condemning it. The MRND took a harder yet position and in late November addressed party militants with the following speech:

> The opposition parties have plotted with the enemy to make the Byumba fall to the *Inyenzi* [cockroaches]....Any person who is guilty of acts aiming at sapping the morale of the armed forces will be condemned to death. What are we waiting for?. ... and what about those accomplices who are sending their children to the RPF? Why are we waiting to get rid of these families? We have to take responsibilities into our own hands and wipe out these hoodlums. ... The fatal mistake we made in 1959 was to let them [Tutsi] get out. ... We have to act. Wipe them all out. (FIDH Rwanda quoted in Prunier, 1995: 172)

It was at this time that Leon Mugesera also made a speech during a MRND party rally proposing a solution to the 'Tutsi problem': "They belong in Ethiopia and we are going to find them a shortcut to get there by throwing them in the Nyabarongo River. I must insist on this point. We have to act. Wipe them all out" (Report of the Commission of Inquiry on Human Rights Violations in Rwanda 1992: 24–25).

Sporadic violence continued in the early part of 1993. Extremist Hutu militiamen went on a murder spree that included torturing prisoners and burning homes for over a six day period killing approximately 300 people, leading to the suspension of the Arusha Accords. On 8 February, the RPF forces broke their end of the cease-fire, beginning the February war.

The February War to Habyarimana's death

The offensive moves of the RPF were successful at the start causing the Rwandese army to withdraw in disarray. By this time the RPF had grown significantly in numbers and the near collapse of the economic situation in Rwanda had led to a deteriorated army. As civil personnel were rarely paid, moral was low. Frustrations manifested in drunkenness and sporadic violence targeting civilians. Consequently, the relationship between the military and civilians disintegrated. The RPF also began directing violence at civilian populations—killing civil servants, women and children. As such, the flow of refugees increased. Hutu peasants continued to flee as they did during the 1990–2 fighting and by late February it was estimated that 600,000 people were on the move, reaching around 860,000 by early March (Prunier 1995). Propaganda exaggerating the RPF's role in the violence exploded, tarnishing their image with liberal Hutu. Additionally, the RPF violence and exaggerated cases of massacres played into France's decision to unite wholly with Habyarimana against the RPF. The French Ministers call for a common front intensified the ethnic tension, which was seen in some quarters as a call to racial war.

Meanwhile hardliners in the presidential circles had lost complete faith in Habyarimana. They believed he should have reacted much stronger against the RPF attack in early February and they began to compile a list of "traitors." Once Habyarimana signed the Dar-es-Salaam cease-fire, the hardliners were outraged and issued a violent communication condemning the act:

> Mr. Habyarimana, Juvenal President of the Republic, has approved the contents of an agreement obviously detrimental to the interests of the Rwandese people. This shows clearly that Mr. Habyarimana does not care any more about the interests of the Nation and is now defending other interests. (quoted in Prunier 1995: 182)

As such, the time was ripe to create a conservative opposition party to the president—the PARMEHUTU. It was instantly popular as the population was more than weary of Habyarimana and the RPF (Gapysis 1993). On 23 June 1993, the United Nations passed Resolution 846 creating the United Nations Uganda-Rwanda Observation Mission (UNUROM). On 5 October 1993, it passed Resolution 872 created the United Nations Assistance Mission to Rwanda (UNAMIR) to ensure progress in the peace negotiations.

The situation in Rwanda became more tenuous with events in neighboring Burundi. In June 1993, Melchoir Ndadaye, a Hutu, was elected president of Burundi. In October, he was kidnapped and killed by extremist Tutsis. Ministers and civil servants used this as an opportunity to encourage the Hutu population to take revenge directly on the Tutsi population. Violence erupted in areas, however the Tutsi-controlled army heavy-handedly restored order. Within days, over 50,000 had died–roughly 60% Tutsi and 40% Hutu (Prunier 1995: 199). Over 150,000 Tutsis fled to army controlled areas while nearly 300,000 Hutu fled across the Rwandan border. For the Hutu extremists in Rwanda, it was yet another example of the "evil Tutsis" reinforcing the genocidal propaganda started in 1992. The death of Ndadaye and the Burundian Hutu refugees, spreading tales of horror at the hands of the Tutsi provided the opportune moment for the Rwandan Hutu extremists to rally even the hesitant to their side. They used their radio station, RTLMC as a base to spread propaganda and a call to action. Increasingly genocidal discourses were spreading quickly even to the remote and rural areas of Rwanda. Coupled with the heightened increase in arms distributions, this should have been a major hint for the UN that peace was far from being restored. RPF sympathizers once again found themselves targets of a death hunt. Other sporadic killings of Tutsi continued with intermittent referencing of the coming genocide. For example, the newspaper *Kangura* (January 1994, 55: 1) wrote, "Who will survive the March War? The masses will rise with the help of the army and the blood will flow freely."

Nonetheless, the UN stood behind the Arusha peace agreements. However, just as other negotiations were postponed, the transfer of power to the new government was slow to nonexistent due to the persistent blockages and proposals by Habyarimana. On 6 April 1994 President Habyarimana was killed when his plane was shot down by two missiles as it returned to the Kigali airport. His death was the final impetus leading to the onset of the genocide.

The Genocide

Almost within minutes after Habyarimana's plane was shot down, militia members set up roadblocks throughout the streets of Kigali. Militiamen and Presidential Guards instantly began house-to-house searches for anyone they had deemed an enemy, killing them on sight. Within days, Commander-in-Chief Colonel Gatsinzi was removed from his position and replaced by General

Augustin Bizimungu, a well known extremist and supporter of the genocide plotting that had been occurring since 1992 (Prunier 1995).

At the onset of the genocide, victims were carefully selected and primarily slaughtered by Presidential Guards. Early victims included: Prime Minister Agatha Uwillingiyimana; President of the Constitutional Court, Joseph Kavarugaunda; several Catholic priests who were believed to be supporters of the democratization movement; Charles Shamukiga, a civil rights activist; Landwald Ndasinga, leader of the *Democratic Parti Liberal*; Fredric Nzamurambaho, Minister of Agriculture; Marc Ruganera, Minister of Finance; and Bonafice Ngulinzira, Foreign Minister and negotiator for the Arusha Peace agreement. This exemplifies the systematic nature in selecting key oppositional leaders within the government, political parties, and/or staunch supporters of democratization. The early killings were being carried out from a list that had been prepared months in advanced. Birara, former governor of the Central Bank, stated in *La Libre Belgique* on 24 May 1994 that General Nsabimana, then army Commander-in-Chief, showed him a list of 1,500 names of individuals in Kigali alone on 24 February 1994 that were slated for death. The list expanded from this to all Tutsis simply and any Hutu who were members of or sympathizers with democratic opposing parties or who were married to Tutsis.

Between the 7th and 8th of April a Committee for Public Salvation was assembled by Colonel Bagosora, the leading organizational figure of the genocide, and Colonel Rwagafiliita. They established a provisional government to act as a front, while the "coup makers remained in the shadows" calling the shots (Prunier 1995: 232). On 9 April, Radio Rwanda announced the composition of the new government by Theodre Sindikubwabo, Speaker of the Assembly and newly named president of the Republic with Prime Minister Kambanda, an MDR extremist. The majority of cabinet posts remained in the MRND hands. All the while, mass killings by militia and army forces reached the interior of the country.

The Radio Rwanda broadcast announcing the interim government drew immediate fire from the RPF. Kagame replied to the announcement by denouncing Bagosora as the real "master of the country and promised to fight on" (SWB Radio Uganda 9 April 1994). As such, RPF troops restarted their military operations on 8 April and the following day began to move down from the north. At the same time, the French Air Force was dropping paratroopers into the Kigali airport with a orders to evacuate all foreign nationals and leading members of the MRND. Many of the dignitaries of the French Embassy were Tutsis and as such were abandoned to meet their fate. Even the provisional government fled to Gitarama to escape the fighting, leaving behind only General Bizimungwa.

By 12 April, the fighting between the RPF and government troops turned into a full-fledged battle and the momentum increased across all of Rwanda where civilian massacres had turned into a full-fledged genocide. The few foreigners paying attention to the events in Rwanda tended to confuse the RPF and Rwandan Government war with the genocide, lending to false accusations that the RPF were the perpetrators of all the massive deaths and violence. Even the UN insisted that the belligerents needed to reach a cease-fire to stop the massacres (*Le Monde* 1994: 1). Yet, such a cease-fire would have done little to stop the genocide.

By the second week of April, the acting militia were 50,000 strong (Prunier 1995). They manned the roadblocks, took part in the house-to-house searches, and acted as executioners carrying out orders from the highly centralized, tightly controlled, central government and local councilors. The massacres spread as officials continued to incite anger and hatred, drawing on the ideology of Hutu supremacy. This facilitated the participation in the genocide by ordinary peasants. While the degree of participation varied from region to region and from individual to individual, a general pattern of widespread involvement of the Hutu population cannot be dismissed. The fear of not participating in the genocide was as much of an incentive as was the prevailing propaganda used to incite the violence from the onset. For example, testimony of one killer captured by the RPF stated,

> I regret what I did. … I am ashamed, but what would you have done if you had been in my place? Either you took part in the massacre or else you were massacred yourself. So I took weapons and I defended the members of my tribe against the Tutsi. (*La Libre Belgique* 1994: 1)

The internal contradiction that affected many of the general peasants can be seen by this testimony. Based on fear that they would be viewed as Tutsi sympathizers and killed and the internalization of the dominant discourse of a Tutsi threat drove ordinary men and women to become genocidal.

Murder was not the only tool of the genocide. Systematic sexual assaults were carried out across the country. Some were spontaneous but most were planned—part of the official battlefield tactics of the genocide. Women and young girls were often killed after being brutally raped. Children were also raped or killed; babies were thrown against walls or rocks. Sexual mutilations of bodies were common including the removal of females' breasts and men's penises.

A Hutu teacher, married to a Tutsi, was forced to watch his pregnant wife be disemboweled and then had his child's fetus pushed into his face while being told to "Eat your bastard." The genocide and violence took on a form of racist sadism that was reaching nearly implausible extremes. A witness stated,

> If you looked, you could see the evidence, even in the whitened skeletons. The legs bent and apart. A broken bottle, a rough branch, even a knife between them. Where the bodies were fresh, we saw what must have been semen pooled on and near the dead women and girls. There was always a lot of blood. Some male corpses had their genitals cut off, but many women and young girls had their breasts chopped off and their genitals crudely cut apart. They died in a position of total vulnerability, flat on their backs, with their legs bent and knees wide apart. It was the expressions on their dead faces that assaulted me the most, a frieze of shock, pain and humiliation. (Irin news)

Meanwhile the Catholic churches, once active in the creation, promotion, and political and religious use of ethnic identities, stood by idly while the genocide was unfolding. Communications with their head offices were limited to informing their Order of the priests that were killed but were silent about the massive killings of their own parishioners or of the perpetrators (Prunier 1995). The only time names were mentioned was when the RPF could be tied to an incident or killing. As late as August 1994, 29 priests wrote a collective letter to the Pope denying any Hutu responsibility for the genocide, attributing it to the RPF. They condemned the idea of an international tribunal to investigate the crimes. As one foreign observer remarked after visiting Kirambo parish after the massacre had ended: "There was not the slightest trace of collective guilt among the Christian clergy" (African Rights (year): 516).

As the genocide continued, thousands of refugees attempted to escape. This amplified the numbers on the road, making them easy targets for waiting ambushes. Few places could offer shelter. Hospitals were no longer a safe haven for the wounded or those seeking shelter. As an employee of *Medecins Sans Frontieres* wrote:

> Any wounded person [Tutsi] was killed. Right in front of our eyes, the army men would come inside the hospital, take the wounded, line them up and machine-gun them down. ... It was also the first time in any of our operations that we saw local personnel being killed on a massive scale. All our Tutsi medical staff, doctors and nurses, were kidnapped and murdered in Kigali in April. Over two hundred people. We had never seen anything like it. (Telerama 1994: 1)

Schools were no longer a refuge place as Hutu teachers denounced Tutsi students to the militias or killed them themselves. A Hutu teacher told a journalist,

"A lot of people got killed here. I myself killed some of the children. ... We had eighty kids in the first year. There are 25 left. All the others, we killed them or they have run away" (Saint-Exupery 1994: 1).

The slaughter continued throughout April. Some areas saw the violence dissipate at the time, but only because nearly every Tutsi had been killed (e.g. Ruhengeri and Gisenyi). Other areas experienced continuous violence well into June (e.g. Kibungo, Southern Kigali, Butare, Kibuye, and Cyangugu). Nearly 80% of the victims, approximately 640,000, were carried out between the second week of April and the third week of May. Mass graves were dug in some areas, while in others the bodies were left in the open or disposed of in riverbeds. Rivers, such as the Kagera, were filled with bodies polluting the river and connecting lakes. 40,000 bodies were picked up out of Lake Victoria, a run off from the Kagera River, and buried on the Ugandan shoreline. During the slaughter in Kigali, garbage trucks were brought in to remove the corpses. By mid May, at least 60,000 bodies had been picked up and buried. It was not until late May that the killings began to subside, though still occurring sporadically (Prunier 1995).

On 23 June 1994, acting under UN Resolution 929, Operation Turquoise, a French mission, was sent to Rwanda to address the violence. Due to the misconstrued observations though, the mission was to help end the war between the Rwandese government and the RPF and to serve 'humanitarian interests' by saving Tutsis. Only 2,500 men strong, they did have considerable fire power (e.g. 100 armored tanks, a battery of 120mm mortars, 8 Super Puma helicopters, two Gazelles, 4 fighter bombers, and 4 ground attack planes), but were controlled by very conservative fire orders. Other states, while voicing their support with promises of troops, never moved beyond the rhetoric except for Senegal. The arrival of the French was welcomed by the local authorities of the former regime, including current FAR members. By this time, the RPF had won considerable territory. Hutu civilians poured out of Kigali to the French Humanitarian Zone or to the Northwest, the government's last refuge. The RPF continued to be seen as the "Tutsi" movement to regain power. As was stated, "They can only do to us what we did to their kith and kin" (Prunier 1995: 295).

Yet, the refugee problem continued. In part this was a direct result of further propaganda by the quickly disintegrating interim government and local authorities. In Ruhengeri, the local authority warned people that "the majority of the population will be massacred" at the hands of the RPF (SEB Radio France International 12 July 1994). Still attempting to convince people their greatest threat was the RPF, in some areas those that did not flee were summarily killed by the militiamen (e.g., Butare). More than one million fled into Zaire in less than a week. As Hutu fled, Tutsis began to filter back in especially those that had sought refuge in Uganda. The eventual fall of Kigali, the center of the RPF war, led to approximately three million individuals fleeing as refugees. With the end of a three month long genocide and civil war in sight, RPF control of Kigali led to a new government being formed on 18 July, headed by President Pasteur Bizimungu, an RPF Hutu. While this was the first sign of normalization for Rwanda since the 6th of April. Yet, the country was far from being a normal state.

With the conquest of Kigali, the previous interim government fled. However, they took with them all the Central Bank foreign currency reserves and very large amounts of Rwandese francs. No monies were left in the public coffers. The policy had been to leave only a wasteland to the RPF which is indeed what they did. The removal of the money, no tax revenues, and the dismantled infrastructure would play a significant role in the near future for rebuilding Rwanda. It was indeed the first steps in an economic collapse. In this scenario, the new government was supposed to manage the population and form a new political structure based on the Arusha Accords.

Rwanda remained in a state of disarray. Thousands were displaced, surviving Tutsis had lost all their possessions including their homes, individuals were in psychological states of shock and denial, many of the raped women were now pregnant with unwanted children. Remaining crops went unattended as population displacement left many areas unpopulated. The situation was quickly deteriorating. The return of Hutus in mass in other areas such as Lake Kivu created another serious problem for Rwanda. Lacking food, sanitation posts, medicines, and water, combined with overcrowding, caused an enormous cholera epidemic. By the first of August 3,000 Hutu died from cholera. However, this tragedy received massive newspaper and TV reports documenting every detail. This twist of fate had a significant impact on how history would try to be told. As noted by Secretary General Alan Destexhe:

> Yesterday the genocide of the Tutsi by the Hutu militia, today the genocide of the Hutu refugees by the cholera? This comparison, which one can see widely used in the press, puts on the same plane things which have nothing to do with each other. Through this confusion the original, singular and exemplary nature of the genocide is denied and the guilt of the perpetrators becomes diluted in the general misery. (Liberation 1994: 1)

While the cholera outbreak is said to have claimed roughly 30,000 Hutus, we cannot forget the fact that the Hutu led genocide on the Tutsi resulted in approximately 800,000 deaths (Prunier 1995).

Summary

The Rwandan genocide serves to remind us of the ethnic, political, and economic conditions that are typical for postcolonial states. Ethnic identities are often manufactured by the occupying forces and then enhanced for political purposes when the state becomes independent. Additionally, postcolonial states often form a one-party government attempting to govern under similar conditions experienced under colonial rule. Thus enhancing the political, economic, and ethnic crisis's that were leftover factors of the colonial powers extrapolation of the lands resources. Inherited from the Belgian colonial period, the same objective of pushing one ethnic group against the other ('divide and rule') was continued within the various 'military', 'human rights' and 'macro- economic' decisions.

As we have shown, the conflict between the Hutu and Tutsi was largely the product of the colonial system; largely the result of the administrative reforms initiated in 1926 by the Belgians which were crucial in shaping the existing socio-ethnic relations. The Belgians explicitly used lineage conflicts to reinforce their control of the territory. The traditional chiefs were used by the colonial powers to requisition forced labor. Under the direct supervision of Belgian colonial administrators a climate of fear and distrust was established, communal solidarity broke down, and traditional relations were transformed to serve the interests of the Belgians. As such, interethnic rivalries were fueled as a means of achieving political control and for preventing the development of solidarity between the two ethnic groups which could have been directed against the colonial regime: divide and conquer. These socio-ethnic transformations of social contracts linking personal and economic dependence played a significant role in the events that unfolded. The Belgians had invented new Hutu-Tutsi categories, one being superior to the other. The problem with racial myths is that once created they take a life of their own. This was the case in Rwanda where by 1940 the myth was a reality. The Tutsi and Hutu conformed to the images that had been forced upon them of themselves and each other. Even the Tutsi peasants viewed themselves as superior beings and the Hutu mass were oppressed (Prunier 1995). Thus, all Tutsis were pictured as oppressors. This led to the 1959 civil war and genocide. However, we cannot forget the role the Belgians and the Catholic Church played in using these ethnic divisions to support the change in power and rule from the Tutsis to the Hutu once the Tutsis were viewed as a potential threat to the occupation and power of the church.

Since Independence in 1962, relations with the former colonial powers and international financial donors became exceedingly complex. The catastrophic impact of structural adjustment policies dictated by the IMF and World Bank along with the fall in coffee prices on the global market, a fall linked to the policies of the Bretton Woods institutions and the United States, played a central role in the Rwandan crisis. The fall of the market in the late 1980's corresponded with the political disintegration of the regime. As such, the massive social discontent from the devastating economic conditions was then channeled by the Habyarimana regime into implementing its plan for genocide.

The Rwandan crisis of the early 1990's became a spectacle in a continuous agenda of donor roundtables, cease-fire agreements, and peace talks. Initiatives were closely monitored and coordinated by the economic donors in a tangled web of conditions. When the RPF and the Rwandan military fighting started, millions of dollars of "balance-of-payments aid" from multilateral and bilateral sources came pouring into the coffers of the Central Bank, later emptied when the MRND fled Kigali. Earmarked for commodity imports, a sizeable amount of these loans were diverted by hardliners within the regime to the acquisition of military hardware. Additionally, since October 1990, the Rwandan Armed Forces expanded from 5,000 to 40,000 men requiring a sizeable influx of outside money to pay the new recruits. The new recruits were drawn from the urban *lumpenproletariot* that had dramatically increased since the collapse of the coffee market in 1989. Thousands of youths were also drafted into the civilian militia. The arms purchases enabled the Armed Forces to organize and equip the militiamen in preparation of the upcoming genocide.

The push for a democratization based on an abstract model of interethnic solidarity, envisaged by the Arusha peace agreement signed in August 1993 was an impossibility with the extant conditions within Rwanda and the lack of true commitment by members of the MRND. Additionally, the impoverishment of the population that resulted from the IMF reforms precluded a genuine process of democratization. Instead, the objective was to meet the conditions of 'good governance' which Habyarimana used as his stage for the international political players. A secondary condition was the installation of a multiparty coalition government under the trusteeship of Rwanda's external creditors. However, this contributed to fuelling the various political factions within the regime, leading to the assassination of Habyarimana.

While the international arena cannot be held directly responsible for the tragic outcome of the Rwandan civil war, the austerity measures combined with the impact of the IMF-sponsored devaluations, contributed to impoverishing the Rwandan people at a time of acute political and social crisis. The deliberate manipulation of market forces destroyed economic activity and people's livelihood, fuelled unemployment and created a situation of generalized famine and social despair.

The mechanics of the genocide also had long historical roots. This included the tradition of unquestioned obedience to authorities, fear of the Tutsi and a general situation of overpopulation combined with economic devastation. All the preconditions for genocide were present: a well-organized civil service sector, an enhanced military and militia fully armed, and a coherent ideology that had been growing since the 1920's which contained the necessary lethal potential: a total dehumanization of the evil other followed by a legitimization of the ideology.

Additionally, the lack of responses by leading international powers to prevent or to significantly minimize the slaughter once it began is another factor of realpolitiks and responses to African crisis. Those who most egregiously failed Rwandans included the Catholic Church, France, the US, the UK, Belgium, and the UN (Berry and Berry 2004).

Note

1. The pattern of political marginalization based on geographic proximity to the center of political power was also evident in the creation of ethnic identities in Darfur: the Arabs versus the African tribes.

· 5 ·

THE UNENDING WAR

Since independence, Uganda has been mired in political conflict and civil war that has produced continuous and widespread atrocities, war crimes, and crimes against humanity. Although Rwanda and Uganda share a history of colonial occupation that led to uneven economic development, a postindependence rule consisting of a one-party system, ethnic preferential treatment, and interstate involvements, notable distinctions have resulted in contrasting etiological aspects associated with the crimes that occurred. The impetus for the crimes against humanity in Uganda are the result of the activities of a militia group, the Lord's Resistance Army (LRA), political party factions attempting to gain political power and control of the state, and of an anomic Ugandan military force practicing sporadic banditry and violence. This chapter begins with a brief historical summary placing Uganda in context with other African countries and with a discussion of the political and economic situation of postindependent Uganda. This includes a discussion of political factions including the Holy Spirit Resistance Movement and the LRA. Finally, the chapter ends with an examination of the charges issued by the ICC.

Historical Context

As with the rest of the region, Uganda has a long history of colonialism and foreign intervention. In the 1880s, following a colonial tactic that had worked well in India, Britain authorized the management of the territory to the East Africa Company (EAC). Such an approach minimized the direct financial risk to the crown, as the EAC bore the financial burden, while allowing the expansion of the British Empire. Early on the company faced major problems owing to an outbreak of civil war between British Protestant and French Catholic missionaries that lead to the British declaration of their authority and rule over the territory (1894). Within two years, the British control expanded to include Toro, Ankole, Buganda, and Bunyoro forming the Uganda Protectorate. Drawing on their well-established strategy of indirect rule, the UK used local African kings to maintain local power. At times this was merely symbolic whereas at other times a king's authority was real and legitimate.

The Buganda Agreement, signed in 1900, acknowledged the status of *Kabakas*, indigenous kings, and their rights to free land. Similar agreements were made with Kenya and other territories held by British authorities. This practice continued until after World War II with the broader drive toward independence that we discussed in Chapter One. By the 1950s, a movement toward independence developed in Uganda. In 1952, the Uganda National Congress (UNC) was formed with Ignatius Musaazi as its president. However, as the party began to reach beyond Buganda in an effort to mobilize support, it had difficulty finding a "national" issue on which it could broadly appeal to the populace. In areas where the party would attempt to use local grievances as a platform, however, the colonial administration would address most of these issues and any support for the UNC dwindled.

In 1956, the Democratic Party (DP) was formed by Matayo Mugwanya. Unlike the UNC, a dominantly Protestant representation, the DP was positioned to attain support of the Catholics of Uganda, who were relatively marginalized in political representation throughout the colonial rule period. The DP was then seen as an outlet to reformulate the political order that had marginalized them. In 1958, the Uganda People's Union (UPU), headed by William Rwetsiba, was created as the independent voices of representation that were allegedly without any religious affiliation. In addition, the Uganda National Movement (UNM) was formed by Augustine Kamya, representing the economically marginalized Bugandans who had long-term grievances against the colonial authorities. However, the party was dismantled after the colonial officials arrested most of the UNM leaders after it had proclaimed a boycott of all non-African goods using violent and intimidating means to break up the Asian monopolies of ginneries and cash crops.

At the beginning of 1959, the UNC split into two parties, as factional fighting set in over the ideological goals of the party. As a result, the UNC, in part headed by Ignatus Musaazi (the Bagandan faction) and the other faction, led by Milton Obote, joined forces with the UPU forming the Uganda People's Congress (UPC) party. With the onset of so many political parties, growing unrest and a growing demand for independence, the colonial powers decided to hold a statewide election in 1961. The UPC won 35 seats, all outside of Buganda, and the DP held 19 seats within Buganda. Benedicto Kiwanuka, of the DP party, was named as the Chief Minister of Uganda. The results of the election caused immediate tension as the Bugandan leaders were not pleased at such a highly positioned Catholic. The Kabaka Yekka (KY) party was formed in an effort to "protect the threatened position of the Kabaka and the Protestant clique at Mengo" prior to the elections for independence that were to be held in 1962 (Uganda History 2007: 3).

The UPC formed a union with the KY believing this was the only way to defeat the DP. Indeed, that is what occurred in the national elections and on 9 October 1962 Uganda became an independent state headed by Obote as Executive Prime Minister, with Mutesa as the symbolic head of state after being appointed by the newly created Parliament. However, the merging of the parties and the union of Obote and Mutesa was not a good combination as they differed profoundly in their ideological views. This led to a political and personal fissure between the two. As Mutesa (1967: 3) claims, "I was supposed to be kept informed of affairs by the Prime Minister, but he gradually ceased to bother to do this. Also I had certain rights such as appointing and dismissing ministers. ... he was not interested in honoring such obligations." Postindependence Uganda was plagued by political antagonisms, with devastating results for the country and the general citizenry. Those who obtained power used the resources of the land for their personal gratification and as a practice of patronage politics, distributing resources to the leader's kin and allies. Once in power, they were ruthless in keeping it. Such intense corruption and internal fighting produced a state in constant chaos and turmoil well into the twenty-first century (see Mwenda and Tangri 2005).

PostIndependence

Intraparty frictions did not cease with the newly independent government or the new constitution. The UPC split into three components with Obote playing the center of the political field. The other two divisions were headed by

Grace Ibingira and John Kakonge. The UPC became known for its conspiratorial nature and flagrant backstabbing, especially among its leaders. Less than two years after Uganda attained self-rule, Kakonge was replaced by Grace Ibingira as the party Secretary-General; members of Parliament crossed party lines from the KY and the DP to the UPC. In part, the switched alliance had more to do with Obote's political promises for key positions than the strength or unity of the UPC. For instance, after ditching DP for UPC, Basil Bataringaya was appointed the Minister of Internal Affairs. There were attempts by the KY and the DP to merge, hoping to attain enough political power to oppose Obote. This failed due to internal rifts within the DP members of Parliament and the party's supporters outside the Parliament. As the government churned in uncertainty and political maneuvering, a well-planned effort was under way to create political confusion as a cover for an attempted coup in 1965.

Obote received a letter suggesting that he issue a statement condemning a planned coup of the government by a group of left-wing individuals. A second letter was sent to the Minister of Internal Affairs, Daudi Ochieng, requesting him to send an official to record a statement from an unnamed person regarding illegal activities of Idi Amin, at that point the Deputy Commander of the Army. Once submitted, the letter was to be used as cause to suspend Amin from his position (Adhola 2006). During a cabinet meeting, Ibingira announced that he had uncovered an assassination plot that was directed at him. The commander of the Uganda army, Shaban Opolot, also sent a report claiming that he had received inside information that Baganda was planning an assassination attempt on his own life and that the Congolese forces were going to attack the Uganda Army Headquarters during the independence holiday. Finally, the brother of Ibingira, Major Katabarwa, told officers in Jinja to report to Opolot at Army Headquarters in Kampala in preparation for the coup. However, the coup failed when Ugandan officers refused to carry out their orders.

Other attempts were made to remove Obote and reorganize the Ugandan government. One such attempt occurred in February 1966 when Ochieng requested an investigation into Obote, Minister of Defense Felix Onama, and Minister of Planning Adoka Nekyon for illegally obtaining ivory, gold, and monies through covert operations with Congolese rebels. He also suggested the suspension of Amin for embezzling 340,000 Uganda shillings (Obote 1968: 24–25). It appeared to outsiders that Amin would be the only individual to receive some sort of reprimand. Publicly, the government claimed to have suspended Amin from his position; rather, he was promoted as the Major-General Army Commander (Mujaju 1987).

After an unsuccessful kidnapping attempt, Obote returned from a tour of the northern regions of Uganda and convened an emergency meeting of the cabinet. He personally called on members of Parliament regarding their "no confidence" and requested their resignations (Obote 1968). On 19 February 1966, Obote returned from a trip to Nairobi to find that Brigadier Opolot had directed unplanned, nonroutine field exercises for the army. Fearing a coup, Obote ordered their cancellation and detained five government ministers on 24 February during a cabinet meeting: Ibingira, Balaki Kirya, George Magezi, Dr. SB Lumu, and Mathias Ngobi (Human Rights Watch 1999). This set the stage for confrontations that would result in the 1966 revolution. With Ibingira no longer able to continue as the leader of the opposing movement, Kabaka Mutesa became head of the opposition. Mutesa played right into the hands of Obote by declaring a need for drastic measures to be taken in the military due to the detention of the ministers, arranging a military takeover with the aid of Opolot. This did not materialize. However, as *Kabaka* of Buganda, he ordered the central government out of the territory of Buganda setting the stage for the secession of Buganda from Uganda. In response, Obote ordered the Uganda Army units, headed by Amin, to take over Kabaka's palace. After a day of fighting between the army and palace guards, Uganda had established control of the palace, but Kabaka disappeared.

Other political upheavals were occurring, including the installation of the 1966 Constitution that abrogated the Constitution of 1962. It made drastic changes to the structure of Uganda including the removal of autonomy for such districts as Buganda, Ankole, Toro, and Bunyoro. Buganda could no longer appoint members of Parliament; the posts of Prime Minister and that of the ceremonial President were removed. Obote created the post of Executive President that he was to fill. This also allowed Obote unprecedented political decision-making power. Revised in 1967, the Constitution abolished the traditional monarchy. From the structural changes and nationalization of the territories came several reactions and counteractions. Those that lost status, political power, and privileges were resentful of Obote and the UPC. Members of the UPC, Parliament, and other factions within Uganda were increasingly unhappy with Obote's political decisions; many of which involved tribal friction between Obote's Lango and Amin's Acholi heritage of the northern region. Obote ensured the army was composed primarily of those from Lango (Fairhall 1971).

Tensions and constant upheavals plagued the state. The government and the UPC were crippled by the power plays, ideological differences, regular accusations of corruption, embezzlement, and assassination plots. There was a failed assassination attempt of Obote in 1969. In response, the UPC banned all political opposition groups thereby creating a one-party state. Obote was preoccupied with consolidating and maintaining his political hold on Uganda. Simultaneously, Amin was covertly establishing control of a large part of the Ugandan army. Tensions between Obote and Amin grew as Obote attempted to limit Amin's power base within the army. Amin grew increasingly convinced that Obote was planning to have him arrested as a political prisoner or have him killed (Human Rights Watch 1999). In 1970, Brigadier Okoya was murdered and suspicion fell directly on Amin.

In January 1971, while Obote was out of the country, Amin led a successful military coup. Obote sought refuge in Tanzania, where he spent the next eight years in exile, with a small force of Ugandan exiles commanded by Tito Okello. There they would wait and plot Obote's return to power. With the successful overthrow, Major-General Idi Amin Dada was acting head of the now military government. The result of long-standing tensions and a rival for political power, Amin rationalized the coup as "necessary to take action to save a bad situation from getting worse" (Short 1971: 1). Although promising a short military rule and democratic elections Amin autocratically ruled his state, using fear, terror, and violence as his primary political tools. His reign was one of the worst that Africa saw in the twentieth century. His widespread atrocities were rivaled only by Obote and, later, by Museveni. Amin lacked legitimacy and had only a very narrow social base of support. To maintain power, he killed many who were suspected of being against him, including Archbishop Janani Luwum, the Chief Justice Benedicto Kiwanuka, the Vice Chancellor of Makerere University, Frank Kalimuzo, Amin's own wife, and numerous others. He also "reorganized" the military: killing Lango and Acholi officers, and enlisted men alike.

In 1972, Amin ordered all Asians—some 60,000 people—to leave the country (Human Rights Watch 1999). This had devastating effects on the economy, as many of the Asians played a positive role in the business and finance sectors (*NY Times 2007*). Their leaving deprived the nation of much needed financial and intellectual capitals. Amin also ordered a governmental expropriation of their extensive property holdings, which included some 5,655 firms, factories, farms, and approximately U.S.$ 400 million in personal goods (Human Rights Watch 1999). The goal was placing these resources in the hands of Ugandans, specifically the state, Amin, and his personal network of cronies and supporters. However, the business knowledge and experiences of the Asian community were lost.

Amin's rule became increasingly autocratic and brutal; 300,000 Ugandans were slain in a short period of time. Amin had created several new governmental security organizations that reported only to him: the Public Safety Unit and the State Research Bureau. With the assistance of the military police, they wreaked havoc on the citizenry, killing more than 10,000 in under a year (Human Rights Watch Report 1999). Refugees poured into neighboring countries.

There were border clashes as tensions with Tanzania escalated. Those Ugandans who were loyal to Obote attempted to gain voice in an increasingly hostile and violent environment. Uganda found itself increasingly isolated form its neighbors. Although Amin attempted to increase his regional power by strengthening ties with Libya, he continued to distance himself from other countries causing further animosity. He accused Israel of undermining Uganda's interests and, in March 1972, Amin ordered that all Israelis leave Uganda. Amin nationalized of all British companies, leading to a break in relations between Uganda and her former colonizer in 1973.

In 1976, Amin declared that he was Uganda's President-for- Life. He attempted to take portions of west Kenya as Ugandan territory, but relented under threat of international trade embargos. His unlimited desire for political power soon ended his rule. In 1978, Uganda again tried and failed to expand its territory when it invaded the Kagera region of Tanzania. President Nyerere countered by ordering his troops to join anti-Amin Uganda militias, including the Kikosi Maluum (Special Force) loyal to Obote, in the Uganda National Liberation Front (UNLF). The sole purpose of the alliance was the ouster of Amin (Human Rights Watch 1999). In January 1979, Obote, still in exile in Tanzania, held a press conference stating:

> Now is the time for Ugandans to close ranks and coordinate their efforts to overthrow the regime of death. I call upon Ugandans in Uganda army and air force to rise up to their national duty by combining their efforts with those of the masses to overthrow fascist and dictator Amin. (Arvigan, T and Honey, M. 1982: 100)

Obote continued his anti-Amin propaganda campaign and consulted regularly with President Nyerere on matters of strategy. On 10 April 1979, Amin's bloody tenure in government ended abruptly when the Tanzanian forces and Ugandan militias successfully forced Amin to flee the country.

Uganda found neither peace nor stability; political upheavals continued. Immediately after Amin's ouster, Ysuf Lule, chair of the UNLA's political arm, became the head of government. However, his rule only lasted 68 days as he was perceived as having a pro-Buganda slant, resulting in tensions between the UNLA's military and political factions. As a result, the UNLA ousted Lule. He was replaced by Obote's former attorney general, Godfrey Binaisa. However, political infighting within the UNLA kept Uganda from stability. In August 1979, Binaisa banned all political parties to avoid "the politics of religion, sectarianism, rivalry and hatred, and be able to work for and even achieve the politics of consensus" (Mutibwa 1992: 134). Less than nine months later, on 13 May 1980, pro-Obote factions within the military of the UNLA placed Binaisi under house arrest, forcefully removing him from power. Elections for a new head of state were scheduled for 10 December 1980.

Even though corruption ruled the political process, the elections proved to be a "watershed event in Uganda's political history" (Human Rights Watch 1999: 4). Four main political parties took part in the elections: (1) Obote's UPC, (2) the predominantly Catholic Democratic Party (DP), (3) the Uganda Patriotic Movement (UPM) of Yoweri Museveni, and (4) the Buganda-dominated Conservative Party (CP). Obote's UPC party won the majority of seats in the National Assembly and he was proclaimed president of Uganda for a second time. International monitors claim the elections were marred by irregularities. This was echoed by the DP and UPM parties, accusing the pro-Obote military commission of rigging the results. In response to the irregularities of the elections and the UPC's return to power, three separate political movements were created to wage guerilla war in an effort to unseat Obote. The largest was Museveni's National Resistance Army (NRA). Museveni's call to arms was simple, "Once again, a minority, unpopular clique was imposed on the people of Uganda, leaving them with no option but to take up arms in defense of their democratic rights" (Museveni 1990: 3).

The NRA routinely conducted violent guerrilla operations throughout Uganda. Once the last of the Tanzanian forces withdrew, the NRA took to attacking former Amin supporters. Although Obote was acting head of state, he could not keep control of the Ugandan military forces (UNLA), most of which did not view him as a legitimate leader. As such, extrajudicial killings became the order of the day as the military forces fought against the NRA guerillas. Obote freely used violence to reimpose his rule. When NGOs and media outlets exposed the regime's crimes, Obote followed Amin's path and secluded Uganda from the international organizations' reach as much as possible. In 1982, after the International Committee of the Red Cross/Red Crescent published a report detailing civilian massacres, Obote ordered all IRCRC personnel out of Uganda. Further, all foreign journalists were forced to leave as well.

In July, the UNLA began a systematic round up of civilians who were then placed in government camps for indeterminate amounts of time. Obote claimed to be directing these detainments at NRA rebels, but in practice the net was pitched much wider and his troops cared little as to who was imprisoned. Under these conditions Uganda continued to experience political and economic chaos as well as being subjected to tribal massacres carried out by armed factions and governmental random violence.

As the struggle between UNLA and the NRA intensified, military barracks and private businesses (e.g., the Nile Hotel, Katikamu, Kireka) became killing centers. The Military's violence and brutality against civilians even exceeded the brutality of the Amin era. Indeed, Obote's security forces had one of the worst human rights records in recent history. In their efforts to stamp out the NRA, they destroyed a substantial section of the country. As such the ongoing civil war was characterized as nothing short of a "wanton disregard for human rights by government troops" resulting in massive loss of human lives (Human Rights Watch 1999: 5). The hardest hit areas included Buganda and the Luwero triangle. Approximately 200,000 Ugandans fled to the Congo, Rwanda, and Sudan.

Despite the repressive measures, the NRA made major progress in its campaign against the Obote government. With Buganda being one of the hardest hit areas, the strong anti-Obote sentiments in that area ensured NRA support in the region. Other rebel groups were actively involved in counter government attacks, including the pro-Amin Uganda National Army (UNA) and the Uganda National Rescue Front (UNRF). The UNLA could not focus all of its resources on the NRA.

Interethnic tensions continued to mount amidst the ongoing civil war, most notably those between the Acholi and Langi. With such mounting tensions, elements of Obote's own army, Brigadier Basilio Okello and Lt. General Tito Lutwa Okello (both Acholi), used the opportunity to depose Obote (a Langi) in another coup in May 1985. Tito Okello became the new head of state. However, the violence did not subside; the trend of extrajudicial killings by government forces continued. The NRA continued its guerrilla campaign to take control of the state. Whereas some of the insurgent groups joined the Okello party, the NRA refused as Museveni was dissatisfied with the representation in the Military Council offered to the NRA. For four months the Okello regime and the NRA engaged in peace talks in Nairobi. However, the Nairobi Peace Accords were never implemented. Violence continued on the part of the NRA and the military forces. By this time approximately

700,000 human remains were buried in mass graves in the Luwero Triangle (Human Rights Watch 1999). In January 1986, Museveni's NRA stormed Kampala and overthrew the dictatorship, effectively establishing itself as the government and Yoweri Museveni as the new president, a position he holds at the time of this writing.

The Museveni Era

Museveni began his rule at the head of a coalition government designed to minimize political opposition. The first step included an announcement that all political party activity was to be suspended during the transition period from the Okella coup to when elections were to be held (Legal Notice No. 1 of 1986). The ban also created the unelected National Resistance Council (NRC) to govern during the interim period. The coalition government had begun to shrink to only Museveni supporters as the other groups that merged with the NRA for the purposes of carrying out the coup began to distance themselves. As noted by Human Rights Watch (1999: 7), "All these groups eventually withdrew from the coalition, citing the government's complicity in human rights violations, official corruption, continuing instability in northern and eastern Uganda, the creation of tribal animosities, and communist and Libyan infiltration of Uganda." Although the NRA faced opposition, its responses were far from moderate. During the course of its anti-insurgency operations, the NRA detained thousands of civilians, holding them without charges at military barracks for undetermined times. Many died in captivity; 69 civilians died at Mukuru, after suffocating in a locked train compartment. Political opponents and critics of the government faced harassment, abuse, and arrest (Human Rights Watch 1999).

The Uganda People's Army was the first armed opposition group that formed against Museveni's new regime. Among the groups opposed to Museveni were numerous Acholi-based remnants of the Ugandan National Liberation Army that had been fundamental in the removal of Amin from power. Unable to mount an effective and coordinated defense against the NRA, various Acholi factions retreated into the northern hinterlands. Later regrouping in Gulu, the UMPA provided patchy resistance. Unsuccessful in their attempts to stop the NRA, defeated and demoralized, most returned to their villages or surrendered to the advancing NRA. Museveni ordered all former soldiers to turn themselves in to the government and receive amnesty. However, as with Amin, those that were detained, were tortured and killed. Military operations continued against those who stayed in the field. Once the NRA regime began transferring detainees to "reeducation camps" in the south, many of the UNLA soldiers fled further into Northern Uganda, regrouping and organizing under former UNLA Military Commander Brigadier Odong Latek and other senior officers. Along with many civilians joining the cause to resist Museveni, the ex-soldiers established the Uganda People's Democratic Army (UPDA). Civilian support for the resistance was initially very high as Acholi regions foresaw negative treatment at Museveni's hands. As Van Acker (2004) points out, since the colonial period the Acholi have long been regarded as a sort of *lumpen militariat*. Little economic development had occurred in the region and the population has been typically drawn upon to fill the ranks of armies organized by non-northern interests, be they the British government, who drew heavily on the Acholi in building the King's African Rifles (Taylor 2005), or later governments of Uganda. In fact, this lack of development has been justified by a set of discourses that painted the Acholi as inherently warlike and perfect for soldiering that originated in the colonial period (see Apuuli 2004; Finnstrom 2006). In consequence, soldiers returning home after conflicts, especially after the 1986 NRA coup, had little in the way of peace-time skills.

The UPDA's attack on Gulu, August 1986, marked the beginning of the current conflict. Primarily Acholi in composition, the UPDA also included northern Ugandans from the West Nile, Teso, and Lango. However, its political faction, the Uganda People's Democratic Movement (UPDM), headed by former Prime Minister Eric Otema Alimada, was mainly operating out of Kenya and the UK. Unlike the UPDA, the UPDM was filled with petty rivalries and factionalism and the influence of the UPDA diminished considerably within a short period of time. Nonetheless, the UPDM/A achieved some early successes. During 1988, the UPDA and the government came to a peaceful resolution; however, this did not include the political arm—the UPDM. Although many of the UPDA soldiers were integrated into the NRA, fundamental political and governance issues and unmet demands led to discontent. Many chose to flee into exile once again. Consequently, the remaining UPDA that rejected the 1988 peace initiative were quickly absorbed into the growing Holy Spirit Movement (HSM).

The Holy Spirit Movement should be viewed as a revitalization movement in that it attempted to recreate the universe and a moral order disintegrated by broader events (typically colonial incursions or major episodes of violence and warfare). Through drawing upon the ideas of purification—of individuals, groups, and the social fabric itself—both the HSM and later the LRA promised an idyllic future created out of a mystical past superior to the chaotic present. Both militias originally gained legitimacy by offering a path forward unrelated to the secular postcolonial governments of Amin and Museveni and one that had purportedly corrected the mistakes of the past that allowed Acholi-land to fall upon ill-fortune.

In the wake of the civil wars, the Acholi regions of northern Uganda were plagued by former soldiers living by looting, pillaging, and harassment of the local populations. Such phenomena are not uncommon in a postwar landscape when a governmental order has not been imposed. Still, the commonality of it was no comfort to the peoples of northern Uganda. Whereas tribal elders attempted to reassert traditional Acholi values of conduct, due to the weakening of the culture during the colonial and civil war period, they were unsuccessful. Yet, core traditionalist values framed the way in which the soldiers were defined and their experiences interpreted within the community. Out of this context emerged Alice Auma and the Holy Spirit Movement. Originally, Auma was not a solider, but a spiritualist and a lay healer attending to the military and civilian persons displaced owing to the civil disorder of the 1970s and 1980s. Before her ascension as prophet, Auma was a healer and spiritual medium in Kitgum. Auma claimed to have been possessed by the spirit Lakwena, from whom she received guidance, direction, and her new name.

The discourse created by Auma/Lakwena—later drawn upon by Jospeh Kony—was an attempt to redefine the moral universe of Acholi-land in light of the failures of older cultural structures to make sense of their current condition. By identifying the *cen* former soldiers were bringing back to the community, as well as their refusal to undergo traditional cleaning rituals, a spiritual source of Acholi ill-luck and domination was identified. Purification was a rallying cry for social change. Alice's status as a medium added legitimacy to the movement. Politically based attempts to protect Acholli-land had failed, but Auma/Lakwena was neither a political leader per se, nor was she even the perceived origin of the ideas, orders, and tactics of the HSM. She was merely the physical conduit for spirit-led communications—a *loar* or spirit messenger.

Alice's troops had to first be cleansed of their perceived impurities. Their histories of killing, looting, raping, as well as their past military defeats marked them as followed by the *cen* or spritis of those they had killed. In general, the *cen* were blamed for the general bad luck and hard lives of the Acholi people overall (Behrend 1998). To join the HSM, soldiers had to be ritualistically cleansed in a practice that was reminiscent both of traditionalist Acholi purification rituals as well as Christian baptism. Yet, each new battle, and associated killings, required purification of the newly acquired *cen*. Lakwena forbade her troops from looting, rape, murder, smoking, drinking, and sex. Although these prohibitions were strongly rooted in the religious-spiritual discourses of the movement, they also addressed the core problems caused by the soldiers before joining. Death in battle was a sign of failure on behalf of a soldier—a spiritually pure solider would be missed by enemy bullets.

After early HSM victories in November and December of 1986, Museveni's forces achieved the upper hand and soundly defeated the HSM. Lakwena fled to Kenya in late 1987. Alice Auma/Lakwena's movement did not exist long enough to devolve into something other than it originally was—a widespread anti-Museveni resistance movement. Her defeat outside of Kampala allowed the HSM to dissolve while still holding onto much of its spiritual and reformatory legitimacy. She died in a Kenyan refugee camp in late 2006 or early 2007.

In 1989, Museveni extended his ban on opposition political parties for an additional five years, claiming that the continued insurgent movements had prevented the NRM from reaching its political objectives for Uganda. The means used to suppress political activity "revealed a readiness to resort to strong shows of force, and had a lasting chilling effect on the willingness of Ugandans to challenge restrictions on political activity which remain in effect today" (Human Rights Watch 1999: 1). Museveni responded to the planned rally by stating in Parliament that those who attended the rally would be killed: "I have told the police to stop political gatherings using force. Tell your supporters that they will be killed if they attend political rallies" (Human Rights Watch 1999: 7). Ugandan forces sealed off the area bringing in helicopters to intimidate any party supporters. Such show of force not only led to a general unwillingness to challenge the political process, it also led to a strengthening of Museveni resistance movements.

Even with the defeat of Lakwena's forces, the Acholi-based resistance to Museveni's government was strong. Shortly after her defeat, new leaders and militias arose to try and harness the same unrest. The militia was reorganized as the United Holy Salvation Army under the leadership of Joseph Koney, currently known as the LRA. From the onset, the LRA committed serious atrocities on both the NRA forces and the general citizenry. For example, between 1989 and 1991, the LRA was responsible for the deaths of hundreds of people and had abducted thousands of villagers in Gulu, Kitgum, and neighboring districts. They subjected innocent civilians to mutilations of body parts, cutting off their hands, ears, lips, or gouging out their eyes (Kasibante 2006).

Most writers on the topic have attributed the widespread brutality visited upon civilians in the north by the LRA as an indirect or direct form of importation of tactics from Sierra Leonne. Such atrocities are interpreted as a way in which the LRA punishes civilian populations for not supporting them and as a form of warning to others. Yet, a deeper reading of the religious beliefs underpinning the movement suggests another potential function: a reconfiguration of a cleaning/purification ritual. As a way to make, what is in the eyes of the LRA, a recalcitrant population atone for their failures to properly support soldiers fighting to bring them a new world, the use of mutilation takes on the form of penance and a violent purification of nonbelievers. This is reflected in a statement by Koney where he later attempted to justify these actions during peace talks with Museveni's administration in 1994, "If you picked up an arrow against us and we ended up cutting off the hand you used, who is to blame? You report us with your mouth, and we cut off your lips. Who is to blame? It is you! The Bible says that if your hand, eye or mouth is at fault, it should be cut off" (Kasibante 2006: 262).

Kony, following the lead of Auma/Lakwean, claims *loar* status and presents himself as a mouthpiece for supernatural forces seeking to remake the world. Although much Western reporting has highlighted the Christian fundamentalism of his discourses, especially his vocalized intent to build a society rooted in the Old Testament's Ten Commandments, the religious underpinnings of the LRA are, like the HSM, syncretic in nature and draw as much on traditional Acholi animism as they do on Christian theology. Further, as the reports of former child soldiers who served with the LRA indicate, Kony is also blending elements of Islam into his discourse and practices—not surprising considering his long encampment in southern Sudan.

We do not wish to present the LRA as a group of religious fanatics, as such an interpretation is not only inaccurate but dangerously reductionistic. The religious ideology at the core of the movement provides a powerful source of solidarity, a central set of motivating elements, and a worldview that legitimates violence. As Van Acker (2004: 349) points out, the religious ideology recreates violence within a "transcendental dimension. ... [wherever violence is] not only ... a necessary expedient ... but [is] divinely decreed, and hence morally justified." Such discourse does not automatically legitimate the army in the eyes of the Acholi people, who have long been victimized by Kony's forces. Support for the LRM/A among the populations of Gulu and Kitgum is significantly less than that previously enjoyed by the UPDM and the HSM.

The LRA has complained about being betrayed by former UPDA combatants and Acholi elders, who they blame for blessing them initially and encouraging them to join the rebellion, but later abandoning them. Owing to the lack of popular support, the LRA resorted to forced recruitment of young people. Those who resisted abduction were brutally punished or killed. In fact, many northern Ugandans see Kony as an *ajwaka*—a witch doctor or someone who uses magic for personal gain not community benefit. His use of *jok* (spirit power) crossed the line in their eyes from an attempt to remake Acholi-land out of its past failures and denigrations into a wide-scale campaign of pure violence and destruction.

The best source of current practices of the LRA came from the children they abducted to serve as soldiers. Human Rights Watch (1997) interviewed numerous former child soldiers. Within their testimonies is a vivid description of the ritualistic and theological aspects Kony uses to structure daily life within the LRA. Molly described the blended nature of the religious practices:

> They prayed a lot, but they didn't pray like normal Christians. Sometime they would use rosaries, but sometimes they would bow down like Muslims. They said they had a *malaika* [spirit angel]. They said the *malaika* said there would be a terrible fight.

Christine described initiation ritual used for new recruits:

> They drew a picture of a large heart on the ground, and divided it into thirty squares. They told us to bathe and to remove our blouses and remain bare chested. They told each of us to stand in one of the squares. They dipped an egg mixture of white powder and water, and drew a heart on our chests and our backs, They also made a sign of the cross on our foreheads and ... across our lips. Then they poured water on us. ... he said they were doing what was written in the bible.

Christine's description highlights the LRA's continued use of the purification rituals originally used by Auma/Lawkena in the HSM. The process used by the LRA holds traditional elements as well as Christian-derived elements. As with the HSM, the continuing religious goal is to purify the solider of prior *cen* or impurities. Also, such symbolic bonding practices help to generate group solidarity and facilitate individual identification with the nature and goals of the LRA itself. Stephen described the prebattle rituals he participated in:

> When you go to fight you make the sign of the cross first. If you fail to do this, you will be killed. You must also take oil and draw a cross on your chest, your forehead, and each shoulder and you must make a cross in oil on your gun. They said that the oil is the power of the Holy Spirits ... also you take a small stone, you sew it on a cloth

and wear it around your wrist like a watch. That is to prevent that bullet might come, because in battle it is acting as a mountain. So those people on the other side will look at you, but they will see only a mountain and the bullets will hit the mountain and not you ... you also have water: they call it clean water and they pour it into a small bottle, If you go to the front, you also have a small stick and you dip it in the battle and fling the water out. This is a river and it drowns the bullet that might come to you. ... finally you wear a cross on a chain. But in the fighting you wrap it around your wrist and hold it in your hand. Should you make a mistake and not wear it on your hand, you will be killed.

The elements of sympathetic magic are readily apparent in Stephen's descriptions. Through symbolic association on item or image (e.g., the oil, the rock) is deemed to transfer the broader qualities of the symbolized item to the bearer. Such ritualism has been transferred to a motivational factor for members of the LRA. As such, their struggle against the NRM government is a divine cause that is being directed and guided by God through Kony. Thus an LRA fighter goes into battle in the firm belief that God is on his or her side and that God will ensure the defeat of the enemy. Consequently, they fight fearlessly, taking undue risks and rarely taking cover, all the while shouting and singing religious songs in praise of God. Although the means of fighting have a religious tone, the LRA operates as an army; it is organized in a military-type hierarchy (e.g., Kony as the Chairman and Commander-in-Chief, Vincent Otti, the Vice-Chairman and second-in-command; the army commander; three senior posts of Deputy Army Commander, Brigade General and Division Commander; and four commanders of equal rank, each of whom leads one of the four LRA brigades) and operates as any army would through subunits and a chain of command. The LRA forces are divided into four main brigades called the Stockree, Sinia, Trinkle, and Gilva (ICC 2004).

By the end of 1991, the tactics of the LRA shifted (Human Rights Watch 1997). The targeting and attacks on civilians increased and a general pattern of abductions of children and females were stepped up. However, there is little publicly available information regarding the LRA's activities during this time. With the increase in LRA resistance, Museveni, unable to conquer the LRA, began Operation North in March 1991, to defeat Joseph Koney's forces. The northern districts of Uganda were sealed off from all external visitors (e.g., NGOs and media), thereby creating an information blackout. Civilians were rounded up and placed in camps, supposedly for their own safety. In reality, the government was trying to remove as much population as possible for the area. This simultaneously prevented the LRA from receiving succor from civilians, and allowed any one encountered by UPDF forces in the region to be identified as LRA.

As both governmental forces and militias continued to commit atrocities on the population, Museveni continued to repress all political opposition in an effort to maintain control of the government and sealed off the northern districts of Northern Uganda for "Operation North." The sealing of the districts essentially kept all external visitors from entering the areas (e.g., NGOs and media) thereby creating an information blackout. As both governmental forces and militias continued to commit atrocities on the population, Museveni continued to repress all political opposition in an effort to maintain control of the government.

At the same time, the regime mandated a widespread media blackout, blocked communications, and a decree forbidding movement between provinces of the north and the rest of Uganda. Operation North included the massive arrest of civic leaders and the creation of placement camps. Human Rights Watch reported that the NRA soldiers were committing serious human right violations in the camps. Human Rights Watch (1997: 84) states,

> People were herded into camps without food, health care, etc. for days at various locations purportedly for screening. Many people died and there were human rights abuses all over. Some innocent civilians were buried alive in Bucoro, while others were shot, crops in the fields were destroyed by the National Resistance Army. The NRA Mobile Battalion nicknamed 'GUNGA' committed homosexual acts even with very old men, raped wives, mothers and daughters in the presence of their families.

At the same time, Kony had also started abducting, raping, and killing of innocent people. The LRA's use of mutilation had also taken off by this point. This was in part a response to the government's attempt to form local militias in northern Uganda. Civilians were seen as being less than supportive of the LRA's mission, supporters of the government, and/or betrayers. As such, arms, hands, lips, and breasts were cut off leaving civilians severely disfigured. This was in an effort also to dissuade any support to the government through generating mass fear and public panic.

In 1994, a constituent assembly was elected resulting in the 1995 constitution that legalized and extended Museveni's ban on political parties. While intermittent militia attacks were an ongoing issue giving rise to counterinsurgency movements by the Ugandan regime, troops were also involved in helping rebel groups to carry out coups in the Congo (including the removal of Mobutu Sese Seko and Laurent Kalila). With the Ugandan army involved in several fronts, some attempts were made by the regime to negotiate with the LRA.

In 1994 negotiations between Museveni and the LRA began. However, these failed to subdue the ongoing violence. The regime claimed that the LRA was not serious about achieving peace, yet, Museveni's opponents claimed that the government was not serious, instead, using peace talks as ambushes to kill rebel commanders. Further, the religious ideology that drives the LRA offered little hope for a peaceful resolution. As their self-professed reason for existence in the purification of the Acholi and of Uganda, they are not amenable to power-sharing agreements or other typical peace accord processes. The fundamentalist nature of their discourse left few options. This held true in the multiple attempts to negotiate peace talks. Upon the collapse of the 1994 peace talks, Kony blamed the Acholi for not supporting him. In February 1994, Museveni announced that the LRA had seven days to surrender or they would face military force that would result in the end of the LRA. In response, the LRA withdrew to southern Sudan establishing bases and reequipping with modern weapons furnished by the government of Sudan.

At this point, Sudan began providing substantial aid to the LRA in the form of weapons and land mines as well as a much needed safe haven. This had a significant impact on the level of violence the LRA could carry out. As such, since 1995, the number of people abducted and killed by the LRA had "dramatically increased" (Human Rights Watch Report 1997: 85). Throughout the Acholi area, the LRA conducted massacres of civilians, more than 200 people died in Atyak alone. They also invaded Kitgum, killing and brutalizing civilians. The LRA practice of abducting children to fight their cause also intensified.

During the resurgence of violence, Uganda's new Constitution took effect which included the renaming of the NRA as the Uganda People's Defense Forces (UPDF). Another active rebel group, the Allied Democratic Forces (ADF), was also conducting raids and instituting violence on the general citizenry. The following year, 1996 saw a rise in the violence on the part of the UPDF, ADF, and LRA. Although instability from the violence kept the population in turmoil, the economy was also in dire conditions as billions of dollars was pumped into the military budget, taking primacy over all other needs of the state.

With the ongoing instability and violence, the regime again reinitiated the practice of "encouraging" rural citizens to move into protected camps where they were again subjected to ill treatment. If civilians were unwilling to go to the camps, the UPDF used violence to ensure their compliance. The UPDF also carried out violence directed at perceived insurgents. For example, in September, a mob lynched alleged rebels in military custody under the supervision of and with the encouragement of Colonial Kazini.

By 1998, UNICEF estimated that over 10,000 children had been abducted by the LRA. Political violence continued to escalate. The majority of the population in the north continued to live in camps and their subsistence remained almost completely dependent on international humanitarian organizations. As such, NGO workers were soon considered to be legitimate military targets by the LRA because of their support for what they called Museveni's "concentration camps." Consequently, they attacked food convoys from the World Food Program (WFP). This coupled with the ongoing violence in Kitgum led to a temporary withdrawal by most nongovernmental organizations during May to June 1998. As we have noted, the violence and crimes against humanity that were occurring were not solely the work of militia groups; Museveni's army, the police, and other governmental security organizations were also responsible. For example: massive numbers of rapes by UPDF soldiers were reported in the north, they continued to detain civilians illegally at army facilities or protected camps and over a thousand persons perceived as rebel supporters remained in Ugandan prisons on charges of treason without legal due process. In addition, government suspects were tortured or executed, beaten with heavy canes, and burned by UPDF soldiers. Young children were detained on treason charges; they were physically abused and/or raped while in police or UPDF custody. By mid-2000, approximately 400,000 citizens of Acholi were in "protected UPDF villages" where they were subject to constant violence.

The following year, Museveni won his second term, under a cloud of voting irregularities and political intimidation. Museveni's governmental agencies continued their violent practices. UPDF units attacked religious leaders who were meeting with LRA leaders to discuss means for reporting under the amnesty granted by Museveni. In response, the LRA again resumed attacking civilians. They launched an attack on Agoro taking the local soldiers who were stationed in the government protection area killing three soldiers and abducting approximately one hundred of the camp dwellers. Reports surfaced of civilians being hacked to death, the elderly were killed with machetes and spears, and infants were reported to have been flung against trees, killing them on impact.

The increase in child abductions continued; their treatments included frequent beatings, being forced to burn houses, and beat and kill civilians including babies and other children. The females were sexually enslaved as "wives" to LRA commanders and subjected to systematic rape including gang rapes, and unwanted pregnancies. By this point, Museveni's army had been fighting the LRA for over ten years. The Ugandan political landscape was defined by the continued violence. Political, civil, and human rights were violated. Uganda was also a major player in armed conflicts in the region.

During 1999 and 2000, Ugandan forces were again involved in international conflicts and were often at odds with Rwanda. However, it was the ongoing intervention in the Congo and general corruption and violations of human rights and abuses that amplified the general discontent of Ugandans. Further, the economic prosperity and security, although lauded as significant progress, was only occurring in certain regions. The southern and western areas of Uganda, especially the Ankole region, enjoyed considerable security and financial prosperity; in the north, conflict continued and poverty grew. In July 2001, Museveni publicly admitted this discrepancy and stated that "while the level of absolute poverty has been reduced from 56 to 35 percent in most parts of the country, in northern Uganda it has instead gone up from 60 to 66 in the last three years" (*The Monitor*, Kampala, 30 July 2001: 1). Nonetheless, in 2001, Museveni was reelected by a narrow margin in an election fraught with fraud.

In 2002, the Sudanese government cut off assistance to the LRA. During March of that year, Sudan gave permission for the UPDF to launch attacks against the LRA in southern Sudan. Operation Iron Fist failed as the LRA fled into mountainous regions in Sudan then crossing back over the border entering Uganda. Not unlike Operation North, Operation Iron Fist had a dire impact on the civilians in northern Uganda and southern Sudan as a consequence of both LRA practices and the UPDF. The LRA increased its attacks in northern Uganda by abducting and killing civilians, looting villages, and attacking camps for internally displaced persons. In August, the LRA declared that all NGO humanitarian workers in northern Uganda had to withdraw or risk becoming targets of attack. In July 2002, LRA forces attacked a refugee camp in Adjumani killing refugees and causing over six thousand of the civilians in the camp to flee. The same pattern was repeated the following month on the Acholi settlement that resulted in the deaths of about 60 civilians and the displacement of approximately 24,000 civilians who were fleeing the camp.

The UPDF forces also continued to commit abuses. Although the LRA forced citizens in the camps to flee, the UPDF were actively abusing them while they were allegedly in protective areas. Forces were carrying out a systematic policy of torture and rape in connection with "cordon and search" missions. Methods of torture included the gang rape of females and attaching wires to, beating, and kicking the male genitals resulting in a loss of penile function. Further, just as the LRA abducted children forcing them to join their cause against the Ugandan government, the Ugandan army also "recruited" children, many of whom had escaped the LRA, in the camps as "home guards" or local defense units (LDU). Yet, the children were used for more than carrying out local watches or security; they were used to fight against the LRA in northern Uganda, the Congo, and Sudan.

The army too began increasing their practice of arbitrary detention of civilians, instituting harsh measures of care including torture, death, and/or rape. Ugandan security and military forces continued to use "safe houses," unauthorized secret detention centers, and, increasingly, civilian police facilities to detain and torture suspected rebels and dissidents. The UPDF continued to maintain its hold in the Congo, supporting rebel groups that were also committing mass atrocities and were engaged in child abduction, becoming child soldiers.

By November 2003, the humanitarian crisis in northern Uganda was proclaimed as the "worst on the planet" by United Nations Under-Secretary General for Humanitarian Affairs and Humanitarian Relief Coordinator Jan Egeland (Global Security Report 2006). Moreover, the Ugandan Human Rights Commission's report stated that the use of torture by UPDF and Ugandan security forces were "presented as part of training" and was "indispensable" to the operations of some Ugandan security agencies. These mass human rights violations continued throughout 2004.

Enter the International Criminal Court

In December 2003, out of options, Museveni referred the ongoing conflict with the LRA and their crimes against humanity to the International Criminal Court. On 29 January 2004 the ICC Prosecutor, Louis Occampa, and Museveni held a joint press conference in London to announce the referral to the court. This caused outrage among Ugandans, NGOs, and militia groups calling into question the legitimacy of the court. Knowing that Museveni and the UPDF were deeply involved in crimes against humanity including child abductions, torture, rape, indeterminate detentions, and civilian displacement, the public announcement appeared as if the court was providing additional impunity to the regime. As stated by Jerome Rone (2005: 1), "Justice in northern Uganda requires that the International Criminal Court thoroughly examine government forces' crimes against the civilian population as well as those committed by the rebels." The court failed to effectively communicate its mandate and impartiality to the civilians of northern Uganda. This has undermined the court's credibility and impartiality in the eyes of many there.

In October 2005, the court announced arrest warrants for Joseph Kony and four of his top deputies. The charges ranged from the mutilation of civilians to the forced abduction of and sexual abuse of children. Less than a year later, LRA representatives again started to participate in a series of peace talks with the government. However, the talks broke down relatively quickly as both sides failed to abide by the conditions of the negotiation process. Both Koney and Vincent Otti were hesitant about meeting their side of the bargain as talks needed to occur in Sudan. As such, it meant that they would be at risk for arrest to appear at the ICC. Since, the LRA refused to engage in any peace talks or other negotiations until the court ceased its instigations and dropped the charges against its leaders. Museveni said he would only talk to the ICC about taking back his request for indictments once the rebels signed comprehensive peace agreement. However, it was no longer Museveni's choice, as the case was completely in the hands of the court.

The Prosecutor of the Court's amended arrest charges against Joseph Koney, Vincent Otti, Raska Lukwiya, Okot Odhiambo, and Dominic Ongwen states that since 1987, and continuing since July 2002, the defendants had been,

> directing attacks against both the UPDF. ... and against civilian populations; that, in pursuing its goals, the LRA has engaged in a cycle of violence and established a pattern of "brutalization of civilians" by acts including murder, abduction, sexual enslavement, mutilation, as well as mass burnings of houses and looting of camp settlements; that abducted civilians, including children, are said to have been forcibly "recruited" as fighters, porters and sex slaves to serve the LRA and to contribute to attacks against the Ugandan army and civilian communities. (ICC 2005: 3)

In all, there were 33 counts of crimes against humanity and war crimes brought against Koney, Otti, and Ongwen, 19 counts against Odhiambo, and 9 counts against Lukwiya. Specifically, Koney, Otti, and Ongwen were charged with sexual enslavement and attempted sexual enslavement; rape, attacks against the civilian population; the enlisting through abduction of children; enslavement of civilians; cruel treatment of civilian residents in camps; pillage;

murder; and inhumane acts of inflicting serious bodily injury and suffering upon civilian residents. Similar, though fewer, charges were brought against Lukwiya and Odhiambo including pillage, enslavement, and cruel treatment, and directing attacks on the civilian population of Uganda.

There is no doubt that such offenses have been carried out by the LRA. However, as we noted, the lack of charges against the NRA and/or Museveni himself seriously jeopardized the court's legitimacy, especially within the Acholi region wherein most of the violence had occurred. In a survey of Ugandan civilians conducted by The International Center for Transitional Justice and the Human Rights Center (2005) when respondents were asked what should happen to UPDF who committed abuse, 51% of respondents stated they wanted them placed on trial and held accountable and 33% wanted to see them punished in some form including imprisonment. At the time of this writing it is unclear whether the ICC Prosecutor will indeed heed the concerns of Ugandan civilians and NGOs and issue arrests for individuals within the Ugandan government who carried out similar LRA atrocities.

Summary

Since the time of independence, Uganda has been devastated by political turmoil, coups, insurgencies, war, and general unrest. Unlike other colonial ruled states, Uganda did not experience the all too common construction of racial identities for political interests of the occupying forces. Religious institutions and spiritual leaders did not play as significant a role in the economic or political sphere as was the case in Rwanda. Although there were fractions based on religious beliefs, they were not used to create a "racial" other (see the Bosnian Muslims genocide).

As such Uganda's troubles since independence in 1962 were primarily the result of politically inspired violence that has been endemic postindependence. The impetus for the political violence is related to the "trickery political legacy" since the beginning of independence and then aggravated further by the political mismanagement and the overtly abusive one-party regimes of Obote I and II, Amin, and Museveni (Clapham 1998: 3). This has resulted in a perpetual practice of governmental coups and the formation of militia insurgent groups vying for political power. Further, it has been northern Uganda that has suffered the most severe violence and additional hardships from the civil unrest beyond other regions since the early 1980s. Recall that among the groups opposed to Museveni were numerous Acholi-based remnants of the Ugandan National Liberation Army that had been fundamental in the removal of Amin from power. Unable to mount an effective and a coordinated defense against the NRA, various Acholi factions retreated into the northern hinterlands and provided patchy resistance. Plagued by former soldiers' looting, pillaging, and harassment, local tribal elders attempted to reassert traditional Acholi values of conduct, yet they were unsuccessful. Out of this context emerged Alice Auma and the Holy Spirit Forces Movement followed by the LRA.

As the most formidable opponent of the NRA and Museveni, the LRA continued with its governmental resistance for the past 20 years. However, as we have noted, Ugandan civilian violence does not rest solely upon the militias operating within Uganda or neighboring states. Indeed, Museveni and governmental forces have committed their fare share of abuses. In all hundreds of civilians have been killed in the rebellion against the Ugandan government and by Ugandan military forces with an estimated 400,000 people left homeless and scores of others that have been subjected to human right abuses, torture, maiming, and child abductions.

· 6 ·

TWO CENTURIES OF HORROR

On 10 February 2006, the International Criminal Court (ICC) issued its first arrest warrant for Thomas Lubanga Dyilo, head of the Union Patriotic Congolese (UPC), one of the major militia groups involved in the ongoing civil war. Dyilo was arrested and charged with the enlistment and conscription of children under the age of 15 and the use of these children to actively participate in the hostilities. As we discuss in this chapter, the illegality of the UPC is not limited to the recruiting and fielding of child soldiers. Further, the UPC is not the only militia group to have committed these types of atrocities. More than a dozen local militia groups have been active in these behaviors since the onset of the Second Congolese War in 1998. In addition, troops from at least six foreign countries have operated within the DRC during this period (Rwanda, Uganda, Chad, the Sudan, Burundi, and Angola). As observers of the conflict have pointed out, everyone involved has violated international law and human dignity through the commission of atrocities, including crimes against humanity.

Since independence in 1960, the country has endured repeated rebellions against the state, experiencing stability only during the corrupt and harsh reign of Joseph Mobutu Sese Seko between 1964 and 1996. Since Mobutu's overthrow in 1996–7 (the "First Congolese War") the region has been plagued by conflict and turmoil. Specifically, the fall of Mobutu's regime ushered in a 20-year period of chaos, violence, disorder, and atrocity. Not unlike the genocide in Rwanda, the roots of the conflict in the DRC stem back to its colonial history. Although the experiences of Leopold II's brutal colonization enterprises did neither directly create the chaos that remains in the aftermath of the 1998 war, nor is it directly responsible for the atrocities seen in the country since 1996, it did establish a pattern of repressive and violent governmental behavior that still reverberates within the Congolese consciousness.

Since 1998, the conflict in the DRC has claimed more than 3.5 million lives. Human Rights Watch (2006c) estimates that more than 1,200 people die per day from direct violence, as well as the indirect results of warfare, for example, starvation and lack of medical care. Tens of thousands of women and girls have been raped; a World Health Organization survey of only two provinces, South Kivu and Maniema, and two cities, Goma and Kalemie, estimated that at least 40,000 rapes have occurred in those places alone. Governmental, rebel, foreign, and militia forces all participate in the ongoing sexual violence against women and children. In addition, there is strong evidence to suggest that, like Rwanda to the east, these rapes are more than war-related; some of the sexual violence is ethnically targeted and motivated, fitting the broader pattern of genocidal rape we discussed in Chapter One (Human Rights Watch 2005c, 2006c).

Although the standing government in Kinshasa is internationally recognized, it has more power in the international political community than it does in its own territory. Much of the east, especially the regions of Ituri in Orientale province, the provinces of North and South Kivu and southern district of Katanga, as of June 2007, remain run by warlords and factional ethnic-based militias. Though some of the militia and rebel groups have accepted a power-sharing agreement with the standing government that included the integration of their troops into the national armed forces, other groups maintain their violent opposition to the government in Kinshasa. As in Uganda, the militias use extraordinary violence—physical and sexual—to terrorize local populations, ruling by force and fear.

Although the Lusaka Agreements, which have brought at least nominal peace to the DRC, bring some hope, there is little to suggest that the end of the war is in sight. Despite the fact that a UN Peacekeeping mission (MONUC) is on the ground, it has had a limited impact on the ongoing conflict. Specifically, the Security Council authorized MONUC to use all necessary means to (1) maintain a presence in volatile areas; (2) protect UN personnel, facilities, installations, and equipment; (3) seize or collect, as appropriate, arms and any related materiel the presence of which in the territory violates UNSC

Resolution 1493; and to support operations to disarm foreign combatants led by the armed forces of the Democratic Republic of the Congo (UN MONUC Department Report 2007: 1). MONUC consists of 18,336 total uniformed personnel, including 16,594 troops, 713 military observers, 1,029 police; supported by 955 international civilian personnel, 2,010 local civilian staff, and 598 UN Volunteers (United Nations 2007: 1).

MONUC has become mired in its own controversies. First, some members of the international community, especially anti-UN groups within the United States, have continued to call attention to an ongoing sex scandal focusing on peacekeepers patronizing prostitutes and engaging the survival sex market. Second, Pakistani forces—the backbone of MONUC—have been observed selling illegally obtained gold in the Mongbwalu area as well as selling arms to active militias that were taken from demobilized militias (BBC 2007a, 2007b). Thus, further limiting its efficacy and legitimacy, and as such, its ability to constrain the ongoing violence in the DRC.

In this chapter, we provide a historical overview of the events leading to the current situation. By tracing sociohistorical forces since the colonial period, we examine the key catalysts that structure the current and ongoing violence. To do so, we explore the experiences of the Congolese during their domination by Leopold II and later the Belgian government. After a brief discussion of the First Republic (from Independence until Mobutu Sese Seko's second coup), we examine the direly purchased stability under Mobutu's regime. From there we then turn to the 1996 and 1998 wars, and the intense internecine violence that the country has seen since.

Historical Background

Colonial Period

The Congo's colonial experience was one of the harshest and bloodiest in Africa. A claimed territory of King Leopold II of Belgium, first as his personal holdings and then in the twentieth century annexed by Belgium, the colonial experience was extremely brutal. The second generation of a monarchy for a newly reestablished kingdom, Leopold II spent much of his early career as a king actively seeking to acquire colonial holdings for Belgium by whatever means he could. Belgium was a small, newly independent state bounded by France, Holland, Germany, and the sea. With a small, poorly trained army Leopold I knew that the only possible location for territorial and economic expansion lay overseas, in the areas of the world being brought under the yoke of European domination. Leopold II followed his father's vision into the heart of Africa.

Much of Leopold II's public rhetoric of expansion combined a patriotic push to better Belgium with a humanistic language of civilizing Africans and protecting them from the Arab slave trade. Yet, his true intentions were far from benevolent. As Ewans (2002: 17–18) notes, "Leopold never genuinely subscribed to the concept that a colonial power had a serious responsibility for the well-being" of its people, rather he was driven to collect colonial holdings as they would provide economic advantages in the "shape of employment, raw materials and markets for its industry ... and ... the transfer of revenue and riches to the metropolis." Failing to find powers willing to sell off holdings, the same problem that had stymied his father's colonial ambitions, his eyes turned toward sub-Saharan Africa. As he remarked to an associate, Baron Solvys, "we must procure for ourselves a slice of this magnificent African cake" (quoted in Ewans 2002: 18). Most of the continent was coming under the rule of major European colonial powers, but the vast wilds that surrounded the Congo River were largely unexplored and unclaimed.

Although known by European naval powers, especially Britain and Portugal, there was never a strong movement toward colonizing the area. Portugal used the location as a source of slaves, but the nature of the terrain foiled most attempts at inland exploration and domination. The main barrier was the Congo River itself: the last two hundred miles of its descent to the sea were marked by huge cataracts. Navigation required many periods of overland travel to reach the inner reaches of the Congo (Ewans 2002). Although many powers struggled to control the accessible ports in the area, the interior was seen as undesirable and unreachable. Thus, it was still "available" when Leopold II began looking for a potential colony site.

The region was essentially unmapped and unseen by European eyes. Henry Stanley, the famous explorer, was one of the few Europeans to have traveled extensively in the region. His dealings with the natives quickly became infamous for their brutality; the British Consul in Zanzibar referred to his behavior as a "disgrace to humanity" (Ewans 2002: 53). He was as apt to attack natives as entreat them. He sold slaves, acquired an African mistress, and reportedly even kicked a man to death (Ewans 2002; Hoschild 1998). Stanley repeatedly tried to interest the British in the region but to no avail. He did find an audience, however, in Leopold II who was eager to hire Stanley to further survey the river and establish a base in the area.

Later Stanley was called upon to negotiate international recognition of the territory as Belgian. As industrialization increased the demand for raw materials in Europe, many powers were beginning to see Africa as a potential source for items other than slaves. Generally, European powers were hesitant to let a new player into the Africa game, and put off Leopold II's attempts to gain formal recognition for his control over the region. Due to essentially a diplomatic accident, the US officially recognized Leopold's claim. With US support, he cemented control over the Congo through the many diplomatic conferences held on Africa at the end of the nineteenth century (Hoschild 1998; Nzongola-Ntalaja 2002). The most important of these, was the Berlin West African Conference.

In 1884, the Berlin West Africa Conference was held to negotiate agreements among European colonial powers vis-à-vis their conduct within the Congo and Niger river basins and the coastal regions. Even before the conference opened, the four major colonial powers were in disagreement as to the nature and purpose of the meeting. For Britain and Germany, the major concern was keeping trade open and free in the region. France and Portugal had more territorially orientated goals. Leopold II was concerned about maintaining access to the Congo River, a Congo Free State, and about having the ability to control trade in the envisioned holdings (Ewans 2002; Hoschild 1998). The meetings lasted until February 1885, but at the end Leopold had what he wanted: a colony in Africa of more than 900,000 square miles. He had secured access to the sea and was able to position Belgium as a neutral power in both European affairs and the unfolding colonial space of central Africa.

L'Etat Independent du Congo

Although Leopold II had gained the international agreements and promises he sought, he still needed support from his own Parliament. Belgium was, after all, a constitutional monarchy. Article 62 of the Constitution of 1830 required that the Belgian Parliament give approval for Leopold's desire to become monarch of another state while remaining monarch of Belgium. Although the debate was widespread, eventually the Parliament acceded and passed the necessary resolution granting the Congo to Leopold II alone. On 1 August 1885 the founding of *L'Etat Independent du Congo*, the Congo Free State, was announced internationally. The agreement gave Leopold II centralized power over everything that occurred in the territory. The Congo Free State was not a holding of Belgium—it was essentially a large private estate of the king, who intended to make it as profitable as possible. Hargreaves suggests that conditions in what would become the DRC were different as "Belgian rule [of the Congo] … was … intensive; in relation to population there were more white officials, more paramilitary forces, more agricultural officers enforcing more drastic programs of compulsory cultivation, than elsewhere in tropical Africa" (1988: 176). The heavy-handed approach would have long-felt ramifications on the region for over a century.

From the start of European interactions in the Congo river basin, the focus was on facilitating private corporations' extractions of the natural resources of the region—especially the highly valued mineral wealth. As we show later, even with independence, this situation would not change. The initial funding for development in the Free State came from Leopold II's own coffers, loans he could raise internationally, and the investment of corporations and individuals who saw unlimited opportunity for wealth in Africa generally and the Congo particularly. The sole goal of the Belgian Congo was profit generation, with a brutal eye to the bottom line. Yet, the costs of transforming the area into a profitable venture were high. As many had noted, until a railway was built, the resources of the interior were essentially cut off from exploitation. Although the financial costs were great, the cost in human lives was even greater. As Ewans (2002: 114) notes, the building of the first rail line "was said to have cost the lives of 132 Europeans … together with those of some 1,800 Africans … the true figures were much greater." In addition, taxes for both the natives and the foreign traders were high enough to undermine the development of export industries themselves once the railways and basic infrastructure were capable of supporting export markets (Ewans 2002; Hoschild 1998; Williams 1985[1890]).

Lands were claimed under long-standing principles of labeling tracts of terrain that appeared to be vacant as "free," granting it to individuals or corporations to use for resource extraction. The European rationale was that unused land was wasted land, yet this perception was grounded in a misunderstanding of indigenous land-use patterns. Lands that Europeans claimed were "vacant" were untilled and on which no village was built. However, especially in the Congo region, many peoples were not farmers, but rather hunters and gatherers. Even those who practiced varying complexities of horticulture and agriculture further supplemented their diets with hunted game and gathered plant foods from the forests. Thus, whereas colonists saw tracts of forests as "unused" they were in fact heavily used by locals in daily food collection—and essential to their survival. Consequently, native subsistence had a different impact on the environment that Europeans did not understand. The goal was to identify land that was of use to them. As such, humanitarian concerns were largely symbolic and reserved for public rationalizations of the colonial mission.

Establishing an economic infrastructure was expensive; the costs of developing an administration were even greater. Compared with other colonial holdings, the official administrative apparatus at best controlled little of the territory leaving much of the Congo essentially uncontrolled by the state. This was noted by George Washington Williams (1985 [1890]), a U.S. Black citizen commissioned by railroad magnate Collis P. Huntington, to visit the Congo to study the possibility of a trans-Congo railroad. Washington not only completed the report he was sent to do, but he also penned an open letter to Leopold II castigating him for the conditions within the Free State. He then sent a report to the president of the United States on the same topic (Franklin 1985). Like Conrad's novel *Heart of Darkness*, these writings provide a first-person account of a Westerner confronted with the horrors of the daily administration of the Congo Free State. When Williams arrived at the mouth of the Loumami River, he noted the presence of armed Arab camps and slave traders uncontrolled by the Belgian authorities. "I saw no where the Congo-state flag, and I know it would be torn down if it were displayed among these ivory and slave raiders. Here the State has no authority, can redress no wrong, protect no life or property" (1985 [1890]: 271). Such conditions would repeatedly affect many regions of the Congo, persisting even until the present day.

Leopold II's rule was plagued by constant insurrection and rebellion, which propelled his founding of the Public Forces (*Force Publique*) composed mainly of Africans led by Scandinavian officers. The largest military force in African history, its cost was "more than half the state's total expenditure" and its men were "[b]adly paid, ill fed, [and] brutally treated" (Ewans 2002: 116). Although designed to secure the ability of business operations to act without interference, the force itself was prone to mutiny and brutality.

The Free State would remain economically problematic and nigh bankrupt until the development of the pneumatic tire; this innovation led to an explosive need for rubber, which was readily available in the Congo. Leopold II lost no time in levying heavy duties on rubber gathered by natives and insisting that they only sell the product to the Free State itself. International economic opposition to the monopolization of Congolese rubber led to Leopold's instituting the infamous domanial system, whereby he cut the territory into zones, some of which were reserves for the state itself whereas others were granted as concessions to companies, such as the Anglo-Belgian Rubber Company.

Yet, due to the integration of royal, social, and economic elite networks, the companies that received these land grants were mostly owned and controlled by Leopold II's supporters and allies. Thus, he silenced any international discomfort with an appearance of free markets, while ensuring that the real profits and control rested with his own network (Ewans 2002; Hoschild 1998). With the land grants in the hands of allies, the brutal conditions could be more easily hidden from the rest of the world.

Rubber and Murder—The Domainal System

The domainal system imposed taxes on local peoples that had to be paid in labor given to the state or its chosen companies. Geographic areas were given specific product quotas to fill and the indigenous peoples pressed into service to meet those quotas. Almost immediately, this destroyed the local subsistence economy. With men in the "tax" labor force, women and children were left to keep to the traditional economic practices, which soon proved untenable and unproductive. In the wake of a lack of food production, disease and famine became increasingly common. Villages were abandoned and the perceptible population in the area dropped. Further, the system made an already brutal administration into an active horror; quotas were to be made at any cost of local life, body, or dignity. Production supervisors, often Africans themselves, resorted to force, torture, and mutilation to generate the production demanded by the companies.

It is in this context that one of the most infamous practices of the Congo Free State developed, one which survives in central Africa today: the taking of hands as a form of terror. To keep costs down, supervisors were warned against wasting ammunition. To account for each cartridge expended, they were required to chop off a hand from the person killed and bring it to their white supervisor. This often led to killing by means other than guns, or simply chopping of people's hands and leaving them to survive, as there were never situations where one bullet equated to one kill. The practice of cutting off hands became, and remains, the strongest symbol of the innate brutality of the Free State. Although often attributed to local customs, as with scalping among native North Americas, this was not a local practice, but one introduced by the white colonizers as a form of social control (Ewans 2002; Hoschild 1998; Williams 1890, 1985). As we discussed in Chapter One, this is a routine terror-tactic used throughout Africa to this day in the DRC, Sierra Leone, and Uganda.

The widespread atrocities in the region led Leopold II to insist that all employees sign promises of secrecy that allowed the state to withhold pay, restrict their movements, and prevent future employment if they spoke of what occurred (Ewans 2002: 175). Yet, news of the horrors of the Congo still made their way to the outside world in the writing of merchants and especially the writings of George Washington Williams. This caused a public uproar in the nascent international community, yet under the terms of the Berlin Act, signatories were unable to involve themselves, save as advisors. The British Foreign Legal Office noted there was nothing they could do to restrain the violence in the Congo, "short of the employment of actual force" (Ewans 2002: 183). Other European powers that could have exerted force or suggestion onto Leopold simply weren't interested. The only real effect the outcry had was in Belgium, where the Parliament was under increasing pressure to exact some form of control over the situation. However, as we see, it took years before real action was taken. In the mean time, the atrocities continued.

Roger Casement, an official in the British Foreign office responsible for the Congo territory, traveled extensively in the area, adding his reports to those of Williams and Joseph Conrad. In his earliest dispatches, he insightfully identified the central problem in the Free State: "The root of the evil lies in the fact that the government of the Congo is above all a commercial trust, that everything else is orientated towards commercial gain" (Casement 1890, quoted in Ewans 2002: 193). With the economic bottom line as the central measure of performance, all other concerns fell to the wayside. Over the next few years, he issued several reports, each more condemning than the last. In a letter to the Governor-General of the Free State, Casement unflinchingly accused the Free State of genocide:

> The system is bad, hopelessly and entire[ly] bad ... Instead of raising the indigenous peoples who are subjugated and who suffer from it, it can only lead, if it is maintained, to their final extinction and to the universal commendation of the civilized world. (Casement 1903, as quoted in Ewans 2002: 195)

His dispatches were so virulent that he was eventually recalled home by the Foreign Office, in the hope that once away from the Congo he could write a more "objective" report of his travels. Apparently either the distance from the Congo or the more immediate influence of the Foreign Office tempered his claims a bit, as the report written in the UK gave praise to Leopold II's administration where it was warranted by politics if not reality. However, he also recorded and railed against the atrocities and abuses that greeted him at every turn. He remarked that in a decade and a half, flourishing villages he had once visited were gone. The inhabitants were either killed by the government for failure to make quotas, died from disease and malnutrition, or had fled to French-held areas on the northern bank of the river. He described the nature of the local economy—the so-called *capita* system. Women and children were held hostage by Free State officials until their husbands and fathers had produced their required quota of products. Like others, he attacked the practice of taking hands as a brutal terror-inducing practice introduced by Europeans but blamed on the "savage" nature of the Congolese by the Belgians (Ewans 2002).

Casement's writings created a public furor over the way in which the Free State was run; international opinion turned decidedly against Leopold II's tactics. The mood was also shifting in Belgium. It was becoming clear to all observers that the days of Leopold's sole control over the Congo Free State were limited. In response to the mounting inquiries, the king delayed inquisitions by not sharing paper work, accounts, and other information at his disposal, while working to reduce the influence that a handover would have in the on-the-ground economic productivity and profitability. He took ownership of mineral rights, created companies and then transferred these mineral rights to them. Although Leopold II held large portions of ownership in these companies, he made sure that they also contained substantial amounts of foreign investment, primarily from France, Britain, and the US. This, he hoped, would prevent the Belgian Parliament from breaking them up or otherwise interfering with the actions of these companies out of fear of creating foreign tensions. He was largely successful (Ewans 2002; Hoschild 1998; Nzongola-Ntalaja 2002). Although he would not be the sole sovereign of the Free State much longer, it could still make him rich.

On 15 November 1900, Leopold II lost his private ownership of the Congo when the Belgian Parliament annexed the territory, making it an official colony of the state. Yet, there were few on-the-ground changes in the day-to-day life in the Congo. Although Belgian rule was not marked by the pure horrors of the Free State, unlike her European neighbors, she did nothing to educate or develop a native administrative class, much less a native investment class. Free trade barriers were removed. Natives could pay their taxes in money instead of labor but would still need to participate in wage labor to meet their obligations. The international political arena seemed satisfied with these changes. However, land policies and the role of corporations in driving the colonial enterprise were unchanged. Further, the first economic crisis of the Belgian Congo was under way: international rubber prices fell drastically as south Asian rubber hit the markets. Nonetheless, the country was mineral rich, which Belgium and other foreign investors quickly moved to thoroughly exploit. At the end of the 1950s, on the eve of the independence, the Belgian Congo produced 70% of the globe's industrial diamonds, 50% of global cobalt and 10% of global copper (Meredith 2006: 97).

Despite large amounts of Belgian investment in industrial growth, the workforce of the Congo was largely not unionized. For example, in 1954 colonial records listed 1,146,000 indigenous laborers; of these, only 7,500 were unionized. This, less than 1%, was in distinct contrast to the 23% of workers unionized in French West Africa and 50% in Nigeria (Nzongola-Ntalaja 2002: 76). Not only did this produce low wages overall, but would leave the workforce without a main principle of organization during the independence era. Despite the lack of educational efforts, a small indigenous elite did develop during the post–World War II years, though like some of their counterparts in Francophone Africa, many did not seek pure independence but membership in a Belgian society and culture (Meredith 2006).

Unlike other European powers, the Belgians were slow to consider independence for their central African holdings. Her economy depended too much on colonial revenues. In the wake of the war, Belgium established a 15-year plan for extracting itself from the Congo region. This changed in response to widespread riots in Leopoldville in January 1959 and a dawning realization on behalf of Belgian ministers that the colonies might be an economic burden rather than an asset, especially when the global copper market collapsed and the value of one of the key exports was severely diminished (Chamberlain 1999; Ewans 2002; Hargreaves 1988). Even though colonial forces brutally suppressed the riots, King Baudoun, the sitting monarch of Belgium at the time, announced that the Congo would be given her independence.

Nous ne sommes plus vos singes

On 30 June 1960 Belgium officially transferred sovereign power to an indigenous government. A ceremony was held in Leopoldville, attended by the Belgian king, his administration, and the incoming Congolese political leadership. King Baudoun gave a patronizing speech, suggesting, among other things, that the new Congolese leadership should be careful not to "compromise the future with hasty reforms, and don't replace the structures that Belgium hands over to you until you are sure you can do better" (quoted in Meredith 2006: 93).

Although the incoming Congolese president, Joseph Kasa-Vubu, made no reference to the king's speech in his own talk, the incoming Prime Minister, Patrice Lumumba, not slotted to give a talk, rose in the audience and delivered a strong but viciously anti-Belgian speech. He highlighted the suffering the Congolese endured under both Leopold II and later the Belgian government. Toward the end of the speech, he directly told the king "*Nous ne sommes plus vos singes*"—We are no longer your monkeys (Meredith 2006: 102). The indigenous subsistence economy was utterly destroyed, as were local political and religious structures. Millions died and the rest had endured starvation, torture, and countless other brutalities.

Despite the horrors of the past, prospects for the new nation were potentially bright, especially economically due to the extensive industrialization program under way. Through the 1950s, industrial production grew to 14.3% of total GDP, a rate equivalent to what China experienced during the 1990s. Belgian financiers had funneled approximately US $1 billion into the colony throughout the decade. In 1960, the GDP was the same as South Korea's. This was an economy built by Europeans, with Africans providing labor (Reno 2006), similar to the situation we examined in Uganda. Belgium divested itself of state-owned holdings by selling them off to Belgian companies while leaving the newly independent state with the lion's share of outstanding debt (Nzongola-Ntalaja 2002). This would ensured that the Belgians would continue to be the beneficiaries of the Congolese economy for the foreseeable future. Further, the peoples of the newly independent Congo not only had to construct basic social institutions but negotiate shared political power and create some sense of shared identity. The latter has proven particularly difficult; similar to most other postcolonial countries, the only thing that the Congolese people shared was a common experience of domination. Almost immediately after independence, regional and ethnic identities asserted themselves, threatening the very foundation of the new nation.

In a week's time the infant nation tore itself asunder—becoming the world's first failed state (Reno 2006). On 5 July rebels attacked remnant Belgian officers, on 11 July Katanga province seceded from the state, followed on 8 August by South Kasai. Even during the colonial period, the Katanga region was loosely controlled at best, though its rich mineral deposits made it highly desired. There were several reasons for these early secessions. Skilled white workers in Katanga sought a state more like Rhodesia to the south—white dominated—than an African-run country. The Kasai conflict was marked by ethnic divisions and tensions, not the first time the Congo would suffer disorder and division on these grounds. This widespread disorder led to one of the UNSC's first peacekeeping missions, which didn't keep the peace so much as it attempted to nation-build by establishing a pro-Western government (Chamberlain 1999; Hargreaves 1988; Hochschild 1998; Nzongola-Ntalaja 2002).

Prime Minister Lumumba ordered the UN to expel all Belgian troops still in the country. When they refused to comply, he threatened to seek the aid of the USSR—beginning a long-standing animosity between him and the West, especially the United States. The United States saw Lumumba's socialism as a threat to their interests in Africa, seeing the new Congo state as a potential Soviet ally. Allen Dulles, head of the CIA in 1960, regarded Lumumba as "a Castro or worse" (quoted in Schatzberg 1991: 15). Eisenhower made his dislike of the Congolese leader well known, remarking, "Can't someone get rid of this guy?" With internal disorder growing, in September 1960 Colonel Joseph Mobotu, the army chief of staff, took control in a coup. He quickly created an interim government that excluded Lumumba. It was during this time that he made connections with the U.S. CIA that would benefit him later, after his second coup. He eventually turned the rule over to a republican form of government, but Lumumba had no place in the new government. Although the stories differ widely as to who and how, Lumumba was assassinated in January 1961 (Meredith 2006; Nzongola-Ntalaja 2002; Schatzberg 1991).

Mobutu's Zaire

Although there was some return to normalcy and stability in the Congo after the 1960 coup, tensions did not abate. The attempted succession of Kantanga was fought until 1963. In 1964, a rebellion broke out in the eastern Congo. Within a matter of weeks, half of the state was under rebel control and renamed the People's Republic of the Congo. Mass atrocities were committed, with at least 20,000 Congolese executed for political or ethnic reasons, with approximately 1 million dead overall (Meredith 2006). The disorder did not subside until 24 November 1965 when Mobutu Sese Seko's second coup swept him into power. This time, he would not step aside for an elected government. Through the consolidation of power and the use of the army, Mobutu was able to achieve some semblance of order. Although initially his reign was widely supported by a citizenry hungry for civil peace and order the following decades found the Congo turned into Mobutu's private bank account.

Despite economic downturns during the chaos, industrial output quickly returned to pre-independence levels and continued to grow. Mobutu had convinced international investors (and states) that he was fully committed to growth and development not only in minerals but also manufacturing (Reno 2006). Although in the interests of his people, if not the Belgians who still owned much of the Congo, in 1966 Mobutu orchestrated the passage of the Bakajika law that gave the state the right to claim land and mineral rights. In January 1967, he nationalized the Belgian-owned UMHK mining company. Belgium responded with an embargo on copper and tried to marshal her European allies to place additional sanctions on Congolese exports. However, the US was undeterred by the pressure extended by Belgium and began a long relationship with Mobutu (Nzongola-Ntalaja 2002). The US saw the Congo as central in the Africa theatre of the cold war. Fearing the spread of Soviet-style communism on the continent, in Mobutu they found an ally who could stand firm against their self-described "red menace." In part, the concern was real, as many of the newly minted African heads of state were pursuing a socialist path toward development and poverty alleviation; many sought aid from any country that would provide it, including the USSR. For the US, Mobutu could hold the center of the African continent for Western interests, and, as in Latin America in the same period, they would support an anti-Soviet leader regardless of human rights abuses (Kalb 1982; Schatzberg 1991).

The combination of favorable opportunities in the world economy (e.g., the record copper prices on the world market), a sympathetic site for foreign investment, and the creation and subsequent devaluation of a new currency (the Zaire), led to economic stability and growth that the state had never seen before or since. However, the Congo could not sustain this potential. In part this was the result of global preferences for certain international exports. Politically, as part of a broader anticommunism effort, the US favored products from East Asian economies (Berger 2004; Haggard 1990; Nzongola-Ntalaja 2002; Reno 2006). In addition, due to Mobutu's continued nationalization of resources, small businesses and land would begin to erode the economic gains that had been made. However, the largest financial burden on the state was Sese Seko himself; Mobutu turned the Congo's natural wealth into his private fiefdom. As the largest shareholder in the Bank of Kinshasa, Mobutu used the national bank as his own financial resource. He grew the bank by requiring all foreign corporations doing business in Congo to bank with the Bank of Kinshasa. He owned multiple palaces and when he traveled, he flew on a privately hired Concord jet. In the 1980s, estimates suggested he was worth US $5 billion, though after his death only US $40–45 million in monies and assets could be accounted for (Meredith 2006). With Mobutu's hijacking of the Congolese economic gains, the country quickly sank into debt.

Due to entrenched U.S. support, the Congo's debt was rescheduled several times by the Bretton Woods lenders, who took the unprecedented step of installing the German financier Erwin Blumental as the head of the central bank. Other debt restructuring agreements required the customs department to be taken over by Belgians and the ministry of Finance by the French. Even this did not constrain Mobutu's corruption; 50–75% of foreign exchange still went into his pockets and those of his cronies and allies (Nzongola-Ntalaja 2002). This was not the last attempt to prop up the regime with favors or foreign aid; the US continued to provide up to one-third of the GNP of the Congo in aid until the cold war was over and Mobutu was no longer useful to US strategic foreign interests. The desistance of support precipitated further economic collapse. From 1988 to 1995, the Congolese economy declined by 40; in 1993 its per capita GDP had declined to US $117, 65% lower than in 1958 (Collins 1997).

Westerners tended to explain these economic failures as the product of underdevelopment process. The standard Western assumption was that due to colonial domination and the lack of a local African technocratic class, much of the waste and corruption in governments was simply the result of incompetence. Western governments and advisors believed all that was needed was the provision of a sound governmental and financial education to turn such states around. As Nzongola-Ntalaja points out (2002: 152; emphasis in the original), "the view that mismanagement in the Congo was a *technical* problem ... was a false view, for what was wrong ... [w]as the use to which the skills available were put." This fatal misperception led to continued programs that did nothing to resolve the economic crisis. It wasn't that the leaders and bureaucrats did not know what they were doing; rather, they knew all too well what they were doing. Long-standing cultural principles and African experiences produced such attitudes. The state has nearly always been viewed as the tool of the elites in charge, a position that can be traced back to chiefly systems that saw no conceptual separation between political parties and the lineage of the chief. During the colonial system, especially the Leopoldian régime, the entire state was bent to the fulfill the desires of a single person. Mobutu inherited a system in which the looting of national treasure for personal and kinship use was a perk of leadership.

In addition to looting his own country, Sese Seko's regime was infamous for extrajudicial executions, civilian massacres, and a host of other crimes against humanity. Mobutu's use of the army and their loyalty to him provided ample opportunity to terrorize his own people. In Kivu during 1983, "soldiers executed all clan chiefs in one locality after forcing them to eat their own ears" because it was thought they sympathized with the Parti Revolutionnaire du Peuple (PRP)—a rebel group that opposed the standing government (Schatzberg 1991: 43). Mobutu also oversaw the creation of the Agence National de Documentation (AND), a secret police force that reported only to Mobutu and acted solely on his orders. AND was renowned for uncovering information, true or false, that linked a given individual to antigovernment activities and views. It was used to investigate university protests, labor movements, and any other group that Mobutu didn't trust.

Mobutu himself was renowned for his public pronouncements of brutality and demands for vengeance. During a public speech in 1988 in a direct response to a group of women who demonstrated against poor living conditions and high infant mortality, Mobutu urged people to take matters into their own hands:

> You see a demonstration ... what do you do? ... you are not going to wait for the soldiers ... you know the meaning of our dearly acquired peace. You have shoes. Kick them. ... You have hands, hit them ... remove them from the road in the name of peace. (Quoted Schatzberg in 1991: 47–48)

When presented with an active and undeniable insurgency, Sese Seko was no less brutal. Not only did he further fragment the diverse peoples of the region and cause widespread economic devastation, but he also provided a model of brutality and corruption that stands out even in the context of central Africa.

After the first Shaba uprising (1977), the army went on a rampage in the Katanga region, causing more than 200,000 refugees to flee. Indirectly the brutal repressions helped the Front de Liberation Nationale du Congo (FLNC) recruit members and prepare itself for the Second Shaba invasion the next year. The Second Shaba war was much more of a real threat to the sitting government and would have been successful had Western allies not funneled aid to Mobutu's government, providing troops, transport, and supplies. "Shaba II nearly toppled the regime, yet it failed because Mobutu's allies emphasized global security considerations while ignoring the conflict's domestic origins in Mobutu's tyranny" (Schatzberg 1991: 58). Nonetheless, the demise of his political reign occurred soon, yet it came not only from within his own state but also from without. As his neighbors Rwanda and Uganda descended into their own civil wars, they were eventually the downfall of Mobutu and his regime.

The Congo Collapses Again: The Contemporary Situation

At this juncture in its history, the Congo had a looted economy, massive resentment throughout the county toward Sese Seko's regime, and essentially empty coffers. Alone, these elements are a recipe for disaster. However, these were not the only sociohistorical forces that came into play. As the 1990s dawned, Uganda was years into Museveni's continued fight against the Lord's Resistance Army (LRA), a fight that, as we discussed in Chapter Five, spilled over into the eastern regions of the Congo. Rwanda was about to experience its genocide; eastern regions of the Congo were used as a staging area of the Hutu invasion and a harbor for Tutsi refugees and resistance fighters. Chad, Burundi, Angola, and Sudan also experienced disorder that spilled over the borders into the Congo. Soon all of these forces came to bear, not only on Mobutu and his regime, but also on the entire territory.

The First Congolese War and its Aftermath

Responding to widespread international and domestic pressures, in 1990, Mobutu allowed steps toward democratization. Opposition parties were legalized and elections scheduled. However, Mobutu and his elite clique maintained control of mineral resources, tax revenues, and the banking infrastructure until he fled the country during the First Congolese War (Nzongola-Ntalaja 2002). In 1996, Uganda and Rwanda invaded the Congo, deposed Mobutu Sese Seko, and installed Laurent Kabila in his stead. To legitimate the international aggression, both countries cited security concerns. Specifically, they stated ipso facto that antigovernmental forces that opposed both governments operated out of the eastern regions of the Congo, some with Mobutu's support, some without. Recall from Chapter Five, remnants of anti-Museveni forces had fled to the Congo after the Ugandan war (though as we discussed in Chapter Four most of them fled into the Acholi regions of northern Uganda). Also as we noted in Chapter Four, *Interhawame* groups had fled Rwanda to the eastern region of the Congo once the RPF consolidated a counter response to the 1994 genocide. The Sudanese People's Liberation Army (SPLA) was also active in the area, with Sudan and Uganda carrying out a proxy war against each other via the funding of rebel groups, many operating within the eastern DRC (Human Rights Watch 2002, 2003c, 2005e; Prunier 2004).

Economically, Kabila took some steps to end corruption and open up DRC's economy for foreign investment. He found many willing investors before the Sese Seko regime was fully overthrown. His administration cut the cost of licenses to trade diamonds, attempting to undercut De Beer's monopolistic control and wrote contracts that insisted on higher levels of local participation and native employment (Collins 1997). Such changes had neither quick nor wide effects. He was never fully supported by the people and never fully in control of the state. Further, Kabila followed in his predecessor's footsteps and engaged in widespread political repression and corruption.

The Second Congolese War

Two years later, in 1998, Kabila attempted to expel Rwandan forces, triggering what is often referred to as Africa's First World War. Like the Great War in Europe at the beginning of the century, it was being fought by numerous armies across a vast geographical area. Uganda, Rwanda, and Burundi poured troops into northeastern Congo, whereas Zimbabwe, Angola, and Namibia came to the aid of Kabila's government. After a series of peace deals, many foreign troops eventually withdrew. Nonetheless, fighting among rival rebel factions and others continued in many parts in the east and northeast. Foreign troops remained in the Congo through 2002–3. During this time, numerous indigenous militia groups rose to positions of power and influence in the nation's hinterlands. Through a series of shifting alliances with foreign powers and each other, these quasi-military groups were positioned to assume control on the ground after the Ugandan and Rwandan troops left. By the time the Lusaka peace agreement was signed in 1999, over 3.5 million people had died. The UN entered into peacekeeping operations that year. On 16 January 2001, Laurent Kabila was assassinated by one of his body guards; the next day his son Joseph Kabila was installed as the head of state, a position he still holds as of this writing.

Postwar Conflict

As we have noted, the signing and implementation of peace accords neither ended the hostilities nor brought peace to the Congo. The government could not assert control over wide areas in both the east and the south. In these areas militias grew strong and for all intents and purposes, became the on-the-ground political and military authority. They held no monopoly of force in their territory and they knew it. More than a dozen different militias have operated throughout the country; each region's conflict is not only the product of the broader state failure but bears distinct local elements and aspects as well. As such, we focus on two areas, and select groups within them, that have been affected by the ongoing conflict: Ituri, the locality of major looting by foreign troops and governments, and the North and South Kivu, places, along with Katanga, that have experienced very little stability since independence.

Ituri

Ituri, a region in Orientale province near the Ugandan border, has been one of the most conflict-ridden and bloody regions of the DRC during the postwar period. At least ten separate armed groups are active or have been active in the area since the Second Congolese war. It is not possible to discuss all combatants, their origins, motives, and atrocities. Consequently, we limit our discussions to the most powerful and their actions, as an exemplar of the general trends and patterns of violence. UN and Human Rights Watch estimates suggest that at least 55,000 civilians have died in this region alone since 1999 (Human Rights Watch 2003). Four structural aspects of Ituri have made it especially prone to continued disorder. First, is its mineral-rich content, with ample gold and colton deposits, among other precious metals. As we show, these resources have been the lure for continued conflict over their control. Second, it is distant from the capital, making it difficult for a tenuous state to exercise full control. Third, it sits on the borders of Uganda and Sudan, with Chadian, Rwandan, and Burundian borders close by. This has facilitated the entry and maintenance of foreign troops in the region as well as their expropriation of Ituri's mineral resources. Fourth, as with other areas on the continent, it houses separate ethnic groups with fundamentally different subsistence patterns that have bred long-term tensions if not outright conflict: the Hema, pastoralists, and the Lendu, agriculturalists. However, like the ongoing genocide in Darfur (see Chapter Seven) and despite some evaluations of the situation, the conflict is much more complex than an ethnic battle between these two groups. In fact, for much of the twentieth century the two groups lived peacefully with much intermarriage.

By the time of colonial incursion into the region, the Hema dominated both economically and politically, leading the Belgian authorities to create separate administrative systems and structures to reduce intergroup conflicts. Although initially sustaining more sociopolitical loss under the colonial system, the Hema quickly took advantage of educational and economic opportunities, eventually becoming the locally favored "elites" (Vlassenroot and Raeymaekers 2004). The Hema further consolidated their economic power after Mobutu's land reform laws that emphasized private (over communal) ownership; Mobutu maintained the colonial and early independence traditions that kept Hema in positions of authority. Once Mobutu allowed a multiparty system in 1990, the most convenient and culturally meaningful source of political orientation was ethnicity (Meredith 2006; Vlassenroot and Raeymaekers 2004). Ethnicity became the most visible site for broader social, economic, and political competition. As we have discussed throughout this book, the conflicts often become misinterpreted as predominately ethnic hatreds originating in "time immemorial" but in actuality, even where there has been a history of struggle or conflict, ethnicity is less of a motivating factor and more of a social organizational factor for bringing together peoples whose autochthonic identity was lost during the colonial period.

The first flare up of Hema-Lendu violence happened during the Second Congolese War, when in 1999 Hema landowners attacked and occupied Lendu lands. Although both sides disagree on the initial catalyst, the result was intense violence. Within the first year, more than 7,000 people had been killed and over 150,000 displaced. Further, throughout the late twentieth century, economic competition developed between the Nande, an ethnic group from North Kivu, and the Hema. Nande traders gained dominance in many local markets, preventing local Itrui populations from gaining strong footholds (Vlassenroot and Raeymaekers 2004). These growing tensions were further intensified by the development of militia groups in the region. After the installation of Kabila, paramilitary groups began to form in Ituri to take advantage of the state power vacuum. The first of these, the Rassemblement Congolais pour la Democratie (RCD) began activities by 1998 and soon fractured into several factions including the RDC-ML (Mouvement de Liberation) supported by Uganda and the RCD-Goma, operating in Kisangani, the capital of the Orientale province.

When Uganda and Rwanda decamped from Congo in 2002 and 2003 respectively, they left behind many factional militias that continued the conflicts. Initially, Uganda supported the Front des Nationalistes et Integrationnistes (FNI), a Lendu-based ethnic armed force; Rwanda supported the Union des Patriotes Congolais (UPC), a Hema group led by Thomas Lubanga. Over time the alliances have shifted back and forth. There is no overpoweringly ethnic or ideological tie between the militias and their neighboring governments; these relationships are based upon mutual need and convenience. In addition, there is a history of conflict over land rights among DRC peoples. This was magnified with the Ugandan occupation of the region wherein the tensions flared. Both Rwanda and Uganda poured arms into the struggle, using the ethnic warfare as a proxy for their own conflicted control of the region. The Lendu and Hema have continued to struggle over control of the rich gold fields, especially those in the Mongbwalu and Durba areas (on the Ugandan border). Fighting has been intense, with war crimes and massive human rights violations committed frequently by all parties (Amnesty International 2003; UNSC 2003; Human Rights Watch 2003, 2005). The central Congolese government could assert no control; Rwanda and Uganda continued to struggle for dominance by providing material support and military advisors to the militias. These militias draw heavily on tactics of terror, genocide, torture, arbitrary detainment, and constant extortion in their attempts to gain and maintain control over a community.

The UPC has been one of the major committers of atrocities in Ituri. As conflicts intensified in the region, UPC leaders began to adopt highly ethicist language, drawing a distinction between so-called originals, meaning the "true" inhabitants of Ituri, or Hema, and "non-originals"—all others including Lendu. Just as this ethnic rhetoric was used for political divisiveness in Darfur and Rwanda, the rhetoric used by the UPC leaders was driven toward ethnic cleansing. In August 2002, it took the town of Bunia, the largest city in Ituri. During the takeover and after, they deliberately slaughtered Lendu, Nande, and Bira. A witness recounted the UPC attack as follows:

> Hema militias chased the Bira and the Lendu ... they knew which houses to go to and whom to target. There was about 200 of them, a mix of those in uniform and civilian dress. They killed a lot of people that day ... men, women and children. The killing went on from 7:00 am 'til about 1:00 pm. (Human Rights Watch 2003: 20)

The next day, Ugandan troops attacked the Governor's mansion. They did not sustain the siege long enough to capture the building and its inhabitants, but did cause more Lendu to flee in fear. Over the course of the next few days, attacks on the Governor's stronghold continued, until it was taken on the afternoon of 9 August. MUNOC estimated the death toll from this attack at 110; locals suggested at least 150. Several mass graves were uncovered; in one

26 women and children had been interred, many of whom had been shot in the back (Human Rights Watch 2003).

In early September, the UPC took the town of Nyakunde and in the process killed more than 1,000 people, mostly civilian noncombatants. Between 8 and 18 November 2002 the UPC attacked Mongbwalu and the RCD-ML forces that controlled the city. The UPC spent five days engaged in the slaughter and rape of Lendu soldiers and citizens. One witness, a man imprisoned during the attack, described what he saw from his cell window, "The Hema militia were killing people from particular groups ... Lendu. They would pick out prisoners to kill ... they tied their arms behind their backs with wires. They slashed their heads with knives. They made them sit down and then they shot them" (Human Rights Watch 2003: 25). At least 800 Lendu were killed, probably more. From December 2002, into January 2003, the UPC repeated these acts in Kilo, where they made Lendu dig their own graves before slaughtering them. Kobu, Lipri, Bambu, and Mbijo were all treated similarly (Amnesty International 2003; Human Rights Watch 2003, 2005, 2006d; Vlassenroot and Raeymaekers 2004).

During the same month, January 2003, the UPC made a formal alliance with the RDC-Goma, further cementing ties with Rwanda. Due to intense distrust and competition, the alliance encouraged Uganda to set up its presence in the region by supporting the Party for the Unity and Safeguard of Integrity in Congo (PUSIC) and the *Forces Armees pour le Congo* (FAPC). In May 2003, when the UPC reestablished control over Bunia, 125 women and girls were raped while the entire village was looted (Human Rights Watch, 2005b). With the population subdued, the UPC began a forced mining practice similar to those carried out by the Ugandan troops. The gold was destined for Rwanda, in exchange, the UPC received arms and munitions.

The UPC is also well known for its abduction of children for use as child soldiers. As we mentioned at the start of the chapter, these acts form the core of the ICC's charges against Lubanga. For example, in November 2002, the UPC kidnapped the entire fifth grade at the primary school in Mudzi Pela; at Salogo they took all children over the age of seven. In 2003, the UPC claimed to have 15,000 active troops; locals suggested that at least 40% were child soldiers. Other witnesses have described a widespread practice at the start of the conflict where every Hema family had to either provide one family member to the UPC or to provide a monetary payment in lieu of a person (Human Rights Watch 2003, 2006d). As with the LRA (see Chapter Five), the UPC used children as frontline troops, human shields, and living land-mine sweepers.

In March 2003, the Ugandan army switched allegiances from the UPC to a coalition of Lendu militias, the FNI, and FAPC. In early March, the combined forces took control of Bunia then drove north to Kilo. Arriving on 10 March, the Lendu groups enacted a revenge slaughter that only stopped when their Ugandan allies arrived and began firing into the Lendu groups to stop the killing. In May, Ugandan troops left the Congo, with their militia allies firmly into control of the gold-rich northeast. The UPC counterstrike in 2003 had returned control of Mongbwalu to the Hema, yet only for approximately 48 hours. The Lendu response was not just to retake the town, but to continue its genocidal retributions against the Hema from July through September of that year. Without Ugandan forces on the ground to stop them, the Lendu slaughtered men, women, and children, including the wounded in the hospital. As with the Ugandans and the UPC before them, the FNI and FAPC took control of the mines, maintained the forced artesian labor conditions, levied random taxes, and maintained a general policy of ruling through the use of extortion, terror, and force (Amnesty International 2003; Human Rights Watch 2003, 2005). Such ventures proved to be wildly profitable for the countries involved, as we discuss below.

Also operating within Ituri is the RDC-ML, a frequent committer of atrocities. Based in Buni, an often fought-over community, it has long positioned itself in opposition to the UPC and tried to limit the power wielded by Lubanga as well as other groups like Bemba's Movement for the Liberation of the Congo (MLC). The RDC-ML specifically has separated its military and political actions. The APC is their military arm, leaving, at least symbolically, RDC-ML leaders to become active within political processes in the future and avoid war crimes prosecutions.

Before the UPC took Mongbwalu, the RDC-ML and the APC carried out wanton violence against Hema typically motivated solely by the fact that the victims were Hema. One person, who witnessed the killing of a Hema woman, provided this description:

> They [the RDC-ML] arrested a woman who was accused of being a witch. But she was Hema and that was the real reason. There were about ten Lendu combatants with machetes and knives. They took her from her house, stripped her and then cut her all over—they cut off her arms and then cut her genitals … and burned her body. (Human Rights Watch 2003: 35)

Unlike the scenes described above when the UPC took the city, RCD-ML leaders did break up the public torture and execution, but no one was ever arrested for the crime.

The Lendu, like every other group, use rape as a weapon in their attempt to control the local population. Human Rights Watch (2005c) reported that between 2002 and January 2004 at least 650 women were treated for brutal rapes by local medical personnel. An NGO representative told Human Rights Watch (2005c: 19) that Lendu combatants "come to houses at night and rape the women, sometimes in front of their husband. Sometimes they stop women as they go to fetch water or go to the fields. They also stop girls coming back from school." As with other incidents, these sexual assaults are more than random soldiers acting with impunity; they are designed to humiliate, terrorize, and destroy a population.

These are just a sampling of the groups that are actively involved in the Ituri region's conflicts and events since the onset of hostilities in 1999. As we have noted, all groups have slaughtered civilians in ways reminiscent of the Rwandan genocide discussed in Chapter Three. All groups have used sexual assault as a tool of war to terrorize and demoralize local populations. Most, if not all, of the groups have abducted children to act as soldiers. Reports have also emerged of some fighters engaging in the ritual mutilation of bodies, both civilian and solider. In some respects, Ituri is a fulcrum for the general violence and disorder in the DRC. Yet, it is not the only locale of such acts. We now briefly turn to actions and actors within the Kivu provinces, which lie directly to the south of Orientale province along the Ugandan and Rwandan borders.

North and South Kivu

The Kivu region, consisting of the North and South Kivu provinces, has also long been a site of violence and disorder in the DRC. The current conflict began in 1993, and has yet to be resolved. Although the RCD has had the strongest position, other local groups also vied for control. Further, foreign troops have contributed to the disorder, including Burundi rebels, remnant *Interahamwe*, and ex-FAR (Brittain 2002). Many of these forces are still active to date, for example the *Interahamwe* still plague the area, intermittently setting up road blocks to kidnap, ransom, and extort the local population (BBC 2005).

One of the local groups is the *Mayi-Mayi* rebels, who organized for self-defense during the period of foreign occupation and remains active to this day. The term *Mayi-Mayi*, Congolese Swahili for "water water," is applied to a whole host of various locally based armed groups. There is no single command structure; no overall coordination of activity. Such groups originally arose in the 1960s conflicts, and reassembled in 1993 in North Kivu to defend their villages against Mobotu's troops, the *Interahamwe* who fled from Rwanda after the genocide, and the RCD. In the Second Congolese War, the *Mayi-Mayi* groups fought against Mobutu and alongside Kabila's forces and allies. After the war, during the scramble for control of resource-rich areas throughout the east, the *Mayi-Mayi* became focused on local defense against the variety of groups that emerged in the fragmentation of forces once Kabila was in power (IRIN 2006b).

The groups have tended to operate out of the forested areas and are easily identified by the locals as they tend to wear skins and other primitive affectations. Like the LRA, they also possess syncretic religious beliefs that unite Christian and traditional spiritualist principles. Kibwe Mwepwe, a *Mayi-Mayi* who surrendered as part of the demobilization program, explained: "To become *Mayi-Mayi* you must first wash in special water; it is part of our Luba culture. The water sprinkled on us to baptize us and protect us so that bullets cannot penetrate our bodies" (IRIN 2006e: 1). A major *Mayi-Mayi* group has recently surrendered and begun the demobilization process after the capitulation of their leader, the infamous Gedeon (aka Kyungu Mutanga), whose group was the target of a major offensive led by General Tshibumbu, assisted by Colonel Siatilo in the Katanga swamps of Lake Upemba. The campaign itself saw atrocities committed on both sides, as the region was where many displaced persons had fled for safety. Skirmishes between the government forces and the militia produced few combatant fatalities, but the victor of the skirmish would then loot the nearby settlements. Such war crimes were glibly brushed aside by Tshibumbu, who told a MONUC officer, "Gedeon is just a bandit but I am the original bandit" (IRIN 2006d: 2). Gedeon's forces arrived in the area in January 2006, and by February the government forces were in place. Gedeon surrendered in the second week of May, bringing with him an entourage of 150 soldiers, mostly children. His surrender broke the local organizational structure of the militia and catalyzed a mass wave of surrenders. He is still in custody while his forces are undergoing the demobilization process (Carroll, 2006; Human Rights Watch 2006e; IRIN 2004a, 2006a, 2006b, 2006c, 2006d, 2006e).

As elsewhere, the *Mayi-Mayi* use sexual assault as a means of instilling terror and humiliation in the locals. One victim recounted the following incident to a Human Rights Watch investigator:

> I was raped by them in front of my husband. They held him down while they did it. I was released afterwards because my husband and children pleaded with them ... I was raped by more than three men. I cannot recall the exact number because I lost consciousness. (Human Rights watch 2005c: 17)

In South Kivu, the *Mayi-Mayi*, remnant *Interahamwe*, the RDC, and governmental troops have all committed widespread sexual assaults in an often brutal fashion. The village of Bukvu has been the location of repeated sexual atrocities committed by essentially every armed group active in the region. Countless reports of the "typical" elements of genocidal rape have emerged: families being forced to watch the rapes, gun barrels being used as tools of sexual assault, and the pattern of moving into a neighborhood and raping every female found. Some attacks have taken on a much more brutal character: women had melted rubber dripped into the vaginas and onto their breasts, other women after being raped, had their legs forcibly spread until their hips or upper legs fractured. Some women reported being raped while lying in the blood of their relatives who had already been killed (IRIN 2004a).

The victimization of women has also taken nonsexual forms. For example, the RDC committed a series of incidents in Mwenga between November 1999 and January 2000. At the time the region was disputed by the RDC and the local *Mayi-Mayi* militia. In November, the RDC buried 15 women alive after accusing them of collaboration with the *Mayi-Mayi*. In February 2000, the RCD beheaded 12 women on the same grounds (Agence France Presse 1999, 2000; Africa News 2000; Brittain 2002).

As elsewhere, much of the conflict in the Kivus has been billed as a deep-seated ethnically based conflict. One main focus on the tensions has been on the *Banyamulenge* (roughly meaning the people from mulenge), formerly, the people were referred to as *Banyarwanda* (people from Rwanda), after the 1994 genocide, they changed their own self-appellation to emphasize their Congolese roots and to differentiate themselves from Rwandan refugees and militia forces. The *Banyamulenge* are descended from Tutsis immigrants from Rwanda who settled in the Kivu region sometime during the nineteenth century. Tensions emerged with neighbors almost immediately. As cattle pastoralists, the *Banyamulenge* came into immediate conflict with the local farmers over land-use strategies. Also, as cattle were the main mark of wealth in the region (as was the case with the Hutu/Tutsis under colonial rule), the newcomers that were also cattle herders received an almost immediate elevation of social status.

During the later stages of Belgian rule, the *Banyamulenge* were politically disenfranchised due to the structural reorganization of political power that resulted in their loss of local self-rule. Instead, they fell under the authority of other ethnic chiefs (Vlassenroot 2000, 2002). This ultimately solidified their position as foreigners—in their own minds and those of their neighbors.

This was one of the first factors that led to the eventual crystallization of a new ethnic identity, one in opposition to and in conflict with other groups in the area.

This new identity was fully constructed during the 1964 Mulele rebellion, locally known as the Simba rebellion. In 1966, with the retreat of the *Armee Populaire de Liberation* (APL)—an anti-Mobutu force—into the homeland of the *Banyamulenge*, the locals found themselves the targets of livestock raids and rebel taxes. Due to the victimization at the hands of the APL, most *Banyamulenge* formed their own militia groups for self-defense, the *Guerriers*, later joining with Mobutu's *Armee Nationale Congolaise* (ANC). The combined forces defeated the APL and spent the next decade and a half hunting down small groups and factions until the APL was entirely eliminated in 1982.

Overall, this conflict served to highlight, intensify, and crystallize ethnic identity differences in the region. The Babembe and Bafulero, who had fought with the APL, saw the *Banyamulenge* as traitors, foreigners, and interlopers on their lands. In return, the *Banyamulenge* saw their neighbors as little more than murderers and thieves after having endured nearly two decades of cattle raids designed to support the APL. Although ethnic and tribal divisions may have been vague and shifting before the war, they were now clear and sharpened by the violence. Whereas under Mobutu's 1981 nationality law, the *Banyamulenge* were considered true Zairians, not aliens, since they were present in the region before 1885. Nonetheless, their opponents used the law, and the ideology behind the law, to undermine their citizenship rights. It was no surprise then, when as early as 1991, young men began to join the RPF, acting as soldiers and ambassadors to *Banyamulenge* villages to recruit more young men into the RPF (Vlassenroot 2002).

During the second Congolese war, *Banyamulenge* participation varied, some still supported the RPF and joined with the RCD, whereas others joined Ugandan-supported forces or pulled back into their own militia groups that focused on defending their own communities and avoiding broader participation in the war (Vlassenroot 2002). The end of the second war did not bring peace to Southern Kivu and the Haut Plateau. Although the DRC military forces were nominally in control, government forces and local militias still predicated upon locals with complete impunity. For example, as elsewhere, women were the frequent targets of sexual violence within the region. *Medecins Sans Frontieres* (Doctors without Borders) reported that in 2005 they treated 1,292 rape survivors in Beni, Kayna, and Rutshuru (*Medecins Sans Frontieres* 2006). As late as 2006, local health centers in the region reported an average of 40 women raped every day; kidnappings, sexual enslavement, gang rapes, and forced marriages remained endemic (Rodriguez 2006).

2006 Elections

On 30 July 2006 the DRC held its first real elections since the first republic immediately after independence. In all, 33 candidates competed for the presidency and thousands ran for Parliament. Predictably, the elections did not go as smoothly as possible. In the days leading up to the vote, the Congolese government claimed to have uncovered a plot for a coup led by foreign security and military personnel (essentially mercenaries). Shortly thereafter, 32 people were arrested, including 3 Americans, 10 Nigerians, and 12 South Africans. South Africa and the UN publicly doubted the government's claims; opposition groups saw this as yet another tactic to again delay the voting process.

Voting itself was largely peaceful, not surprising considering there were 17,600 UN peacekeepers, and an additional 2,000 EU troop in Kinshasa alone, to dissuade violence. Many opposition groups claimed mass fraud. The Carter center, which had 58 observers in the country, did state that there was disruption to legitimate campaigning in the run up to the election, but overall they felt the voting was carried out as well as could be hoped for, even with some problems (e.g., polls opening late, long lines, etc.). Citizens reported that in the eastern part of the country there were incidents of voter intimidation, especially by *Interhawme* forces that threatened to mutilate those who did not vote for Kabila. There was no clear winner in the first ballot, but the top two candidates, according to the votes recorded, Kabila and Bemba, stood in a run-off election in October 2006. Joseph Kabila was declared the winner in November. In response, Jean-Pierre Bemba alleged mass vote fraud. When the Supreme Court of the DRC met on 20 November 2006 to hear the case, riots broke out in the streets and the court building was attacked, leading the UN security forces to evacuate those inside (AP 2006; Harris 2006; Isango 2006a, 2006b). This has allowed the rebel and militia groups an ideological justification to continue their operations.

Mineral Expropriation

One of the widespread criminal actions within the DRC has been the wholesale looting of the country's rich mineral resources by foreign powers and regional ethnic militias. The brief period of economic growth that the state experienced in the late 1960s and early 1970s was the result of its mineral resources. As we have noted, the region possesses large deposits of diamonds, copper, gold, colton, zinc, and silver among others. Shortly after independence, 80% of industrial diamonds used in the US came from here; in the early 1970s more than one-third of total global diamond production was Congolese (Goreux 2001; Samset 2002). The major reason this region has been so heavily contested is the mineral deposits, which represent a major source for profit in an overall, destabilized African economic system.

During the Second Congolese War, Uganda occupied gold-rich lands in the north, establishing control over the Gorumbwa, Dubra, and Agbarabo mines. According to Human Rights Watch (2005), almost a ton of gold was extracted during a four-year period (1998–2002) worth approximately US $9 million. Without the resources to engage in industrial mining practices, they forced miners to engage in artisanal labor practices—generally low-technology efforts using little more than picks, shovels, pans, and screens. Typically, this approach is used to take advantage of alluvial deposits of precious minerals—those that have washed out the bedrock due to the erosion action within river beds. Here, a shovel and pan is all that is needed. In some cases, underground mining operations have been run with low-technology approaches; such actions are highly problematic and highly dangerous. At the Gorumbwa mine, these practices led to the collapse and loss of the mine itself in late 1999. Ugandan soldiers frequently beat and extorted the local miners by required monetary payment to enter the mines and taking a percentage of the ore that they mined (Human Rights Watch 2003, 2005). Not only was the treatment of miners and the local communities a violation of human rights laws, their destruction of the mines and surrounding infrastructure constitute war crimes—specifically violations of the provisions of Geneva conventions which insist that occupying powers protect nonmilitary assets of the occupied territory.

Much of the territory's mineral production was severely reduced or outright ceased as a result of the multitude of conflicts experienced—not only the First and Second Congolese Wars, but also the Katanga succession, the first and second Shaba conflicts and the loss of order in both North and South Kivu provinces. Further, Mobutu's Zairization policy not only replaced skilled foreign workers with less-skilled nationals, but the nationalization of mineral fields enhanced corruption and reduced production. Mobutu's legalization of artisanal mining practices in 1981 served to reopen the industry. Artisanal practices, while less safe and less productive in general than industrial mining operations, allowed peasants to enter the industry with essentially no capital and no training. Further, as seen elsewhere in Africa (e.g., Liberia and Sierra Leone), the ease of this type of mining has led to intense exploitation of the resources by militias and other nonregular military forces. Artisanal mining typically involved the exploitation of alluvial deposits—those in river beds that are widespread throughout the region. Often the only technologies that are used are shovels, pans, and screens. The diamonds are light and easily transportable—which not only enhances legal mining but facilitates smuggling and illegal expropriation. Some gains from illegal smuggling have benefited the government of the DRC, some of its officials and still more foreign powers (especially Angola, Uganda, and Rwanda).

Taking advantage of the chaos surrounding the Second Congolese War, Uganda established patterns of illegal resource appropriations, especially in the areas of gold and diamonds. In 1995, 3.09 tons of gold was exported from Uganda totaling US $23 million, although only 0.0015 tons were produced within the legal borders of the state. In 1996, exports increased to $60 million, valued at US $105 million in 1997. Ugandan gold production peaked at 0.0092 tons in 1998 and its export of gold peaked in 1999 at 11.45 tons. Similar gaps between production and export have been noted in diamonds as well. Uganda has no indigenous diamond production. According to the Diamond High Council, Uganda exported US $120,000 in diamonds in 1997; US $1,440,000 in 1998; US $1,810,000 US in 1999; and US $1,260,000 in 2000 (as of October of that year) (UNSC S/2001/357).

Recall also that 1997 was the year that Uganda invaded the DRC in the Second Congolese War. Rwanda exported approximately US $720,000 in diamonds in 1997; US $20,000 in 1998; US $440,000 in 1999; and US $1,790,000 in 2000 (as of October). As with Uganda, in 1999 and 2000, Rwanda had entered into agreements with local militias to smuggle diamonds over the border. By comparison, the value of DRC diamond exports were US $752,800,000 in 1997; US $879,000,000 in 1998; US $520,100,000 in 1999; and US $210,500,000 in 2000 (UNSC S/2001/357). Thus in a two-year period the country's diamond exportation fell by almost three-fourths. In part, this was a result of military hostilities reducing production (though note the increase between 1997 and 1998—after the start of the second Congolese war), but it was also the result of foreign troops and local militias taking control of mineral fields and smuggling the proceeds across borders for exportation.

There is little debate over the source of these minerals. Indeed, the government of Uganda acknowledged to the IMF that the volume of gold exports does not mirror production levels and may indicate that some exports are "leaking over the borders" (UNSC S/2001/357: 19) from the DRC. However, this did not prevent the IMF from conveniently proclaiming the increase in exports as a strengthening of the Ugandan economy, thus increasing its assessment grade for balance of payments status. Also, due to these revenues, the World Bank lauded Uganda as a success story for what its structural adjustment programs (SAP) could accomplish. The paradox is that the SAPs did nothing to increase Ugandan economic health and can be seen as providing motivation for the government's engagement in illegal mineral expropriation. In fact, the UNSC cites internal memos establishing that the World Bank was well aware of this, yet didn't seem to care. In fact, the World Bank "not only encouraged Uganda and Rwanda indirectly by defending their case, but equally gave the impression of rewarding them by proposing these countries for the Highly Indebted Poor Countries debt relief initiative" (UNSCs/2001/357: 39). Thus, not only did these countries profit from their organized criminal activity, but were rewarded by the World Bank for doing so.

Similar patterns have been established with Rwanda's exporting of minerals. For example, as with Uganda, Rwanda readily acknowledges that it has no indigenous diamond production. The UNSC, the WTO, and the Diamond High Council have established that starting in 1997 Rwanda began a major export enterprise of bringing rough diamonds to the international markets. Between 1997 and 2000, the Diamond High Council estimates that Rwanda exported a total value of US $2,964,414 (UNSC S/2001/357: 25). The same processes have occurred with niobium, colton, coffee, timber, and cassiterite have been noted by international agencies. Colton, an essential ingredient in portable electronics, became the focus of smuggling across the border into the eastern part of Rwanda and the southern region of Angola.

During 1999 and 2000, world prices of colton exploded, increasing nearly tenfold (Jackson 2002; Samset 2002). Rwanda reaped massive benefits from this, exporting US $250 million in that period, again with little-to-no indigenous sources of the mineral. These revenues were used to maintain military control over portions of the eastern DRC, especially in the Ituri region. As Samset (2002: 477) points out, at least half of colton production in the eastern regions of the Congo were expropriated to Rwanda and Uganda.

In the Kivu areas, an entire informal economy developed around colton for a brief period in 1999 and 2000. Intermediaries would buy colton ore from locals, transport it to urban areas, then sell it to *comptoirs*, who then clarified, processed, and sold the ore to interests in London, Brussels, and Amsterdam.

This local boom economy created a dollar economy and encouraged the development of local markets for brewing, prostitution, and other petty goods and services. It did not take long for young men to abandon subsistence production for dollar-generating endeavors. Local estimates suggested that up to 90% of young men were "chasing dollars," leading to large reductions in the production of beans and manioc, the two main regional food staples. These shortages led to inflation in food markets. In November 2000, seeing enormous profit potential, militias assumed monopoly control of the colton market in the Kivu region. Although this cut out the *comptoirs*, locals still engaged in the production and distribution of the mineral (by choice or force) until the global collapse of the prices in early 2001. Even with a drastically reduced price, most locals still focused their economic endeavors to some degree on colton as there was not the available capital to reestablish livestock herds and seed stocks for widespread planting (Jackson 2002).

Although these mineral resources, especially those easily transported across porous borders, have an obvious value, that value cannot be realized unless the commodity can be sold. Uganda, Rwanda, and Angola do not have large refining industries or large manufacturing sections that demand such goods. The demand comes from Western and Asian economies. We now examine how these stolen goods made their way from the African states that illegally expropriated them into the hands of those who were willing to purchase them.

The International Context

Owing to the highly valued mineral wealth found, especially in the northeastern part of the nation, both transnational corporations and Switzerland were either implicitly or duly complicit with the violences in northern Congo (Human Rights Watch 2005; UNSC 2003). Gold, silver, diamonds, colton, and other precious minerals constitute the major exploitable natural resources of the area. As we have noted, with the political and economic chaos instigated by the civil war of 1998, and the continued unrest since, these mineral resources are effectively controlled by militia groups. Although the sitting government can, and has, issued contracts and deeds for mineral extraction, such official permissions are meaningless in the hinterlands. To actually take advantage of these economic agreements, companies must also negotiate with the on-the-ground powers or establish relationships with neighboring states to purchase raw materials illegally taken over the border and then shipped into major global markets (Human Rights Watch 2005; UNSC 2003).

Involvement in this sort of trade violates human rights laws when the nature of mining and export operations fails to follow existing international guidelines. This is precisely the situation that has widely existed in the northeastern region of DRC. The UN Panel of Experts (UNSC 2003) named over hundred corporations with problematic or suspect dealings within the DRC during the chaos of the past eight years (see the UNSC 2003 report for a full accounting of those involved). Although the majority of these were African-based companies (most based in neighboring countries), major transnational organizations, such as De Beers, were also named. Belgium, Canada, Germany, Israel, the Netherlands, Switzerland, the UK, and the US all have multiple companies on the list.

After the June 2003 establishment of a DRC transitional government, transnational corporations almost immediately began seeking the state's license to pursue gold extraction in the north. Anglogold Ashanti Ltd. (AGA) has been given the sole mineral extraction rights in the Ituri region by the sitting government (Human Rights Watch 2003, 2005). Yet, as both the government and Anglogold Ashanti acknowledge, since the mines are in militia-controlled regions, these allowances mean nothing on the ground. In order to activate the governmental contract and to begin gold extraction, AGA had to enter into negotiations with the individuals who controlled actual access to the mines: the FNI and its leader Floribert Njabu (Human Rights Watch 2005). In an interview with Human Rights Watch, Njabu was perfectly clear about the nature of mineral concessions and the way in which any economic activities would work in his (or any other) militia-controlled area:

> I am the one who gave Ashanti [AngloGold Ashanti] permission to come to Mongbwalu. I am the boss of Mongbwalu. If I want to chase them away I will ... The contract for Ashanti is with the government but we [the FNI] control Mongbwalu so they need to come see me if they want to work there. (Quoted in Human Rights Watch 2005: 62)

When such militia groups are involved in war crimes, forced labor, and other crimes against humanity, this makes the transnational corporation both complicit and responsible for these crimes. In general, these actions may potentially violate specific UN Security Council or General Assembly resolutions, such as arms and other trade embargoes. Specifically, such actions violate the Norms on the Responsibilities of Transnational Corporations and Other Business Enterprises with Regard to Human Rights. Engaging in, supporting, or taking advantage of the forced and otherwise exploitative labor practices identified with the DRC constituted a crime against humanity. This opens up a new realm of jurisdiction for the ICC—the behavior of transnational corporations. Someone has to buy the minerals and either refine and manufacture them or sell them to those who have the resources to do so.

Metalor Technologies, a leading Swiss refinery, is responsible for purchasing Congolese gold from Ugandan sources (Human Rights Watch 2005). Although claiming to follow all Swiss and international laws, Metalor's due diligence is problematic; they knew the gold was coming from Uganda. It is also well known that there is essentially no indigenous Ugandan gold production and Uganda does not import gold from other countries. This leaves one likely source of the metal: northeastern Congo. Metalor's purchases were facilitated by the Swiss freeport system. Freeports provide a place for the importation of goods that are legally outside the realm of governmental control. No duties or tariffs are applied to goods brought in through these zones and thus no governmental record keeping or oversight occurs. A company like Metalor can buy gold within a freeport zone with no official taxation and, more importantly, with no tracing of its origins. Although aware of the military and humanitarian crisis in the region, and fully cognizant of the illegal gold trade across the DRC-Uganda border, the Swiss government has shown no interest in altering import laws to shut down the market. This is not the first time that the Swiss financial system has been implicated in facilitating criminal action, or even the first time it has been linked to crimes against humanity (e.g., the now infamous use of the system to hide Nazi gold and other wealth extracted from nations conquered in World War II). The Swiss are not the only world power to be complicit in this case. The UNSC has identified numerous companies benefiting from the illegal mineral exploitation, including those based in Belgium, Bermuda, Burundi, Canada, China, Germany, Finland, Hong Kong, India, Israel, Malaysia, the Netherlands, Pakistan, the Russian Federation, Rwanda, South Africa, Thailand, Uganda, the United Arab Emirates, the UK, the US, and Zimbabwe. Essentially all do so with full knowledge of the source of what they are purchasing.

Summary

The territory around the Congo River has suffered one of the longest and most intense periods of disorder, terror, and atrocity on the African continent. From the early days of Leopold's Free State to contemporary events, the land and her peoples have faced almost constant violence, subordination, domination, and warfare. The greatest asset of what is now called the Democratic Republic of Congo is also her greatest curse—the rich mineral deposits in the north and the south. The sheer brutality of Leopold's rule devastated the population and eradicated indigenous lifeways. Under the rule of Belgium, though there was not the raw number of atrocities, conditions improved little. Independence and the way in which it was delivered, brought no hope of stability. Within days the new state was sundered by civil war; since, internecine conflict has been one of the hallmarks of the Congolese national experience. Although stable under the reign of Mobutu Sese Seko, the government and the country was turned toward lining the pockets of the president and his network of kith and kin. Congo's resources steadily flowed out of the country into European markets with little benefit to the local population, as they had throughout the nineteenth century. With the ouster of Mobutu, the country again fell into civil unrest, warfare, and outright invasion by her neighbors. Now, as then, the lure was the same: abundant natural resources to be expropriated. As Reno (2006: 53) points out, "Congo is marginal to the global strategic and economic interests of powerful countries." There has not been a strong motivation or desire in the international community to strongly intervene in the Congo. Currently, these state's businesses profit from the disorder and there is no strong interest or will among the governments or citizenry of the West (or the East for that matter) to intervene and bring the situation to resolution. With no cold war–style foreign policy imperatives, central Africa is now politically irrelevant (at least until it begins to harbor terrorists).

The problems of violence and disorder continue. Every time the area seems on the verge of a real peace agreement, be it the signing of the Lusaka Accords, the power-sharing agreement between the standing government and militias, active demobilization and disarmament of militias, or the recent elections, violence quickly arises and questions the legitimacy of the entire process. At the time of this writing, the DRC is not a state in the classic or contemporary sense. There is a government that is internationally recognized providing a legal existence. Yet, on the ground, the government does not monopolize the use of force in the territory, nor does it exert widespread influence on policy or living conditions. It does not control its entire natural resource base and, at least as of now, does not possess widespread legitimacy among the population.

· 7 ·

AGAIN THE WORLD STOOD BY AND WATCHED

To date, internecine violence within the Darfur region of Sudan has claimed the lives of over 400,000 civilians (Coalition for International Justice March 2006); more than 2 million people have been displaced and countless more have been raped, robbed, intimated, and suffered other depredations of a collapsed social structure. Since the 1980s, the people of the region have been subjected to national and international military abuse and political marginalization. Despite massive amounts of public discourse, both raising awareness of and calling for a stop to the violence, little has been done by any sociopolitical actor to either resolve or remediate the situation and improve the lives of Darfuris. The origins, and continued enactment of the conflict, is far more complex than is currently reflected in either the discourse of the Sudanese government or the international political arena. There has been serious debate within the international arena, especially within institutions focused on international legal issues, as to whether these actions are genocide or crimes against humanity. Political and media discourse has generated several characterizations and rationales for the mass murders, rapes, and population displacements. Though driven by long standing political conflicts with the Sudanese government and limited humanitarian interest, Colin Powell, former US Secretary of State, *did* characterize the acts as genocide in a speech before the United Nations. The Sudanese government blames rebel factions, the Sudanese Liberation Movement/Army (SLM/A) and the Justice and Equality Movement (JEM) faction of the SLM/A, and random opportunistic bandit groups for the atrocities, denying the involvement of its own armed forces. The government has also suggested that the mass killings, rape, and torture that have occurred over the past several years are the result of ethnic tensions between "Arabs" and "Africans." However, as we show, these labels are not only misleading but also the product of a historically recent social construction process. The assumption is that the Arab-dominated government in Khartoum aligned itself with Arab-ethnic militias against rebels descended from African Groups. This allowed the framing of the issue as having its ultimate origin in "time immemorial" as Arab peoples have held a presence in this region for centuries. However, historically, "Arab" herders and "African" farmers generally coexisted peacefully. Moreover, the existing ethnic consciousness is the result of political manufacturing of the Sudanese government during a time of intense political power struggles.

Others suggest that the violence and deaths of hundreds of thousands of Darfur citizens is the result of desertification, producing a struggle over scarce resources that include intense violence (Lobban 2004). This interpretation has led many to view the situation as a humanitarian crisis rather than a human-generated set of atrocities: broader issues of intentionality, corrupt regimes, and the express promulgation and manipulation of these events by the Sudanese state. Moreover, the focus on desertification assumes that this is a natural and uncontrollable process. Although this is true to a degree, the major droughts of the 1970s and 1980s did expand the scope of the Sahara, human action has played a role as well. For example, as populations grew in Sahara border states, marginally arable lands previously used for grazing and ranching were tilled for agriculture. The soil was too thin and nutrient poor for these uses, leading to erosion and growth of desert (Meredith 2006).

The symbolic value of political and legal labels within the international context is significant to the way a given phenomenon is perceived by the international society that directly affects the likelihood and nature of international intervention. These labels also have severe ramifications for a state's political and legal culpability on the international stage. In this chapter, we take the position that although many of the existing explanations of the Darfur crisis are partially correct, none are fully so. Indeed, there is an ethnic and tribal element to the conflict; the process of desertification has also indirectly contributed to the violence. As with other cases we have explored here, the effects of colonialism are important in understanding the backdrop and the way in which political, economic, and military power is distributed, both ethnically and regionally, as the crisis evolved in the 1980s and 1990s. Now we turn our attention to the history of Darfur followed by the subsequent genocidal actions of the Sudanese government and the *Janjaweed*.

Historical Context

Colonial control came later to Sudan than the rest of the African continent. The region remained essentially autonomous of Western control until the early years of the twentieth century—1916. The Anglo-Egyptian takeover was both direct and indirect. Although ultimate authority was held by the dominating state powers, the new Sudan Political Service was not keen to do anything that represented any form of change or break with the traditional means of governing (Prunier 2005). The plan was to continue the use of tribal administration, a typical UK approach. However, this glorification of Tribal Administration and the "hands off" policy led to the general neglect of any development in education, health, transportation, or the economic system, save the north and the areas immediately surrounding Khartoum, the capital.

By the end of the colonial rule, 56% of all state investments were concentrated in Khartoum, Kassala, and the Northern Province, with only 17% going to Kordofan and Darfur. Only 5–6% of all investments reached Darfur, despite the fact that more people resided in the West (including Darfur) (Prunier 2005). This investment and infrastructural inequity is critical to understanding how the crimes we explore are organized in time and space.

The first postcolonial elections were held in 1958; they were won by the Umma—the political party of the *Madhist* (roughly meaning "community of Islam believers"). The general Darfur population supported the *Madhist* party. Despite this, they failed to gain the recognition or political clout to address the growing economic crisis of Darfur. As Prunier (2005: 39) states, "The Darfur *Madhist* devotees were good enough to carry spears in the *Madhist* militia and to vote for the Umma Party ... but this did not earn them the right to claim a fair share of the budget from the government to whose election they had made a decisive contribution." The divisions of power and representation began to surface more clearly during the 1960s.

By 1965, the Constitutional Committee was created to devise a governmental structure for Sudan. Three positions emerged: a secular constitution supported by the southerners of Sudan, an Islamic Constitution supported by the Islamic Charter Front, and an Islamic-oriented Constitution supported by the Unionists. Darfur was generally opposed to an Islamic Constitution;

although Muslim, they regarded it as a "ploy for consolidating the hegemony of Northern and Central Sudan under the umbrella of an Islamic and Arabic culture that would perpetuate the marginalization of Sudan's Southern, Western, and Eastern populations" (Warburg 2003: 148). It was at this juncture that the perception of a united Islamic front began to deteriorate causing a slight, but persistent, split in the Muslim majority in the northern Sudan along ethnic and regional lines. The goal was not the establishment of an Islamic state for the sake of pure religious ideology and advancement, but an identity used politically to unite a diverse population. Since the region was under Egyptian control, these discourses and identity processes were central to sharing and maintaining legitimacy, the government, and the wealth of the country (Prunier 2005). This demarks the first of "Arab" used to denote and denounce what was viewed as the ruling "elite."

By the 1968 elections, the Umma had separated into two parties—one supporting Sadiq and the other Sadiq's uncle Imam al-Hadi. Darfur was a staunch supporter of the Umma and it became the battleground between the two parties. To gain support, Sadiq, after calculating that demographics would favor the Fur and other "African" tribes, made an alliance with the leader of Darfur leaving his uncle with the "Arab" tribes. An exaggerated racial-cultural rhetoric emerged as a political tool to solidify support in the area. Due to years of favoritism out of Khartoum for the north, such an ideological vision found ample support (Prunier 2005). The "African" electorate was told that if Darfur had been marginalized and neglected, it was the fault of the "Arabs." Fur, Masalit, and Zaghawa eagerly accepted this belief, given that historically their presence and representation was absent from the power center of Khartoum; however, the marginalization had not really been racial or cultural, rather it was regional. Nonetheless, the Arab discourse offered a hope for the Arabized tribes to be co-opted into the "Arab elite" ruling group that had historically remained at the center of political power (Prunier 2005). The political manipulation of these divides began to take on more than a symbolic meaning; it set the stage for later ethnic politics and violence.

These increasing tensions were exacerbated by the drought and famine in neighboring Chad during the 1970s. Although France shipped 50,000 tons of food to Chad during 1973, the southerners who supported the Tombalbaye regime received the aid first. Little food reached the north. Consequently, the northern Toubou and Zaghawa tribes fled to Darfur for support. There they were perceived as "Arabs" that were armed and angry. Moreover, Sudan became heavily involved in anti-Libya rhetoric and gave full support to the upcoming

Chadian leader, Hissen Habre. Within a short time, Habre's Forces, the *Armee du Nord*, settled in Darfur to harass and skirmish with the already present Chadian Army. The manipulation and handling of Darfur by the Chadians, Lybians, and Khartoum forces only worsened the regional ethno-political landscape that was being ideologically distorted via the evolving political discourse. Darfur tribes found themselves in a broader interstate conflict where they were "summoned to declare themselves as either Arab or Black Africans" (Prunier 2005: 46).

Although these labels were attributed to them by outside forces, acts of nature further nurtured the ethnic dichotomy. The recurring droughts of the 1970s and 1980s initiated a process of desertification, creating a significantly degraded ecology that further polarized the politically manipulated ethnic identities. In 1986, Kutum had only 197 mm of rainfall compared to 295 mm in 1976. El-Fashir received 162 mm of precipitation, 108 mm less than in 1976. El-Gencia's total was 373 mm versus the 510 mm of 1976 (Prunier 2005: 49). These climatic changes altered local plant life and water supplies, making pastoral lifeways that much more precarious and unpredictable. The drought played havoc mostly with the Arab tribes' means of subsistence—horse and camel herding. The nomadic lifeway of pastoral peoples encouraged and perpetuated the view that they were indeed different from the African neighboring tribes.

In 1977, President Nimery began a "patriotic reconciliation" project in which he called out to fellow Arab leaders and parties, once his opponents, to stimulate Arab unity. Nimery also became heavily connected to neighboring oil monarchies (e.g., Saudi Arabia), thereby benefiting from massive profits. By 1980, Sudan sought to become "the future breadbasket of the Arab World" (Prunier 2005: 51), however, this productivity never fully materialized. Although massive investment in machinery to industrialize the farming base was made, production actually declined, leaving Sudan with US $12 billion in foreign debt. The droughts of 1983 and 1984 further undermined the hopes of building a strong agricultural basis for the nation. Nimery did his best to ignore the destabilizing consequences but the combination of famine, unemployment, massive foreign debt, and widespread corruption produced widespread protests (Meredith 2006). The famine was at its peak in 1984 and Darfur was considered a disaster as the death toll escalated and mass displacement occurred. It has been estimated that between August 1984 and November 1985, 95,000 people died (Waal 2005: 88). In April of 1985, Nimery was overthrown.

In addition to the drought and ensuing famine, through the 1980s, other factors solidified the politically drawn ethnic identities. The Chad conflict continued to spill into Darfur. Internal political tensions were compounded with the ongoing international involvements, for example, the ongoing Libyan interest in Darfur and support of the north in the larger Sudan conflict. The presence of the Libyans also reinforced the ethnic divisions by favoring the Arab tribes. As a result of the famine, resources were scarce and divisions were strengthened between the Fur and the Arabs. The famine sharpened the geographic and economic divisions between nomadic herders and sedentary farmers that was increasingly being defined by the peoples themselves as an Arab/African dichotomy. The new government in Khartoum did not address the problems of Darfur; rather it began a campaign of incitement to ethnic hatred. The Arab center in Khartoum automatically sided against the African periphery. Moreover, the north/south conflict was in full force and Darfuri conscripts represented an exceedingly high proportion of those going to fight in the South (Prunier 2005).

By 1986, resistance to the Khartoum regime's policies started forming. Riots took place as many Fur conscripts refused to fight their "brothers" in south Sudan (e.g., Nyala). Libyan troops were still present in Darfur and the conflict in Chad continued to spill over into Darfur. This not only brought on the ground violence, but also exacerbated the increasing ethnic hatred that outside forces were encouraging in support of their larger goals. For all intents and purposes, Darfur was now in a state of civil war. Between 1985 and 1988, approximately 9,000 deaths occurred (Prunier 2005: 65). The instrumentalization of ethnic divisions was still rather limited during this civil war. However, it was during this period that the term *Janjaweed* was first used to describe the Arab horsemen. The spring of 1989 saw Darfuri tribal leaders begin their own peace efforts. In part, this was due to a growing awareness that domestic clashes were being manufactured by Libya for its own interests in Chad. Moreover, by this time Libya asserted Darfur as its own, based on a long territorial dispute between the leaders of Libya and Sudan. During the second half of that same year, Libya claimed victory in Chad; Darfur slowly began to experience a modicum of peace. This temporary peace allowed the Khartoum government to again ignore Darfur leaving it in a state of chaos. Correspondingly, Libya also lost interest in the region as it was no longer of tactical value.

In 1989, General Omar al-Bashir seized power in a coup, installing an Islamist-orientated government. Almost immediately, the intended brutality of his regime was evident as political, religious, and civil dissent was crushed. Hundreds of people disappeared (Human Rights Watch 1994). Two years later, he replaced Sudanese law with a rigid Islamic penal code and a host of repressive laws and regulations. The government quickly became known internationally as a supporter of terrorists, allowing Hamas training camps to be set up and providing a safe haven for Osma Bin Laden and Sheikh Omar Abdel Rahman (Meredith 2006).

In July 1991, Khartoum assigned al-Tayib Sikha, a National Islamic Front (NIF) activist in charge of Darfur to regain control of the province using militaristic means. With the resolution of the international conflicts, Darfur and the rest of Sudan's domestic ills were labeled as a "Sudanese problem." Moreover, the interest in Darfur was secondary, merely a means to gain political capital internationally by appeasing the Arab League, US, and the UN. This would frame Sikha's operations politically as the long-awaited addressing of the needs of the marginalized areas of Sudan. The center of the militaristic approach was operations against the Zaghawa and the Fur. Nevertheless, such actions were overlooked due to the intense slaughter in the south, an internecine conflict that quickly turned international. Uganda began supporting southern rebel groups; el-Bashiri responded by supporting Kony's LRA (as we explored in Chapter Four). The US then provided aid to Museveni to counter Khartoum's influence (Meredith 2006).

Up until 1991, Sudan was a federal state. The central government in Khartoum selected gubernatorial delegates and redrew state boundaries as each regime saw fit. During 1994, the acting Minister for Federal Affairs, Ali al-Haji, changed the divisions of Sudan, dividing each of the nine states (excluding Khartoum) into three—making 26 new states—and reestablished the traditional tribal administration previously used during the British rule. In early 1995, the Governor of West Darfur restructured the Administrative allocations filling most positions with friends, relatives, local Arabs, or associates from Khartoum. Protesting their continued marginalization, the then Governor Fadl was replaced by Hassan Hamadein, who ruled with military force when needed. The years 1996–8 were filled with low-intensity warfare. This ended in 1999 when clashes between Massalit and Arab herders were used by the government to propagate the view that these groups were part of an antigovernment rebel group (the SPLA). Consequently, Khartoum sent in troops and helicopters killing thousands and displacing at least 100,000, with nearly 40,000 forced to flee to Chad (Prunier 2005). Although temporarily subduing northwest Darfur, nothing had been solved.

Although the conflicts in northern Darfur were suspended, and the south was under enough nominal control to allow development of an oil industry, the underlying tensions remained. In December 1999, Sudan was proclaimed a state of emergency by President Omar el-Bashir. The following month the parliament of Sudan was dissolved. Once again, the focus, internationally and domestically, was on the north/south conflict in Sudan ignoring the western region: Darfur. Several peace agreements between the north and south were signed over the next couple of years. Although this did not produce the peace the international arena assumed it would, progress appeared to be made. With all the focus on peace negotiations, Darfur was again neglected and left at the margins of the political spectrum.

Meanwhile, the situation in Darfur quickly grew worse. In November 2002, the Khartoum regime's "strong arm" visited Darfur, warning the people that any insurgency should stop and gave symbolic promises of development in an attempt to appease the growing disgruntlement (Prunier 2005). Within weeks 11 South African police officers were killed in southern Darfur. In February 2003, a group of 300 insurgents organized an attack that killed nearly 200 soldiers. With this event, Darfur could no longer be politically dismissed as violence from armed looting or rogue bandits. Instead, the Government of Sudan decided that a quick and sharp domestic response would be the only way to minimize the growing unrest in an effort to assure Sudan was making progress in the larger north/south peace process. In response to the uprising, the Government of Sudan sent the President of Parliament Transport Committee, Idris Yusaf, to negotiate with the armed group from Jebel Marra. Yusaf gave the group an ultimatum to surrender in 10 days or "suffer the consequences," adding that they felt "the Army can solve the situation in 24 hours" (Musa 2003). The next few years brought the deaths of at least 210,000 and the displacement of hundreds of thousands, bringing an estimated total of 2.2 million Darfuris affected by the war (UN 2004).

The Crucial Years: 2003–7

> When the problems with the rebels started in Darfur, we in the government of Sudan had a number of options. We chose the wrong one. We chose the very worst one.
> (Lt. General Ibrahim Suleiman, 17 October 2004)

2003: Kill the Fur

The Sudanese government's initial response to the insurrection was both a symbolic political gesture and hard-lined covert military response. Several symbolic attempts were made to settle the growing insurgency. The Sudanese government spokesperson Ali Osman Mohammed Taha promised that the government would build 100 km of good roads and increase Darfur's budget for water connections threefold. As in the past, the monies were never actually allocated. Economic and social grievances remained unaddressed; the insurgency was still depicted in the media as disorganized bandits attacking the government. The Government of Sudan continued direct combat against the insurgency as well as unofficially using the *Janjaweed* militia. By this time, many of the governors of Darfur had also been replaced with Khartoum supporters. A task force, set up by the Government, also began exploring the possibilities of formalizing the government's relationship with the *Janjaweed* militias to extend government military power and response capabilities, while simultaneously masking it from any international political repercussions by being able to deny involvement in actions committed by the militias. Although publicly denying such a relationship, militia were paid a salary, provided regular army uniforms with insignia of rank, and received weapons directly from the Khartoum government. Subsequently, they operated in direct cooperation with government forces. For all intents and purposes, international law would now recognize them as state troops under the command and control of Sudan, with all legal obligations.

By June, full repression was being implemented against the Darfuris. President Omar el-Bashir dissolved previously set-up special courts to address the ongoing human rights violations by the *Janjaweed*, allowing all military bodies to operate without obstruction and with full impunity (Prunier 2005). In late July 2003, the Sudanese Army was using aircraft to release bombs on villages, destroy local public institutions (e.g., schools), and to perform reconnaissance in the region to identify targets suitable for *Janjaweed* raids. The typical approach to carrying out these raid included cordoning off villages, looting all belongings, raping the females, stealing the livestock, shooting anyone unable to run away, and then burning the villages and the young. Human Rights Watch reported that they were told by a former Sudanese soldier that the captured livestock were given to the *Janjaweed* and "large army trucks would transport the looted livestock back to *Janjaweed* camps" (Human Rights Watch interview, north Darfur, 14 July 2005). According to an interview with a former soldier conducted by Human Rights Watch, July 2004, the government's first major campaign using the military and Musa Hilal, a *Janjaweed* leader, was devastating. He stated,

> We were asked to clear the way and the area for the *Janjaweed* to attack, burn, and loot the village ... that day too, Antonova [a military plane] came during the attack and dropped three bombs on the mountain near the village. People were running away. I saw villagers being killed ... soldiers burned huts and buildings in the village along with the *Janjaweed*. Three hundred and fifty soldiers participated in the attack.

Only five refused to shoot or shot in the air. Three of the five were later arrested, court martialed and sent to jail. There were no SLA (Sudanese Liberation Army) only civilians.

In August 2003, several Darfuri residents living in Khartoum petitioned President Omar el-Bashir to open political dialogue with the insurgency, begin a ceasefire, free Darfuri political prisoners, send humanitarian aid before the rainy season was to begin, and to stop using the militias for repression (Prunier 2005). In response the government declared a state of emergency in Darfur and stepped up arrests of people who associated with, or were suspected of sympathizing with, the insurgents. State-supported militia activities against the Darfurians also increased; the government abandoned any symbolic negotiations and was fully committed to its military response. As Ahmed Harun, State Minister of the Interior from Khartoum, stated in a speech to the military, "Kill the Fur" (Human Rights Watch, January 2005: 27). Now, the violence was directed toward ethnic cleansing; a genocide was under way.

By late October, the parties to the Darfur conflict met again with Sudanese representatives. However, the Chadian government was now feeling the impact of the crisis as the *Janjaweed* and the Sudanese Army were routinely crossing the border of Chad. In addition, Khartoum began intensifying its genocidal measures by targeting the livelihood of the remaining civilians as well as blocking food and aid supplied by the international arena (e.g., USAID, US Charge d'Affaires). In an attempt to provide international cover, Sudan's Minister of Humanitarian Affairs declared there was no food emergency in Darfur. In December, the government increased the quantities of troops to the area while decreasing them from the south of Sudan. President el-Bashir also proclaimed the war in the south and all other areas had come to an end (Prunier 2005). Meanwhile, a third round of talks was supposed to have occurred between the el-Bashir's administration and Darfuri representatives. Publicly, Sudan reported that the insurgency wanted oil money, their army, and separation from Sudan. However, the true demands were that international observers be present during the talks, an international investigation of the war crimes be initiated, and a military force be set up to protect civilians.

2004: The Janjaweed *Ride Free*

At a time of international concentration on peace talks for Sudan, the killings and masses of refugees from Darfur continued unabated. A US $10.3 million relief fund from the UNHCR still had not made its way into Darfur and President el-Bashir was claiming "an end to the military operations now that the Armed Forces are in full control of all theatres of operation" (Prunier 2005: 113). In addition, el-Bashir promised unimpeded access in Darfur for all UN Agencies and NGOs. Such agencies found it next to impossible to provide aid. Fighting prevented the safe passage for aid workers and individuals who had spoken to any aid workers or the USAID representatives were arrested. Meanwhile, the killings continued.

In February, the Naivasha Peace Talks resumed and the killing of Darfuri civilians continued. Refugees continued to flee to El-Fashir. Testimony from a schoolgirl reported to Amnesty, "The *Janjaweed* entered my school and caught some girls and raped them in classrooms. I was raped by four men inside the school. When they left they told us they would take care of all us black people and clean Darfur for good" (AI Wire, May 2005: 1). Other schoolchildren did not fare as well as reports claim, children were often raped and then thrown back into the building once the buildings were set on fire. Villages continued to be destroyed and people were forcefully displaced. Those that remained met terrible fates. As one refugee stated,

> The *Janjaweed* came to my house and asked me why I was not gone like the others. I said I had been in Mecca and I could not flee from a person. Then they shot me on my back. I fell. Then they cut my skin on the top of my head and my ears. Then they picked me up and threw me into the fire. They looted everything, the market, everything. They were as numerous as ants. (Human Rights Watch, 27 June 2005 interview)

Other testimony given to Amnesty International (November 2004: 30) alludes to the mass rapes that occurred as a means of demoralizing survivors. He stated,

> In February I left my home to flee "exactions" [evacuations]. In the bush, I was intercepted by six Arabs; I tried to take my spear to protect my family, but they threatened me with a gun, so I stopped. The six Arabs then raped my daughter in front of me and my other children.

Human Rights Watch also stated that a 35-year-old female interviewee told them that when the *Janjaweed* militia attacked her village, many of the residents gathered in the police station seeking protection. However, the civilians were held there while "militia selected young women for rape and men were shot and tortured if they protested" (Human Rights Watch, April 2005: 3).

The tensions with Chad also increased at this time as cross-border raids by the *Janjaweed* continued. It was during this month that the UN Humanitarian

Coordinator for Sudan stated, "the only difference between Rwanda and Darfur now are the numbers involved" (UNHRC). The government retaliated by claiming that the statement was nothing but political lies and lodged a protest against the UN.

The intensity of violence continued into March as did the connections between the Sudanese government and the *Janjaweed*. A 22-year-old Zaghawa man was arrested after a joint-army *Janjaweed* attack in the village of Omda Dabo. He was then turned over to the *Janjaweed*. In testimony to Human Rights Watch he stated,

> They hung me with hooks piercing my chest. They also burned me. I was arrested with thirty other men. They tied us together and interrogated us about animals. We said we did not know so they called us liars and shot and slaughtered some of the men in front of my eyes.

On 8 April 2004, the Khartoum and Darfuri representatives agreed to yet another round of peace talks and a ceasefire for 45 days. This was again broken within hours of the agreement. By this time the UN was requesting that a fact-finding mission be implemented. Khartoum asked for more time to "prepare" for the mission's arrival. Sudanese forces began emptying mass graves and moving bodies to Kordofan for incineration. The *Janjaweed* were being issued official army identity numbers and those killed were ex post facto put on the army casualty lists. Once the UN team arrived, it was hampered from entering certain regions, including the Wadi Salch area where some of the recent atrocities had occurred.

With the increased humanitarian presence and emerging international awareness the systematic massacres and repression began to shift from overt slaughter into low-intensity counterinsurgency. This included less military intervention but more focus on sabotaging food and medical aid. The government's move toward a more covert role was reinforced by the incorporation of the *Janjaweed* into the regular army. It was subsequently placed in charge of securing the refugee camps and protecting the civilians. By this time, there were over 1.2 million displaced peoples in Darfur, 120,000 in Chad and over 1 million others that were deeply affected. As a result of the food shortages, ethnic clashes began to occur as tribes turned on each other in their struggle to obtain subsistence resources.

On 22 July 2004 the UNSC adopted yet another resolution trying to bring the Khartoum government in line with the desires of the international political society: Resolution 1556 that gave Sudan until August to disarm the *Janjaweed*.

The Resolution neither acknowledged the role of the government nor that it was simply not realistically possible to separate the militia forces from the regular army forces. At this point the two forces were fully intertwined, as noted by a confidential Sudanese government document, "Its absurd to distinguish between the Sudanese Government Forces and the Militias—they are one" (Takirambudde 2005: 1). Although there were symbolic arrests of several alleged *Janjaweed* in an effort to appease the international arena, all were petty criminals or were already in jail, for example, one was the Nyala town drunkard arrested for violating alcohol laws (Power 2004).

Instead of reigning in its death squad, el-Bashir drove the genocide onward; he would complete in Darfur what he tried to complete in the south—elimination of all opposition. According to a document dated August 2004 seized from a *Janjaweed* official, the "execution of all directives from the President of the Republic. ... Change the demography of Darfur and make it void of African Tribes." It continues with a general encouragement to "kill, burn villages and farms, terrorize people, and confiscate property from members of African Tribes and forcing them from Darfur" (Kristoff 2005: 2).

With the arrival of the rainy season, humanitarian supplies were cut off and the civilian deaths were tallied simply as "crude mortality rates." This confused those who died from natural causes with those who perished from starvation with those who met more violent ends. Meanwhile, another peace negotiation was under way in Abuja. The el-Bashir regime asked the African Union to disarm the "rebels" while they promised to disarm *Janjaweed*. However, by this time, skepticism of the sincerity of the government was present. To put additional pressure on the process of foreign diplomacy, Khartoum's Minister of Information declared that Sudan would not sign the Naivasha (north/south) peace talks before the Darfur question was solved. By September, the Abuja peace talks collapsed and the Darfur situation was declared by the European parliament as tantamount to "genocide." On 18 September 2004, the UNSC passed Resolution 1564 demanding the end of human rights violations and to create a "Commission of Inquiry" to determine whether genocide occurred.

The focus now shifted from the actual crisis and systematic deaths that were occurring in Darfur to a conflict of discourse: genocide, ethnic cleansing, or humanitarian crisis. Meanwhile, Sudan began "repatriating" displaced Darfuris even though they had no homes to return to. This included bulldozing refugee camps and the use of violence against anyone who attempted to stay or resist the Sudanese efforts to "return home." By November 2004, the UNHCR withdrew its staff from south Darfur after the government refused to let them work because they had protested the forced relocations and repatriation programs. On 19 November, UN Resolution 1574 was implemented calling an end to violence. However, Khartoum continued to use the north/south Naivasha peace talks as symbolic good faith attempts knowing actions in Darfur would continue as part of the status quo. Darfur was descending into "total anarchy and warlordism" (UN Special Envoy, Jan Pronk, 2 November 2004).

2005: Genocide By Any Other Name ...

On 9 January 2005, the Comprehensive Peace Agreement was signed effectively bringing an end to the north/south conflict. However, the Darfuri situation in the west was omitted from the agreement. With the general satisfaction of the international society regarding peace, the focus on Sudan was alleviated. Again acting with impunity, the Khartoum government resumed its offensive. Within one week of the Peace Agreement, *Janjaweed* militia, in coordination with Sudanese government forces, attacked the village of Hamada. As residents were detained in the village, men and women were separated into groups, many of the males were executed, women and children were killed, and others were repeatedly raped (Human Rights Watch 2005). Those who managed to flee reported they were told by the *Janjaweed* they were "cleaning the land from Shariya to El Fashir through Shangi Tobaya."

In the same month the UNSC Investigatory Commission completed its report and determined that the actions within Darfur did not constitute genocide; rather they were crimes against humanity. In its determination of whether or not the actions in Darfur constitute genocide, the UNSC's Investigatory Commission essentially had three questions to answer: (1) Did the actions exist on a widespread and systematic level? (2) Do tribal groups constitute a protected population under the genocide and crimes against humanity conventions? (3) Was the specific intent of destroying an entire category of persons present?

Answering the first question is a matter of empirical investigation. The UNSC established that the regular Sudanese Army and their *Janjaweed* allies were primarily responsible for these behaviors. Hence, it was not a question of *if* atrocities occurred, but rather the appropriate legal label applied to them. The second question was also noncontroversial. Drawing upon case law established in the ICTY and ICTR, the commission established that tribal groupings did qualify for the status of a group as a protected category of persons as we discussed in Chapter Two. Under international humanitarian law, to qualify as genocide, the targeted group must represent a distinct national, racial, ethnic, or religious category of person. In the case of Darfur, the vast majority of the victims of atrocities have been members of the Fur, Massalit, and Zaghawa tribes. There are few, if any, objective distinctions among these populations; as we have discussed, these ethnic differences were fabricated and highlighted in political discourse in order to solidify the el-Bashir regime's hold on political power.

The third question has produced the most controversy. The UNSC investigatory commission has concluded that the actions in Darfur do not reach the threshold of genocide because the express *intent* to eliminate a protected group of persons could not be established. Their findings on intent rest upon several claims. First, the UNSC investigatory commission denies genocidal intent because during the course of attacks on civilian populations not everyone was killed. To establish this interpretation they cite only the attack at the village of Wadi Saleh where 800 survivors were left and a singular case from the Abu Shouk relocation camp where *Janjaweed* members attacked a group of brothers, robbed them of their camels, and left one alive. The logic behind their claim is that genocidal intent would not allow for the leaving of survivors. This assertion is problematic in a number of ways. Moreover, such a claim ignores precedent law. In the Akayesu Trial held before the ICTR in 1998, paragraph 497 of the ruling states that "genocide does not imply the actual extermination of [a] group in its entirety, but is understood as such once any one of the acts mentioned in Article 2(2)(a) through 2(2)(e) is committed with the specific intent to destroy 'in whole or in part' a national, ethnical, racial or religious group" (see also Rutaganda, 6 December 1999, para. 48–49).

There has never been genocide without survivors. Even the Nazis kept some Jews alive to be used as forced labor (e.g., Volkswagon and Ford auto plants used Jewish slave labor, see Matthews 2006). The Japanese did not kill every Chinese prisoner of war and civilian during their infamous Nanking campaign (Chang 1997). Although the rhetoric of genocide suggests the complete destruction of a population, this is never fully accomplished. Primarily, the necessary organizational apparatus rarely exists to do so. Even for a supremely centralized nation-state (i.e., Stalin's USSR or the United States during the post–civil war "Indian" war period), the organizational capacity necessary to fully exterminate a population is unattainable. Although Stalin killed millions, many survived. Similarly, although the US devastated its indigenous populations, representatives of most of these groups still survive. In this finding of fact, the UNSC Investigatory Commission is producing a narrow definition of genocide based almost solely upon the intent of the Nazi Holocaust and uses of the death camps as its model for enactment.

The Abu Shouk case is similarly nonconclusive. This was an example of banditry associated with a general chaos produced by unrest. Because a small group of *Janjaweed* bandits simply stole some camels and then failed to kill everyone does not deny the enormity of the atrocities in the nation. It means that a small group of militia opportunistically robbed a group of brothers and for whatever reason left a survivor. It is clear that in this example these bandits were not operating at that moment as agents of the state in the ongoing military actions but rather on their own in a violent, acquisitive crime. At best, the tie of this specific action to a broader genocidal intent would be to place it within the broader campaign of terror that often accompanies genocides. A common tactic within such campaigns is to leave survivors to spread news and enhance civilian terror.

The second point the UNSC investigatory commission uses to deny genocidal intent is the creation of camps for displaced persons rather than outright execution of those persons. Again, the logic is that if utter destruction were desired, they would simply kill rather than confine group members. Yet, the historical record clearly shows that genocides involve the construction of camps that first serve as places of confinement, then, as the Nazi Holocaust demonstrates, turn into places of mass execution once the organizational capacity for mass slaughter is produced. In Germany and Yugoslavia camps were antecedent to slaughter. Further, the vast number of human rights violations committed against camp residents by the *Janjaweed* and the Sudanese Army strongly establishes that these camps were not created out of humanitarian interest in the groups. Rather, by collecting the populations in one place they are easier to control and victimize.

The UNSC commission's third major claim points to the fact that the Government of Sudan allowed for Non Governmental Organizations (NGOs) to provide humanitarian assistance to displaced peoples. Their logic is that if utter annihilation were the purpose, then Khartoum would not allow humanitarian relief efforts to move forward and minister to the needs of the Darfuri population. Such a position assumes that the Sudanese government either makes decisions in a complete sociopolitical vacuum or has no desire to interface with the rest of the globe. International pressure has essentially deprived the Government of Sudan with a choice in this manner. If Sudan desires positive interaction with other nations and wants to be considered part of the "community of nations," it must abide by such pressures. As we have explored, the el-Bashir regime has also been infamous in its lack of cooperation and its attempts to disrupt the services provided by those NGOs.

The Commission's final piece of evidence for failing to find genocidal intent is that villages inhabited by both "African" and "Arab" tribal groups have not been targeted. There are numerous reasons why such villages may not be targeted, the least of which is geographic location. Moreover, such an argument falls back to the previous point that genocide need not be directed at a group in whole. As noted by the UNSC's own report, "in some instances individuals, including government officials, may commit acts with genocidal intent." We have catalogued in the chapter evidence of genocidal intent.

The focus from the Darfur crisis to a focus of political discourse and labeling of the atrocities had devastating effect on future events. The UN Commission of Inquiry compiled overwhelming documentation of crimes against humanity; however, it absolved the Sudanese government of the crime of genocide. Although seemingly a mere linguistic turn, this legal labeling is highly significant. The Commission's decision to use the term "crimes against humanity" absolved the Sudanese government from its role and culpability in the ethnic cleansing (Jafari 2004). In addition, by charging crimes against humanity versus genocide, the international society was not obligated by treaty to respond. According to the Genocide Convention, a finding of genocide leads member states to call upon competent organs of the UN to take action appropriate for the prevention and suppression of acts of genocide. As we have seen, the international community showed itself unwilling to intervene, through not using the sociolegal label of genocide, they allowed themselves to limit their behavior to finger wagging and the sending of food aid, thereby avoiding military or other actions. The strongest argument against labeling the actions in Darfur as crimes against humanity rather than genocide continued to play itself out. Although the UNSC bickered about how to get a force on the ground and awaited the approval of the Sudanese government to do so, the Bashir regime escalated its attempts to eradicate those populations that it labeled as undesirable.

Following the UNSC Investigatory Commission's finding, the Resolution 1591 was passed that strengthened sanctions imposed by the UNSC and provided an agreement to forward Darfur to the International Criminal Court (ICC). On 31 March 2005, the UNSC, following procedures outlined in the Rome Statute of the ICC, referred the case of Darfur to the court to conduct an investigation to see if (1) crimes mentioned in the Rome Statute occurred and (2) there is ample evidence to prosecute the individuals responsible.

In response, Sudan announced that it had arrested and charged 15 members of its military and security forces with war crimes (Silverstein 2005). This claim remains unsubstantiated.

In April 2005, the UN released its report to the ICC with 51 alleged Darfur war criminals noted. Nonetheless, the Sudanese government claimed the list of alleged perpetrators was only a guide; the list includes senior government officials. On 14 June 2005 Sudan opened a Special Court to try alleged Darfur war criminals; however, as Amnesty International (AI) noted, the establishment of such a court may be reminiscent of past governmental inquiries and may represent a tactic to avoid prosecution by the ICC (AI, 13 June 2005). In addition, the announcement of the creation of Special Courts came one week after the prosecutor of the ICC announced the opening of investigations into the war crimes and crimes against humanity committed in the Darfur region (ICC 2005).

To date, the Special Criminal Court has handed down several verdicts, however, none of the cases were related to the conflict in 2003 or 2004 nor did any verdicts convict any high-level officials. Thus, it remained a symbolic gesture by the al-Bashir regime to ensure impunity (AI, July 2005). In addition, Article 60 of the Interim Constitution for Sudan, ratified 6 July 2005, contains a provision granting immunity from prosecution to the president and vice president of the Republic of Sudan. Similarly, Article 92 grants immunity to members of the National Legislature.

The UN secretary general's monthly report continued to note the inaction of the Sudanese government declaring that Sudan "had taken no steps to stop the ongoing violence" (UN S/2005/821). Women and children continued to be raped and mass killings remained common practice by the *Janjaweed* and the Sudanese Army. In October, AMIS increased its forces to over seven thousand personnel. Its mandate was expanded beyond ceasefire monitoring to include securing the environment of humanitarian aid relief and the return of refugees to their homes. Nonetheless, violence continued to escalate.

During November 2005, southern Darfur experienced the highest rate of violence. As Kofi Annan noted, "Large scale attacks against civilians continue, women and girls are being raped by armed groups, yet more villages are being burned and thousands more are being driven from their homes" (UN News Service, 29 December 2005: 1). As of December 2005, militia activities continued and in some areas, namely southern and western Darfur, they have increased (UNMIS). Specific areas targeted included Bajo and Duwanan (UN News Service, 27 December 2005). In all, more than half of Darfur's population of 6 million civilians continued suffering from the effects of a collapsed economy, lack of mobility, loss of livelihoods due to the looting and destruction carried out by the army, and *Janjaweed*. Likewise, over 2 million individuals remain displaced and confined to camps.

2006: A Question of Will

The New Year brought little change to the people of Darfur. The government's facilitation of violence continued unabated. The refugee crisis continued to grow as refugees continued to cross into Chad. The *Janjaweed* pushed their way once more into Chad continuing the devastation beyond borders, denying Darfuris any safe haven. The UNSC did agree in February to send troops to protect Darfur civilians, but on 1 March 2006, the plan was rejected by Sudan. Khartoum insisted on African Union forces not an international UN force. In fact, Sudan portrayed the UN entry as a precursor to a Western takeover.

The important, yet politically charged task of counting the precise number of victims remains an arduous task. The death toll has most recently been estimated to be between 60,000 and 160,000, according to Deputy Secretary of State Robert B. Zoellick. However, the Coalition for International Justice reports estimates near 400,000. Hundreds of thousands remained displaced and the region of Darfur was in an economic and social crisis. In August 2006, the *Associated Press* reported that in the five weeks prior, over 200 women in Darfur refugee camps had been raped. The government began a fresh assault on rebel groups, delivery of humanitarian aide ceased, and the recent peace accords did nothing to stop the violence (Polgreen 2006). Although recently, there has been substantial media and political dialogue over ending the genocide, little has been done to remedy the situation, improve the lives of Darfuris, or enact legal controls against those responsible for such acts. As major political actors took up discussion of the situation in Darfur, a debate of terminology emerged. Although some actors have used the term genocide (be it honestly, as with some NGOs, or cynically, such as the US State Department who in all likelihood use the term due to its long opposition to the el-Bashri regime dating back to the first Gulf War), the UNSC still insisted the atrocities were "merely" crimes against humanity.

The selection of terminologies here is critical, both legally and politically. The terms "genocide" and "crimes against humanity" have vastly different sociopolitical and legal connotations. Recall that crimes against humanity refer to acts committed as part of a widespread or systematic attack directed against any civilian population. In addition, it is a less restrictive definition than genocide because the criteria of intent to destroy an entire category of persons is absent. Although the UNSC insists that it is not downplaying the severity of the crimes through labeling the incidents as crimes against humanity, the significance of the legal label is crucial.

Genocide weighs heavily on the consciousness of international political actors, especially in the wake of Rwanda and Yugoslavia. If the UN were to label a situation as genocidal, and then if the UNSC were to stand either idly by or establish an underdeveloped response, the global response could be powerful. This would be tantamount to admitting that genocide really was not a concern and that the lessons of the 1990s were insignificant. By labeling the actions of the Sudanese government and the *Janjaweed* as crimes against humanity the international society was able to treat the incident as it has other African crimes against humanity (e.g., Uganda, Sierra Leonne, the DRC), either by doing nothing or dispatching a small UN peacekeeping force with a weak mandate and insufficient human and military resources (as they had done in Rwanda a decade earlier). Although denotatively calling something a crime against humanity does not lessen the severity and horror of the actions, as the UNSC has pointed out, it does connotatively characterize the atrocities as less-than-genocide. The moral weight attached to the terms differs profoundly.

As we examined in Chapter Two, according to the Genocide Convention, a finding of genocide morally requires member states of the UN to call upon competent organs of the UN to take action for the prevention and suppression of such acts. Specifically, Article VIII states: "Any Contracting Party may call upon the competent organs of the United Nations to take such action under the Charter of the United Nations as they consider appropriate for the prevention and suppression of acts of genocide or any of the other acts enumerated in Article 3." In response to the United Nations' failure to label and prevent such acts as genocide, Kofi Annan (2006) remarks: "[I]t is a question of will, the will of the member states to move. ... The international community has an obligation." Further, Article 39 of the UN Charter empowers the Security Council to maintain or restore international peace and security by determining the existence of such a breach and decide what measures to take.

UN Resolution 1366, passed in 2001, acknowledged failure in the prevention of genocide in Rwanda. Specifically, it requested that the Secretary General of the UN refer to the Security Council all situations that "risked deteriorating into genocide unless urgent action was taken" (Mendez 2006). In a 2006 press conference, UN Special Advisor Juan Mendez reaffirmed to the UN and member states that the Genocide Convention requires states to prevent genocide. Further, the "duty to protect" language was repeated in the 2005 World Summit's Resolution that declared an international consensus that governments would take "collective action" in a "timely and decisive manner" to protect populations from genocide. Conversely, there is neither a written nor understood morally binding agreement for state intervention in crimes against humanity.

By labeling the acts of the *Janjaweed* and the Sudanese government as crimes against humanity, the Commission ensured it would be impossible to mandate UN member states to take action with an international force. Despite the UNSC's insistences to the contrary, such a label not only diminished the gravity of the crimes but also placed a roadblock for meaningful immediate action—that is, the UN's military response. Moreover, according to the hierarchy of international law, failing to label the acts as genocide has an impact on the punitive decision-making for those who may be brought before the ICC. Although the prosecutor of the ICC can bring whatever charges he or she sees fit, it is highly unlikely that he or she would counter the definitions of the UNSC, especially since the UNSC forwarded the case to the court to begin with—an unexpected instance of this authority under the Rome Statute.

International leaders' failure to request UN action is highly symptomatic of states' military and economic interests overriding commitment to international principles and values. Specifically, if states have no political or economic interests in regions, they often fail to provide the necessary support or aid required by the UN to respond to such atrocities (Rothe and Mullins 2006a). As noted by UN Special Advisor Mendez (2006), all states "bound by the genocide Convention were not living up to their obligation to prevent the violations from happening." In addition, due to the complimentary system of the UN—one that requires support by states for the UN's mission and any proposed actions—the UNSC was not in a position to send a large peacekeeping mission to Darfur. As Annan (2006: 1) states, the UN is "in the hands of our member states, yours, and mine, and the others ... since we don't have a standing army." As we have seen, the international arena showed itself unwilling to intervene in the atrocities in Darfur, limiting their behavior to finger wagging and the sending of food aid while avoiding military or other actions.

2007: The International Criminal Court Investigates

The ongoing violence against the Darfuri peoples continues, as does the impunity for the head of state of Sudan. However, on 27 February 2007 the prosecutor of the ICC concluded that there were reasonable grounds to believe that Ahmad Muhammad Harun and Ali Muhammad Ali Abd-Al-Rahman (better known as Ali Kushayb) bore criminal responsibility in relation to 51 counts of alleged crimes against humanity and war crimes. As such, two summons to appear were issues for one Ali Muhammad Ali Kushayb (militia leader), and the former Minister of State for the Interior of the Government of Sudan, Ahmad Muhammad Harun. This was the result of 20 months of investigations since the case was referred to the court by the UNSC. The charges are limited to crimes that were committed during August 2003 and March 2004 including the attacks on the village of Kodoom, and the towns of Bindisi, Mukjar, and Arawala. Although this is progress toward ending the violence and some form of justice for the victims, it should be noted that at this stage the announcement of appearances are very limited in scope, especially since the UNSC provided a list of 51 perpetrators including many within the Sudanese government. However, the court based their decision to charge the two defendants on the grounds that

> After, Ahmad Harun was appointed Minister of State for the Interior of the Government of the Sudan and tasked to head the "Darfur Security desk." His position as head of the "Darfur Security desk" became critical. Why? State and Locality Security Committees in Darfur reported to him, especially on matters relating to the staffing, funding, and arming of the Militia/*Janjaweed*. The Security Committees were comprised of representatives of the Sudanese Armed Forces, Police and Intelligence agencies plus the Governors of each state. Shortly after Harun's appointment, the recruitment of Militia/*Janjaweed* greatly increased, ultimately into the tens of thousands. (ICC-OTP-20070227-208-En)

Further, the court found that Ahmad Harun and Ali Kushayb acted together with the common purpose of attacking the civilian populations of the villages and towns.

In March 2007, the human rights and humanitarian situation in Darfur remains catastrophic and continues spreading into eastern Chad where 230,000 Darfur refugees now live. The violence in Chad is being carried out mainly by the *Janjaweed* some of whom come from Sudan and from Chad, along with other Chadian armed militia groups. As we have pointed out, the cases in this volume all have interconnections between states. This is a typical pattern of the failed, weakened, or delegitimized states and ongoing violence in sub-Saharan Africa. This situation is lending to another potential interstate crisis as the climate of insecurity continues to increase the already existing political tensions: Sudan and Chad both accuse each other of sponsoring, harboring, and arming opposition armed groups. On 28 November 2006, the government of Chad declared that it was in a "state of war" with Sudan. In addition, the international political actors continue to fail in any meaningful way to intervene in the ongoing violence in Darfur or the Chadian borders. Although, the African Union (AU) peacekeepers are in Darfur, they do not have the resources or manpower to cease the daily atrocities. The mass rapes, killing, looting, and acts of torture continue by both the Sudanese government and its sponsored *Janjaweed* militia.

The situation evolved again in April of 2007, when the two main rebel groups in the region joined forces. Meeting in Chad, the SLA announced that it joined forces with Yassine Yousef Abdul Rahman's Arab insurgency group. Shogar, the current head of the SLA, explained, "We are brothers for Darfur ... we are in the same struggle for our rights" (Polgreen 2007). Although this does provide more strength for the anti-Khartoum resistance, in all likelihood it signals more violence for Darfur, as the el-Bashir's regime is likely to further step up their anti-rebel and genocidal program in the face of the newly allied rebels.

Summary

As with other cases in this volume, international political forces, environmental crises, and widespread institutional disorganization created an environment wherein conditions became ripe for the vast atrocities that have befallen the civilian Darfur population. However, as we noted one cannot reduce these complex events to bare political motivations realized in an environment of ethnic hostility or as hostilities arising out of a humanitarian crisis. The evolution of both the social conditions behind them and the events themselves are much more complex. The Sudanese government was attempting to maintain both, international legitimacy during peace negotiations and domestic power and control over the population in Darfur and the growing insurgency. In addition, the opportunity for such atrocities was created by the state's political exploitation combined with geographically constructed ethnic divisions. International involvement in the peace negotiations indirectly provided the Khartoum government with additional motivation to quell the uprisings without much external scrutiny. Further, as a state, the government was in a position to define the events that were occurring as banditry and ethnic tribal conflicts. The militias were clearly motivated by self-interests and as state sponsored, they operated within a structure with little constraints or controls.

On a positive note, the investigation into and subsequent summons to appear by the ICC represents hope that justice will be done for the victims. In addition to the other current investigations that are covered in this volume, once the ICC begins to adjudicate cases and levy sentences, the impunity that drove the opportunity factors here (and in many similar cases) will cease to be. As warlords, militia leaders, and political heads of state begin to be tried, convicted, and punished, the institutional validity of the ICC will be established. In and of itself, such an international order will bring order to disorganized nation-states in many parts of the world, but hopefully Africa specifically. As this, and other cases have emphasized (see Rothe and Mullins 2006), militia leaders frequently scoff at investigators working for AI or Human Rights Watch who suggest that what they are doing could lead to their imprisonment. They perceive impunity; they perceive themselves as the only legal order extant in the countryside. One of the strongest results of ICC prosecutions will be to disabuse them of such notions.

· 8 ·

EXPLAINING ATROCITY

The preceding chapters focused on the description of four key African-atrocity producing events in the late twentieth and early twenty-first centuries. By exploring the sociohistorical context and the enactment patterns of the Rwandan genocide of 1994, the 20-year war between the Museveni government and the Lords Resistance Army (LRA) in Uganda, the complete collapse of social order following the Second Congolese War in the Democratic Republic of the Congo, and the Darfur genocide in the Sudan, we have provided rich narratives of atrocity-producing events. Although the description has value in and of itself, the main drive for examining the four cases in this volume is the attempt to build a criminological theory that is capable of explaining the phenomena. It isn't enough to simply describe: explanation is necessary, not simply for raw and removed academic understanding, but also to critique and design structures capable of containing, if not preventing, mass violations of human rights.

In Chapter One, we presented an integrated theory of supranational crimes. This theory attempts to parsimoniously unite several extant threads and themes in criminological and sociological theory that, when brought together, provide an adequate explanation of crimes against humanity and other atrocities, though it should be generalizable enough to cover other state crimes that we do not focus on here (e.g., corruption, crimes of aggression, etc.). The theory centralizes two core elements of a criminal action: motivation and opportunity.

All crimes require both these factors. Hence, the understanding of any crime calls for exploration of both as well. We also examine two key aspects that can prevent crimes outright or at least modify enactment patterns: (1) constraints, those elements that can constrain an actor from committing an offense or to which offenders have to successfully negotiate to accomplish a crime and; (2) controls, those elements that can prevent a criminal action or are ideally represented by formal legal sanctions. The second component of the theory insists that these elements be examined at four levels of analysis: the international, macro, meso, and micro.

In this chapter, we thoroughly apply the supranational theory we presented earlier to the cases examined. As discussed earlier, we follow an exemplar tradition of case studies. Meaning, we use the narratives to test the power and boundaries of the theory and use the theory to illuminate central features of the cases. As such, we hope to take criminological theory further along that road in the process.

International Level

For centuries, the world has been global in some manner or form, not merely local. Although many commentators seem to think this is a recent phenomenon, the past 400 years have shown a world growingly integrated in its political and economic functioning. Specifically, although the intensity and number of these global connections have grown over the past decades, the process has accelerated in the past 120-odd years since the Berlin Conference, especially for African nations. Indeed, the conditions within states are central to the etiologies of any atrocity, however, the space between the states, loosely referred to as the international community has a strong influence as well. After all, states do not exist within a vacuum; they clearly influence the conditions and behaviors of both their immediate and distant neighbors. Concerning this point, Seeley (1986: 133) states, "Never be content with looking at states purely from within; always remember that they have another aspect which is wholly different, their relation to foreign states." Intrasocietal interactions as well as interstate relations entail highly complex processes in which not only "economic and security interests but also moral interests play a prominent role, in which the actions of states must be understood as the culmination of both external pressures and domestic political struggles" (Nadelman 2004: 2). A state's immediate international context, for example, what is happening in one's immediate geographic vicinity, is often central to understanding a given set of war crimes, crimes against humanity or other widespread atrocity. As all four cases we have discussed have shown, they were not limited to actions within one single state, but the events were motivated and enacted across regional borders. Rwanda, Uganda, the DRC, and Sudan all share common borders and crossed those borders in military conflicts.

In addition, states are imbedded in a global network of social forces and influences. Transnational corporations and fully internationalized markets tie the African countries discussed to major Western and Asian states in import/export as well as debtor relationships. Trends in global commodity prices have had huge impacts on the nature of life in many local single-commodity markets (e.g., the effect of falling coffee prices on Rwanda as explored in Chapter Four). As such, we cannot ignore the larger context within which states exist. Simply, ignoring the international influences and conditions would lead to a partial understanding of the phenomena under examination.

Motivation

At the international level, the main driving motivational elements of most of the cases at hand are reverberations of postcolonial global economics. However, political and ideological factors were at play during the historical periods of colonialization that set a portion of the conditions for the latter motivational factors leading to the crimes. For example, ethnic divisions in Rwanda under colonial rule were shaped by economic and political forces into the precise form that motivated the 1994 genocide. Similarly, the colonial preference for the "Arab" speakers and the north in Sudan shaped the nature of the Darfur conflict. In addition, there are a number of instances wherein political ideologies have factored directly in to other countries' participation in the atrocities. For example, Sudan's economic and military support of the LRA in the Ugandan conflict is based on political and ideological interests. Further, international involvement in Sudan's north/south peace talks, Comprehensive Peace Agreement, produced additional motivation for the Sudanese government to pursue its genocidal plan in Darfur in a more timely and covert manner. The same holds true for the Ugandan involvement and support of the Rwandan refugees who fled after the first Tutsi/Hutu conflict of the 1960s. The behavior of international actors toward these events requires a thorough historical and contemporary examination of international politics and relations (e.g., why the US strongly supported Mobutu Sese Seko despite his dictatorial behaviors), but the focus of the criminality we examine here is primarily directed toward a nation's own citizens. The groups here, be they governments or paramilitaries, are not responding to international drives and forces, but internal forces.

When these crimes occur they are also motivated via resources and resource extraction factors. As shown in the Democratic Republic of Congo (DRC) case, the systems of forced labor and illegal mineral expropriation by Rwandan, Ugandan, and Angolan forces were economically driven. Internationally, the way in which the World Bank and International Monetary Fund (IMF) calculated economic health and development allowed these neighboring states to satisfy internal economic needs (e.g., additional monies for military spending) while simultaneously improving the international assessment of their economic health. Similar processes are seen in Rwanda, where the role of Bretton Woods organizations and the crash of the coffee market provided motivation for the Hutu. As the DRC case also illustrates, there are a plethora of international corporate actors willing to facilitate economic gain from violence and genocide. The presence of the Free Port system, as well as numerous transnationals who are willing to obtain a commodity from anyone, as long as the price is right, function strongly to motivate individuals to seek economic gains from these events (they also provide opportunity to do so, as we discuss below).

Opportunity

Markets for misappropriated goods are a powerful international opportunity driving some of the atrocities explored here. Companies willing to buy stolen minerals and other commodities from war zones are the fuels that drive the practices. Whether it be De Beers, AngloGold Ashante, or Metalor, without buyers commodities are worthless. Mineral wealth could not drive civil conflicts if there were no buyers for them. As we examined in Chapter Six, the Swiss Freeport system has been central in the illegal mineral trade from central Africa. With no checks on source and no verification of legality of possession of good, the free ports have allowed essentially legal smuggling. Metalor announced on 20 May 2005 that it would no longer buy Ugandan gold. This has come more than five years too late; illegally obtained minerals are no longer flowing over the DRC borders into neighboring states like they were in 2001.

As most of the conflicts examined here have had some international flavor, a key opportunity factor for many militias is their level of access to foreign support. Such support can be the provision of a safe haven out of their enemies' reach (e.g., the LRA in Sudan, the *Interhawme* in Congo, the ADFL in Rwanda and Uganda). It also takes the form of supplies and armaments. As we explored in the DRC, such relationships of support were highly intricate and fundamentally economic in nature—with Uganda and Rwanda buying minerals from militias and further facilitating their purchase of food, weapons, and other necessities to continue their existence. Such opportunities are not hard to come by, as the international relations in the region have long been troubled and filled with distrust. Due to porous borders and cross-border ethnic ties, many resistance groups find natural allies a few miles away protected by the sovereignty of another country. A neighboring state could be eager to take advantage of an allied armed force operating in a contested border region, especially if the group manages to assume power at some point in time allowing the succor-providing state to call in "favors." Recall that this is how Uganda originally became established in the Ituri region of the Congo.

An equally important opportunity force within the international context comes from the existing complimentary legal system. As explored in Chapter Two, all international law exists in adjunct to existing state law and legal systems. Even with the International Criminal Court (ICC), the court does not step in to engage in the enforcement of international criminal law unless the signatory state is unwilling or unable to, or unless the case is referred to by the UNSC. Although the later are the specified conditions for the ICC to act under the Rome statute, other international legal mechanism informally follow the same pattern. Most crimes against humanity and other wide-scale human rights violations tend not to draw international legal attention. In the history of international law, only four ad hoc tribunals have been established, three of which were established in the wake of the end of a Western-led military action (e.g., Nuremberg, Tokyo, and the ICTY). The fourth, the ICTR, was created out of strong international pressure for some global institution of justice in the wake of the genocide.

International relations, especially the lack of intervention experiences, strongly provide opportunity to commit atrocities as the lack of global will to protect citizens creates a space of impunity in which genocideiers can operate. This is a factor in all four cases we explore in this book. In the case of Rwanda, it was clear that the West was not interested in intervening in events in Africa, at least not while hostilities were occurring. The world knew what was happening and allowed it to continue. This provided a strong message to those in the region that they could act with impunity in pursuit of their political, economic, and ideological desires. Similarly, there has been little international concern about the situation in northern Uganda or throughout the DRC. Although there has been quite a bit of symbolic attention paid to Darfur, little formal intervention has occurred; the genocide has not been stopped. If anything, the al-Bashir regime has at times stepped up the speed at which it has carried out the genocide in response international pressure brought to bear by the UN and other major states like the US, the UK, and most recently China (also due to international pressure).

Constraints

There has in general been a lack of international action opposing these sorts of crimes. Although there is an endless debate, posturing, and symbolic gesture toward constraining such actions, especially with the situation in Darfur, none of this has saved a single life nor removed a single solider from the field. Hypothetically, international public opinion could act as a constraint on crimes against humanity, but the world community has done little in terms of actions against governments that engage in such behavior. At best these forces seem to push for the signing of peace accords between disputing parties (e.g., the LRA and the Ugandan regime; the SLA and the Sudanese government). However, these agreements are of little value if they are not implemented. International attention and will has not forced the implementation of these compacts as signed and this serves to undermine any potential constraining function that world opinion or international relations could have. In and of itself, international attention has not ended impunity and perpetrators of atrocities know it.

The Bretton Woods' lending institutions (the IMF and the WB) are uniquely situated to act as a potential constraint upon the behavior of states that depend upon foreign aid. As the source of substantial amounts of the GNP of many developing countries, if these organizations would go beyond their rhetoric of anticorruption and democracy-building and truly support these principles, they could substantially reduce the likelihood of widespread atrocities such as those discussed here from occurring. Leaders and parties who knew that massive human rights violations would make its regime ineligible for loans from these states would have to consider other paths. The past 50 years have shown that these organizations can influence the behavior of states. Especially, IMF's SAPs have shown, countries tend to implement the policies demanded by the IMF and the WB. As we have shown in the cases of Rwanda and Uganda, when threatened with a loss of necessary aid, governments will modify their policies and readjust elements of their social structure that can affect the ongoing conflict or facilitate conditions.

Unfortunately, in the African context, SAPs have served as a criminogenic force rather than a deterrent force (see Rothe, Mullins, and Sandstrom 2008; Rothe, Muzzatti, and Mullins 2006). The typical demands of SAPs (i.e., increased private ownership, reduced social spending, and currency pegging programs) work to create environments conducive to crime, rather than reduce such motional forces. State-run industry has indeed shown itself highly susceptible to corruption, but the demands of opening such enterprises to private ownership is really an opening of these systems for foreign investment. High levels of foreign investment, while potentially providing much needed financial capital, reduce the amount of local control of the economy—especially the distribution and use of profits from economic labors. It is another form of labor and resource expropriation cloaked in the language of international capitalism.

When industry is owned by non-Africans, and profits are diverted to those nonindigenous investors, both the economy and the government lose legitimacy in the eyes of the people. Creating anomie in a Mertonian (1938) sense, this can become a motivating force for individuals and organizations to seek criminal paths to resolve the anomic tensions. Although this can manifest as petty theft, prostitution, robbery, and other street crimes, it can also lead to the creation of militias and the drive to other large-scale crimes. Anomie is also increased as social programs are undercut and infrastructure investments do not occur. Educational, transportation and healthcare systems are neither expanded nor repaired, reducing overall social health. As scholars working with the concept of crimes of globalization have shown, conditions imposed by Bretton Woods–lender institutions can produce states crimes through their effects of local social structures, as well as the organizations and states themselves ignoring basic legal and human rights protections (Friedrichs and Friedrichs 2002; Rothe, Mullins, and Sandstrom 2008; Rothe, Muzzatti, and Mullins 2006).

Nongovernmental Organizations (NGOs) are situated to serve as a strong constraint on the behavior of both states and militia groups. By being present in a region, NGOs are able to transmit information out of the country concerning what is occurring including increasing public and/or political pressures as well as the United Nations Human Rights Committee who answer to the General Assembly. Such actions also circumvent forms of government domination of the media and/or external contact. NGOs such as Amnesty International and Human Rights Watch have done admirable work in recording and transmitting information about events in these countries, as well as lobbying national and international organizations to take action to end the conflicts. However, as with our discussion of international relations above, it has not created a general will or widespread drive in the international political community to do anything forceful (or meaningful) to counteract states' perceived self-interests. As such, other countries refrain from providing troops for an international armed movement or unilaterally, at least any sizable numbers, or financial assistance to bring peace to a region.

International media can also serve to bring information to the rest of the world regarding atrocities. The BBC, Africa News, and the Integrated News Integration Network run by the UN Office for the Coordination of Humanitarian Aid report thoroughly and frequently about these events. They have staff on the ground in these countries and report back events to the rest of the world. As with the NGOs though, this information is not enough to compel action. Further, many states use their own media to place counter messages into the international discourse, creating debates out of the reporting of facts and presenting alternative realities for international consumption. Both the el-Bashir regime in Sudan and the Museveni regime in Uganda have actively produced counter discourses that, while carry seemingly little currency overall, do seem to add just enough legitimacy to the positions they advocate to delay and/or weaken international responses to ongoing situations.

Controls

As of now, there is little in the international realm that has power to operate as a complete blockage as we defined in Chapter One. We have conceptualized international law as potentially capable of fulfilling this purpose ideally in the form of deterrence. As we have noted in Chapter Two, the extant body of international criminal law is present and clearly criminalizes the behaviors and atrocities that have been occurring within the DRC, Uganda, Rwanda, and Darfur. Yet, many jurisdictional gaps remain and as such international legal codes do not possess the enforcement power of domestic legal codes. The control is present; yet, without the ability to systematically enforce it, potential deterrence is compromised. As we have noted, the potential of the ICC to fill this gap is promising. However, even with the ICC in place, conducting investigations, and handing down indictments, control is not yet fully operative. Indeed, there does seem to be a deterrent effect of the courts' operation. For example, the ICC claims that their indictments have simultaneously reduced the violence within northern Uganda (Agirre 2007). With the indictment of Joseph Kony of the LRA, the LRA has reduced its violent actions. Was this a pure result of the ICC's actions? Maybe, maybe not. In all likelihood it had some influence as the timing is undeniable. Yet, we should also realize that by the time of Kony's indictment, the war had been going on for 20 years, the LRA had worn out its welcome in the northern territories of Uganda and the political situation in Sudan began to shift as the al-Bashr regime came under the scrutiny not only of the international community in general but of the ICC in particular. For years, the main source of new recruits for the LRA has been child soldiers. In and of itself, the messianic fervor of such a movement cannot burn forever. But, even with this skepticism, the court's actions seem to have had an influence on the LRA's thinking.

Obviously, time will tell how influential the ICC will become and how much deterrence it will be able to generate. This is indeed an important area for future studies. It is possible that such deterrence will only be effective for actors that currently operate with a higher level of impunity. After all, as street crime research has shown, social location and position strongly influences deterrence (Paternoster and Piquero 1995; Paternoster and Simpson 1992; Piquero and Paternoster 1998; Sherman and Berk 1984; Stafford and Warr 1993). Those actors most likely to be involved in these types of supranational crimes would seem to be those who are most influenceable by law. However, the social positions and general practices of militia leaders would suggest that they would not be as likely to be deterred by the law. Consequentially, deterrence could potentially only serve as a control if continued prosecutions for these types of crimes occur via the ICC.

The UN, as an internationally sanctioned body, holds the power to apply sanctions to states that violate either international law or are overly abusive of their own citizens. Such has been the case with some of the countries examined here. However, the ability to back up sanctions with coercive force is limited to members who are willing to volunteer the necessary force to act in the organization's name. For example, the UN Security Council can, and has, sanctioned states endlessly, but without formal mechanisms to enforce those sanctions, there is nothing to compel compliance, thus providing further opportunity for state criminogenic behaviors.

Macro Level

Most sociological analysis has seen the macro level as the main focus of social forces and the location where most determinations play out or view the state as rather nonempowered entity within the global context. Simply, in general, sociological models of the state either focus on domestic affairs or on international relations and/or globalization. There are few accounts of state theory that are capable of addressing both without reducing one or the other to a point of irrelevance. Moreover, the few theories that do address both usually focus on the Western capitalist state to do so (Barrow 2005; Cox 1987; Whyte 2003). Although we reject a singular focus on this level of analysis, as we do those that omit the state within the international context, clearly, what is happening at the level of society/state is essential in comprehending the nature of these crimes. Owing to the fact that states hold a certain level of legal accountability coupled with the fact that they operate within a larger construct, we conceptualize the macro level as representing a country itself that is, specific, legally defined territory, laws, and subsequent culture and ethos of that region. Whereas this is generally an artifact—as there may or may not be anything inherent within a set of geopolitical boundaries that serves as a social demarcation in terms of social forces—it is a convenient one that is well recognized within the literature that we use.

Motivation

All the cases examined in this volume occur within states that experienced colonial domination at some point in their more recent histories. Save for Sudan (1916–58), the colonial domination originated in the nineteenth century and lasted until after World War II. Colonial experiences have had a number of effects within each of these territories that directly or indirectly produced the crimes explored here.

Economically, colonialism devastated indigenous communities. As detailed in Chapter Three, local means of subsistence as well as divisions of labor were ripped asunder by the imposition of colonial export economics. With independence, states were left with little choice but to try to reestablish local economies and infrastructures that quickly led to the need to compete within globalized economic systems, drawing upon whatever desired resources their country possessed. Such a situation produces large amount of social anomie that generally destabilizes a social system. These conditions are then often increased through states' need of international finance institutions that, as we have noted, can lead to additional anomic conditions. Weak economies produce high amounts of social disadvantage that generate social disorder at the community level (see meso-level catalysts below) and motivates individuals toward acquisitive crimes or to join criminal organizations, militias, owing to a lack of other present opportunities. Economic scarcity enhances intergroup competition for access to resources and play into broader trends of ethnogenesis and the harshening of ethnic tensions and rivalries. Further, the ideologies of hypercapitalism were introduced to these areas by colonial authorities, which further amplified the anomie and drives toward using criminal activity to obtain financial resources. This was especially the case with the DRC.

Both states and militias commit atrocities to achieve political goals and cement political power. For sitting governments, the use of illegal tactics in internecine warfare is a direct attempt to stabilize power through the removal of an opposition group. This was the case with Sudan and its genocidal actions against the Darfurian peoples and the insurgency that erupted due to the lack of political power and general marginalization. Further, none of the states explored in this book could be termed truly democratic. They are quintessential African one-party states; opposition groups are a threat to the regime's existence. From the standpoint of many militias, their goals are similarly political, at least rhetorically. The LRA, most of the DRC groups, the *Interhawme*, and the SLA directed, at least at the start, their activities toward the overthrow of a government that either saw them as undesirable or which they saw as problematic.

Cultural systems were also widely denuded of meaning under colonial rule. As cultures are holistic schema that connect with, reinforce, and are reinforced by other institutional practices and arrangements within a social order, the widespread structural transformations of colonialism served to undermine, if not outright destroy, extant cultural beliefs and practices. This process directly occurred when colonizers selected a portion of the population to be trained as social elites and administrators, providing opportunity for Western education and the partial assimilation into Western worldviews that this produced. Widespread Christianization (or Islamicization in northern Africa) also hastened this process through its direct attempt to eliminate indigenous religious systems and structures. Indirectly, economic and political transformations, as well as increasing contact with Europeans through interactions with colonizers, trading companies, and other parties, transformed the cultural climate of these geographies. In essence, these forces eroded the legitimacy of traditional worldviews and, especially in a postindependence environment, left nothing in its place. Such a vacuum allows for the ethnogenesis processes we discuss below as well as other cultural innovations that can catalyze atrocities. For example, this cultural reconfiguration produced Alice Lakawena's Holy Spirit Movement, parts of which would become the LRA. In Chapter Five, we outlined belief structures in the LRA that produced many of the atrocities. In addition, recall from Chapter Four that the tradition of Kubandwa, a devotion to the Lord of Spirits that centered on spirit possession, played an important role for social cohesions among the Tutsi, Hutu, and Mutwa. It was a local cult, trans-ethnic, and personal. However, it was destroyed by the imposed religious practice of Christianity and as such destroyed important social glue between groups.

Although we reject a simplistic modeling or learning theory, we can't discount the fact that all of the countries under examination were brutalized during colonial rule. Regardless of what a given peoples in these regions thought the state may be or what a given political institution was suppose to do, all experienced the situation where a colonial power ruled the geography for the sole purpose of the economic benefit of the dominating power. No colonial experience was without harsh, violent repression of civilians; no colonizer kept their agents in line at all times. Simply put, colonized peoples see in the state an instrument of violence and oppression, one that subsumes the natural resources of an area (including human capital) for the benefit of a leadership cadre and those connected into an elite social network. The sort of atrocity that is examined in this book was part and parcel of the domination experienced; the peoples under this domination saw governmental appartuses use violence as needed to extract value from the area. Is it so surprising when taking the reins of government themselves they continued the past practices?

The indigenous populations that endured colonialism and then took the reins of state in the mid–twentieth century are complex and nuanced social actors possessing agency. Yet, seeing the state used in a given way for generations assuredly generated within the cultural landscape a set of ideas and ideologies that defined, at least in part, the state as a tool of domination when required. Further, upon independence, some elite actors combined neo-traditional practices of a territory's leader, such as a king, which provided them the ideological and political power to expect all resources, goods, and loyalty to be bestowed onto them. Such was the case with Rwanda and the unquestioning obedience to the state as well as Amin claiming his presidency for life and during 1994, when the acting Minister for Federal Affairs of Sudan, Ali al-Haji, changed the divisions of the federal, dividing each of the nine states (excluding Khartoum) into three, making 26 new states, and reestablished the traditional tribal administration previously used during the British rule.

Whereas the opportunity for corruption works at the meso level (see below), the existence of intense corruption in a government has motivations and influences on the macro level also. As seen by the number of coups and insurgency efforts undertaken against highly corrupt regimes, political and economic corruption undermines a government's legitimacy. Even where citizens welcomed an insurgency, they lose faith in the regime as it mires itself deeper and deeper in the abuse of its own peoples and economy. For example, this was seen in many of the postindependence regimes in both Uganda and the DRC. Amin's takeover from Obote was hailed by the people as their liberation and a second independence until Amin turned the state into his personal tool of economic advancement and repression of his enemies. Similarly, Mobutu's overthrow of the first republic was widely supported by the general Congolese population. After he too had succumbed to the lure of absolute power his citizenry welcomed his overthrow by Kabila's forces in the First Congolese War. However, support for Kabila was short-lived as his administration soon turned to corruption and looting his own country's resources.

State corruption reinforces ideas held by the general public defining the state as useless and predatory. A fairly common view among Africans, rising out of both colonial and early independence experiences, this translates into high levels of political skepticism and alienation. Not only does this lead to general political disengagement among the general population, it also creates an environment, especially in the rural areas, that generates initial toleration, if not outright support, of rebel or resistance groups. Further, as surveys of attitudes toward post-conflict justice suggest (see Arzt 2006; Drumbl 2002; Gibson 2002, 2004, 2006; Shaw 2005) even the most intensively victimized civilians in a conflict do not fully trust a government to engage in prosecution or other mechanism of adjudication. It also seems to have a bleed-over effect onto how citizens perceive international organs of criminal justice (e.g., the ICC and other international criminal tribunals). It will take time and exemplary service for new governments to overcome these deep and long-held attitudes.

Intensely corrupt governments also motivate opposition groups, both at home and abroad. Widespread corruption and abuse of power in Uganda, under Amin and Obote, and in the DRC, under Mobutu and the Kabilas, acted as a strong motivator for the formation of resistance groups, whose presence or actions would then lead to atrocity-producing circumstances. Due to the diversion of funds, corruption also undermines economic health and infrastructure development. Projects do not get completed; citizen's needs go unmet. This not only generates meso- and micro-level motivations through the promulgation of a poor economy, it also enhances general social anomie, which serves to encourage criminal responses among some groups and people. Such conditions also reinforce colonial, or in the case of Sudan—postcolonial, constructed racial identities, or ethnic divisions.

Ethnogenesis has been a fundamentally central process in the conflicts within Rwanda, the DRC and Sudan. The intensification of ethnic identity as a solidarity-producing mechanism has been seen in these cultures since the colonial era and has served to separate groups and place them into opposition with each other. In the colonial period, this was done to, first, reduce opposition through a divide and conquer strategy. For example, when the French favored the Tutsis for administrative jobs, the British favored the Acholi for military membership, and the Anglo-Egyptian powers in Sudan favored those people living near the capital and ignoring those in the hinterlands. This had the function of directing unease, tensions, and hostilities away from the colonial power and on to another indigenous population. Second, favoritism toward one group creates loyalty among that group to the colonial group (or at least a realization that the group had a vested interested in maintaining some level of the status quo social organization), which simultaneously reduced resistance at least within one segment of the population and motivated a group against their fellow indigenous population and in defense of the government.

As we discussed in Chapters Four, Six, and Seven intensification of these ethnic identities, if not the genesis of them in and of themselves, (e.g., the *Banyamulenge* of the DRC, the Hutu/Tutsi divide, or the Arab/Africa split in Sudan), occurs more strongly in the postindependence environment. Divided populations with little in common, save having suffered under the same colonial power, do not make for the most stable of states. Political leaders throughout Africa (and elsewhere) find that ethnicity is an easy tool to create division in populations. Just as the colonial powers used ethnic favoring policies to divide and conquer, postcolonial leaders use ethnicity to cement political support and/or government legitimacy within a given population base. Simply, it is the easiest and most readily apparent way to create social solidarity.

Ethnogenesis is not only essential in the building of support and opposition population groups, but the nature of these beliefs construct a set of values and ideologies that facilitate atrocity-producing environments. In the process of constructing groups as essentially different, members of other "ethnic" groups are Otherized. Such conceptualizations allow for the dehumanization of an entire category of people, which, when further developed and taken to extreme, allows for their being defined as more akin to animals than people. For the Hutu, Tutsis were cockroaches to be slaughtered; for the "Arab" northerners, the "Africans" in the south of Sudan were "black" subhumans and a drain on "Arabic" Sudan; the *Banyamulenge* were aliens to be driven out of the Kivu regions. Such ideological perceptions facilitate, if not being outright necessary, for the attempted genocide or crimes against humanity.

Similarly, when these ethnogenic discourses tap into concepts of autochthonic populations—the idea that there is a "true" population that has lived in an area from time immemorial—motivation arises for the elimination of the "alien" population as well. At their core, autochthonic discourses define one population as the rightful inhabitants of an area, with a historical (if falsely constructed) and moral superiority of claims to the land and resources. All others become "aliens" and "intruders." In a postcolonial environment, these populations are directly or indirectly associated with past colonial experiences. In a direct sense, the defining population will attempt to associate the outsider population with the former colonial order or other intrusive power. For example, Tutsis were defined by missionaries and colonial authorities as the "superior" race and of another region. This resulted in the Hutu claims that the Tutsi solution was to send them back to Ethiopia using a shortcut by throwing them in the Nyabarongo River. In the DRC, local groups were able to associate the *Banyamulenge* with the invading *Interhawme* and RPF due to the association of them with Rwanda, even though that connection was more than a century in the past.

Indirectly, the cultural consciousness of being dominated by foreigners is strong within a postcolonial national consciousness. Such cognitive categories allow the development of a rhetoric of exclusion and fear of any group not defined as indigenous, thus providing motivational factors. In any former colony, there will be easy targets of this discourse. For example, in Uganda there were remnant English populations as well as large groups of South Asians. During the rule of Idi Amin, the ability to marshal and direct those innate tensions was central in Amin's assuming control of private, foreign-held business and his expulsion of Asians. Similarly, the same structures allowed general support of Mobutu's seizure of Belgian-owned companies in the DRC.

Opportunity

Owing to the weakened, if not outright failed, nature of most of these states, there is a general lack of law, law enforcement, and adjudication, especially in hinterland areas where militias tend to operate with the greatest frequency. Naturally, in the absence of local controls, opportunity is rife. Further, control of the apparatus of the state itself brings a host of criminal opportunities. First, the bureaucratic structures are available to be turned toward criminal activity; this provides a host of people, technologies, information, and organizational locations. In addition to the raw empowerment of controlling a government, an offender or offending group also has control of the instruments of secrecy and privacy associated with a state. The best examples of these processes are the regimes of Mobutu Sese Seko in the Congo and Idi Amin in Uganda. Both used their positions as head of state to gather information about those who might oppose them and used that same position to either imprison or eliminate them. They were able to keep the majority of such incidents from the eyes of the public. They drew upon their control of financial and taxation organizations to become wealthy—hiding much of the ostentation of their spending behind the veneer of being a head of state and thereby entitled to some degree of pomp and circumstance.

Controlling a state also allows the creation and control of a military or policing arm that can direct itself toward rooting out and eliminating opposition. Controlling military forces, be they regular or irregular, provides the essential opportunity to commit crimes against humanity, war crimes, and other atrocities. Having a group of armed troops willing to carry out specific orders given is central to the enactment of these crimes. Clearly, states wield this opportunity with near impunity, as we see with the Ugandan Army's (UPDF) campaign against the LRA and the Sudanese Army's actions within the Darfur region. As heads of state, the ability to rule military forces can easily be ensured. Such was the case with Amin in Uganda in 1972 wherein his authority lacked legitimacy and had only a very narrow social base of support. To maintain power, he reorganized the military by removing the Lango and Acholi factions—by having them killed and then replacing them with members of his own social network.

All four of our cases highlight that control of the media provides a strong opportunity factor to encourage and orchestrate the types of crimes examined here. Media control provides opportunity in a number of ways. State-run media curtails that amount of public opposition that can communicate its message throughout a state, hence increasing the opportunity structures for regimes to continue such actions. Seen most dramatically in Rwanda, media control can be used to amplify ethnic and other tensions as well as actually direct an atrocity event as it occurs. Hutu media control was central in the accomplishment of the 1994 killings. For months before the genocide, a constant barrage of anti-Tutsi propaganda was broadcast on Hutu-controlled radio, as was the trigger of the genocide itself. Troops were directed to specific locales and constantly encouraged to quicken the killings. In the DRC, radio stations owned by Jean-Pierre Bemba, head of the MLC, similarly devoted themselves to broadcasting propaganda. Controlling media also allows a group to control the messages that get out to the rest of the country. Where events are limited in their geography, as is the case with Uganda and Darfur, this is central in creating public support for a given regime's actions.

As noted above, media itself can propagate a sense of nationalism based on the ideology of Hutu supremacy facilitating the already divisive situation. Further, nationalism can be used to ensure a regime's legitimacy and as such, its opportunity for corruption and/or continued violence onto the peoples. We see the use of nationalism being used this very way in the case of Sudan and the call for a United Islamic front in Sudan.

Constraints

Most state-level constraints have failed to be useful in the curtailing of the types of crimes we explore here. Although in more democratic states, citizen and media groups can act as watchdogs and place pressure on governments, in weakened and failed states even if these organizations are allowed to exist and publicly state an opinion—which is often unlikely—the amount of constraint they can place on the state is minimal at best. There are often no political opposition groups, thus, little in the way of national political pressure to end the illegal actions. Even if public opinion is strongly against a given regime, or militia for that matter, as we saw in both northern Uganda's lack of support of the LRA, and numerous villages spurning the militias within the DRC, in and of itself in nondemocratic environment public opinion will not serve as a control. The regime will have no desire or obligation to honor these protests as it monopolizes political voice and power. Public opinion, as well as potential social movements, only serve as control when they reach the level of armed resistance.

Whereas the need for state legitimacy can work as an instrument of constraint, in the four cases drawn upon here, we find that the need for legitimacy has instead acted as a facilitator for more violence and repressive forms of rule. Other constraints we have noted include internal opposition. With the cases at hand this has typically come in the form of coups. Such was the case throughout Uganda's postcolonial history wherein an authoritarian regime was ousted from within; often using the existing military apparatus that was no longer loyal to the acting head of state.

The same is true for the proposed constraint of counterinsurgencies. The strongest macro-level constraint on a state engaged in these behaviors is a strong rebellion that can force the negation of the end of the atrocities. However, for an antigovernment movement to build itself to that stage, it is likely to catalyze a number of crimes against humanity and atrocities, often committed by the both the government and the rebel group itself, before it reaches the level of empowerment necessary to force negotiations. Within the cases we have explored here, no single group has been able to do this. The histories we recounted show numerous governments overthrown and replaced by rebel groups, often with the result that the remnant governmental forces simply reorganizing as militias to continue the struggle. Clearly present in the cases we have explored, (i.e., the Hutu revolution in Rwanda and the NRA in Uganda), these have typically resulted in a replaced system of marginalization either politically or socially further facilitating divisiveness and/or violence.

Controls

Ideally, domestic law can serve to control actions, but, due to the unique position of a state vis-à-vis its own law and the problematic ways in which it is enforced, law may not hold the same deterrent power over a political body or its citizenry in states where anomic conditions, social disorganization, lack of legitimacy, and/or general thuggery rules with authority. There are two central issues with the macro-level controls concerning the four cases examined here: (1) the ability of the state to legitimize the atrocities and (2) the ability of the state to enforce the extant laws.

When laws are present and able to be enforced, regimes are in positions to ignore, or at best use symbolic means to appease, countering pressures. For example, in Sudan, although there were symbolic arrests of several alleged *Janjaweed* in an effort to appease the international arena; all were petty criminals or were already in jail. Then, on 14 June 2005 Sudan opened a Special Court to try alleged Darfur war criminals, yet the Special Court handed down few verdicts, none of which were related to the conflict in 2003 or 2004. Standing regimes are able to manipulate domestic laws to ensure immunity for themselves. Again, we saw this occur in Sudan when the Interim Constitution contained the provision granting immunity from prosecution to the president, vice president, and members of the National Legislature.

On the other hand, the ability of the state to bring enough force to bear to enforce the existing laws and reassert a monopoly on the use of force is indeed a crucial control. However, as we have noted throughout these cases, the government is often unwilling or unable to do so. Governmental forces are too few and too scattered across a landscape to effectively bring militias under control (e.g., Uganda's inability to control the LRA for 20-odd years). It is often precisely the fact that the government cannot exert control over the hinterlands and monopolize the use of force that catalyzes the development of militias at the start. Until the on-the-ground government in each of these countries is strong enough and willing enough to craft and enforce national laws curtailing these actions, there will be little in the way of macro-level controls in operation.

Meso Level

The meso level of social organization includes complex organizations (e.g., governments, corporations, paramilitaries), nonformal social networks (familial and friendship networks), as well as other elements of a more immediate social environment (e.g., village or neighborhood-level experiences). As discussed in Chapter One, there is a long tradition within Western criminology of identifying and examining criminogenic forces at the meso level. Within the white collar and state crime literatures, much attention has been paid to organizational context and organization decision-making processes. Throughout the case studies, we have highlighted the role that both state and nonstate organizations play in producing the crimes against humanity and other atrocities we explore. Thus, attention must be paid theoretically to dynamics and processes at work within these organizations. Further, there is a similarly rich criminological tradition that examines how social forces work within communities that are disorganized to produce criminal actions and actors. Due to the state of social organization within many communities that have produced and experienced such atrocities, these aspects of meso-level influence need discussion as well.

Motivation

As sociologists of bureaucracy (e.g., Perrow 1986; Weber 1946) and scholars of corporate crime (e.g., Gies 2007) have pointed out, within complex organizations the needs and desires of the organization often take precedence over individual desires. Minimally organizational environments simultaneously possess goals and other objectives that members strive to fulfill (this is *the* basic characteristic of bureaucracy as per Weber 1946). Throughout this book we have highlighted numerous organizational goals and drives that generate criminogenic impulses. As paramilitary organizations, militias have the primary goal (like all organizations) of survival. Further, as military organizations, their immediate goal accomplishment mechanisms are innately violent and thus prone toward slipping into atrocity when unchecked and constrained by extant command structures.

Organizations also possess cultures that can motivate individuals to engage in offending behaviors. Since Sutherland (1949), corporate crime research has strongly established that unique meso-environments exist within complex organizations. As individuals are brought into these environments, they acquire criminal values and attitudes via association with others in the organization. Even if they don't internalize them, they learn that such actions are standard operating procedures in the organization and will confirm their behavior to them if they desire to remain associated with the group. Thus the bulk of organizational energy can be devoted toward the attainment of a criminal goal even if most people are not criminally inclined when they join the organization, or even when they are assisting in the actions themselves. Further, due to a bureaucracy's ability to control information flow within itself as well as what information gets released to the outside, it can hide the true nature and extent of certain actions from members in other subunits as well as the world at large.

These environments are also important when we take into account cases of forced inclusion within these organizations. For example, the incorporation of child soldiers into the organizational culture. The assimilation of them to the organizational goals and practices, while done harshly, does replicate in an extreme form the impact an organizational culture can have on individuals that are not prone to such criminogenic tendencies if removed from the group. This also is directly related to leadership pressure. Pressure to adhere to organizational culture and practices is clearly seen in the use of child soldiers' obedience, albeit through fear, to leadership.

Organizations possess reward structures as well that can serve as motivators to commit atrocities. In a military or militia situation, soldiers who fulfill organizational goals, even when doing so required law violation, may be rewarded with promotions, additional pay or better living conditions, loot or other rewards by their commanders. For example, the LRA is known for its tendency to reward soldiers by giving them child brides abducted during raids on communities. The ability to rape and loot is, inter alia, a motivation to not only engage in military violence but also engage in crimes against humanity. Other examples include the *Janjaweed's* rewards in the form of cattle looted from villages and then transported by the Sudanese government as a reward for raiding Fur areas. If military units allow and reward such behaviors, they will be far more common than if the organization attempts to control said acts (see below).

In addition to organizational environments, the meso level of analysis includes neighborhood/village-level structures and forces. The international and macro forces discussed above come to bear on immediate communities creating socially disordered environments. In the ensuing gap of normative and structural order present within a disorganized environment, motivation to join paramilitaries emerges as a path to adult statuses (see discussion of micro-level motivations below). Further, the immediate anomic environments can encourage the development of ethnicist ideologies as a way to explain community problems and to direct the strain individuals experience due to community anomie. Simply, communities without strong economic and political structures create space in which resistance groups can thrive and encourage belief systems that support atrocity events.

Social scientists working in more stable African countries have noted a crisis in African masculinity coming to the fore in the past few decades. Recent work done in South Africa, Kenya, and Mozambique (see Ager et al. 1995; Campbell 1992; El-Bushra 2003; Jacobson 1999; Sideris 2003) shows how widespread social transformations in economic and family structure have constructed a situation where men are unable to engage in traditional (in the colonial/postcolonial sense) masculine practices. With economic collapses, men have more and more difficulty finding wage labor employment. Without access to wages, men cannot fulfill broadly expected roles within local communities and households as breadwinners and providers of economic support. In the absence of male labor, women's labors—traditional and nontraditional—have become even more essential to the survival of communities, which further undermines men's positions in their own communities as well as their own perceptions of their ability to enact appropriate masculine attributes and structural imperatives.

As a result, marriage rates in many southern African communities have dropped, alcoholism among men (especially unemployed men) has increased, and domestic violence is apparently on the rise. These forces simultaneously increase community disorganization (see our discussion of meso-level forces below) as well as operate on individuals as a form of motivation into criminal action (similar processes have been noted by scholars of street-life subculture (criminal and non) in the US and UK as well—see Anderson 1999; Hobbs et al. 2005; Mullins 2006; Winlow 2001; Wright and Decker 1994, 1996). With hegemonic masculinity denied to them, such men will look for other ways to reinforce masculinity and, as gender is fluid, situational and contextual (see Connell 1995, 2000; Miller and Mullins 2005) they will also look for other masculinity constructions to enact.

Specifically, in the absence of the ability to enact breadwinner masculinity, men will turn toward other avenues of gendered performances. As many scholars have noted (see Arkin and Dobrofsky 1978; Barrett 1996; Campbell 1992; Connell 1995; El-Bushra 2003; Jacobson 1999; Sideris 2003), military units are intensely gendered environments with their own specifically situated masculinities and, of course, the opportunities to construct them. These displaced and emasculated men can join militia or regular army groups to not only gain access to financial resources but are also entered into a ready-made set of gendered structures and expectations that allow a nigh-immediate resolution to their prior problematic experiences of being unable to engage in adequate gender performances. In this context, one's manhood is primarily determined, not by usefulness to the productivity of a household, but by the value they contribute to their military or paramilitary unit. Thus, toughness and viciousness become much more highly valued and therefore more intensity (re)constructed within individual action, increasing the number and magnitude of atrocity-situations. The brutality of some of the attacks and the high prevalence of sexual assault across the board within the conflicts examined in this book are in part the more visible indicators of these gendered processes. Proving one self in battle either through normal combat behaviors or atrocity commission is a clear way to construct and reinforce masculinity in the eyes of oneself and others.

Sexual assault further highlights these processes, as the soldiers (re)create masculinity in the process of the brutal victimizing of women. Due to the generally dichotomous nature of gender definition processes (see Connell 1995), in the process of attacking and denigrating women, the literal (and figurative) destruction of the other assists the creation of the masculine. Within genocidal rape this intersection of creation/destruction processes is intensified as not only is the object of destruction oppositional in gender, it is oppositional in ethnicity. Although rape itself is brutal enough, the processes of masculinity generation in all likelihood increases the number and the intensity of the attacks (especially when combined with other factors we discuss elsewhere in this chapter).

Opportunity

As with the ability to control a state discussed above, controlling any organization provide a host of opportunities as one is able to bend the capacity of the organization itself to the fulfillment of goals. Human and other capitals are at the leadership's disposal to further their agendas and to engage in genocidal and other endeavors. Further, within organizations the innate division of labor, role specialization, enhances opportunity provision as one can use these basic dynamics to avoid both legal and moral culpability. In a large amalgam of people, it is difficult to identify specific perpetrators within actions, especially when one tries to trace chains of command to uncover who designed and orchestrated a specific event. Such impunity is ample opportunity to pursue or continue illegal actions as social actors perceive a high level of personal safety in doing so. Even when it is clear what group was responsible for a given action, it is not exactly clear where full accountability lies.

In addition, when there are multiple organizations involved, one being the state, the relationship of the secondary organization to the regime provides additional opportunity and impunity for criminogenic behaviors. This was the case with the *Janjaweed*. As we discussed in Chapter Seven, the relationship between the el-Bashir regime and the *Janjaweed* provided opportunity for the militia to conduct raids, rape, and pillage with the assistance of state military forces and aero support. Economic support for the organizations is also fundamental to the opportunity structures. Whether this be in the form of state economic support: as is the case with the *Janjaweed*; interstate support: such as Sudan's support of the LRA; or transnational support: as we have seen in the DRC. Within state organizations, subunits are also afforded opportunities that may not be present under other conditions. For example, the UPDF has successfully carried out atrocities and general banditry and thuggery sanctioned and protected by the larger state apparatus.

Constraints

Within regular or irregular military organization the most obvious constraint upon behavior are extant command structures. Even militias have chains of command; officers can stop incidents while under way and can either turn over soldiers who violate the law for civilian prosecution or enact punishment in a military context, either through a more typical trial or through summary executions (an atrocity in and of itself, but a potential behavioral constraint). As we have shown within the DRC, militias have attempted to become part of the mainstream power structure by cementing their control over specific communities and territories then use this power base to argue for inclusion in a power-sharing agreement. In these locations, leaders have used their forces to break up atrocities in action and have arrested specific soldiers for specific atrocities. This does serve as a constraint on particular behaviors, especially when troops on the ground are aware of the leadership's desire to normalize their activities. The main weakness in relying on this form of constraint has been the generally symbolic use of these methods of social control. Realizing the need to gain support from local community members and from the other powers in play (e.g., the sitting government and the international actors of interest), military leaders make token efforts to show a level of control of their troops, but fail to systematically enforce these rules as their overall goals are better fulfilled by committing atrocities.

Within communities, the overall loss of informal social control, conceived as a constraint, in communities makes local constraint difficult. If there were local value systems that emphasized the value of local and traditional leadership mechanisms, such tools could be brought to bear to control the actions of troops. Yet, what evidence has been gathered from communities within these territories suggests that local and traditional loci of power and authority have long been denuded of legitimacy and thus their ability to constrain behavior (Arzt 2006; Shaw 2005).

Controls

Few controls operate at the meso level. Most external legal controls operate at the international or the macro level, while idiosyncratic internal controls operate at the micro level. The main control at the meso level is organizational leadership—for our cases, the warlords themselves. Militias tend to be charismatic organizations (per Weber's (1963) conceptualization) focused on the innate ability of a given leader to draw people and maintain their loyalty. If the leadership of these paramilitaries, or legitimate governments like the el-Bashir regime in Sudan or the Museveni government in Uganda, decides to end the commission of atrocities and war crimes, then a control at the meso level has emerged. However, as we have seen throughout this book, organizational leadership drives the crimes to the point that raison d'etre of most of these military organizations is innately criminal.

Micro Level

Ultimately any discussion of criminogenic forces has to identify and examine issues at work within individual decision-making processes. All criminal action is the result of agentic action committed by individuals. This principle was codified in international jurisprudence by the Nuremberg tribunal and is central to the adjudicatory actions of the ICTY and ICTR (see Mettraux 2005). While our theory heavily emphasizes the various contexts at all levels of analysis, ultimately these forces come to bear on social actors and influence choices. Individual agency is indeed modified or even extremely constrained by the social conditions; nonetheless, no actor is a mere automaton. In many ways, most of the forces we have discussed so far not only have an existence at higher levels of analysis but are recreated and reformulated by individuals within interactional contexts. For example, although ethnogenesis is a sociohistorical process operating at the macro level, it is (re)created at the micro level when individuals: (1) internalize these new ethnic identities and (2) draw upon these activities when determining behavioral paths and responses.

Motivation

When examining motivation for this sort of criminal activity at the micro level, we begin with individual gain. As with participation in street crimes or occupational crimes, a primary motivation for criminal activity is the satisfaction of individual desires. Actors involved in crimes against humanity and other widespread human rights abuses are no different. Within this context there are numerous desires that can motivate people toward and through the commission of an atrocity: social meaning, indoctrination, economic gain, ethnic identity, immediate peer group membership and influences, political or religious ideology, fear or situational security, obedience to authority, and gender construction will all, to some degree, work within the perceptions of individuals to motivate the sorts of criminal actions we explore here.

One element that all of the cases discussed in this volume exhibit are the generally high levels of banditry and thuggery in which both militia and regular army troops engage. Prior chapters have documented general theft, intimidation, enforced slavery, and other crimes being committed by essentially every armed group discussed. Such actions are often committed for a variety of individual reasons including economic gain or peer membership prestige: such processes were at work with the *Janjaweed* and their role in committing atrocities as well as their general banditry and thuggery.

Revenge also becomes a frequent motive for individual's joining groups that engage in atrocity-generating behaviors. Recent street crime work has firmly established the role of retaliation in motivating criminal endeavors (see Brookman et al. 2007; Jacobs and Wright 2006; Mullins, Wright, and Jacobs 2004; Wright et al. 2005). In any long-term conflict, individuals will develop personal grudges or perceived (or real) slights. Villages are destroyed, family members are killed, robbed and raped, and property is stolen or commandeered. All of these experiences motivate some to join a group in opposition to one which aggrieved them out of a desire to gain retribution. At the level of atrocities discussed in previous chapters, revenge is often related to the social meaning and/or ethnic divisions that had been preconstructed and later internalized by individuals. Further, revenge, fear, and the need for security can combine to provide the necessary catalyst to commit acts that otherwise individuals could not. We saw this occurring with some of the Hutu and their role in killing Tutsis.

Individuals are not necessarily fully committed to an army or militia's mission and tactics upon joining. People join these groups for a number of reasons arising out of their local environments and personal experiences. Although data is not available, it would be surprising if every new recruit was willing and capable of genocidal rape, murder, and mutilation the day he or she became a member of an armed group. Just as any military has to convert a citizen into a solider, state and nonstate armies must not only train new recruits in the tactics and techniques of warfare, they must also inculcate the basic values of the organization in the newly joined member. Recruits learn from others around them—formally and informally—what behaviors are desirable or at least required. As military members, regular or irregular, experience atrocity-situations time and again, eventually initial compunctions and negative reactions against these acts become diluted and less intense. Sociologists have long referred to this process as the normalization of deviance. As the testimony of child soldiers serving with the LRA in Uganda show, at the start of their military experience the children are often horrified by the actions they are ordered to commit and those that they routinely observe occurring around them. They are desensitized to these actions as they continually observe, and are forced to commit, them. As we discussed in Chapter Five, the abducted children are ordered to harshly discipline their peers as well as kill captives and civilians. Such requirements ensure motivation for obedience and to participation in the actions (e.g., indoctrination, fear, obedience to authority, and definition of the situation at hand). Once loyalty has been achieved—by conversion or force—the processes of desensitization occurs. As has been noted in other conflicts that produced criminal atrocity (e.g., Japan's China campaign in World War II, Sierra Leone's civil war), it is the field experiences that inure soldiers to the horrors around them. Further, these same processes apply to noncriminal wartime actions.

As we noted at the meso level, joining militias or armed forces can also be motivated by a lack of other opportunities within communities for both economic gain as well as the attainment of adult and gendered status within that community. With little in the way of work or other socially approved way of constructing and enacting those adult statuses, especially for men, being a solider is not only a job, but it is a path toward the creation of an adult-gendered identity. Money and other scarce resources (food, drugs, valuable artifacts, and sexual access) can be obtained via military service as can prestige and a place within a community network or social group.

Opportunity

At the individual level, being a member of a military or paramilitary group is in and of itself ample opportunity to commit the crimes we explore here. Empowered by group membership and the sheer fact of being armed, soldiers are free to violate law with little immediate recourse foreseeable. No one can, or will, stop such events while under way. Other aspects of organizational conditions will also arise at the micro level. Social processes long known to bureaucracy scholars play out within an individual context to create opportunity for offending. Group think and the general diffusion of responsibility within organizations open up spaces for offending without immediate consequences. Being able to claim that the entire organization though a given set of actions were the best course of action or being able to hide the actual committers of atrocities within a boarder organizational framework all add to the widespread situation of impunity that regular and irregular military personnel experience during conflict actions.

Constraints

On the micro-level constraints present themselves as an influence on an individual's decision-making process. Once a potential offender is motivated and is either seeking an opportunity or structuring a set of behavioral processes to take advantage of that opportunity, constraints are those things that modify an individual's actions to account for the potential deterrent influence. Recent studies in white-collar crimes in an American context have emphasized the importance of moral views and stand points in the criminal decision-making process. Simpson (2002) has found that one of the strongest predictors of offending behavior among potential white-collar offenders is one's moral view of the correctness or wrongness of such actions. One of the strongest potential controls available on the micro level then is individual rejection of the appropriateness of these behaviors. However, much of the book to this point has directly or indirectly examined how those individuals involved at all levels in atrocities perceive what they are doing as appropriate and legitimate.

Controls

As indicated in our causal model, we see all potential controls operating as moderating influences on the relationship between an individual's criminal motivation and their taking advantage of a criminal opportunity thereby producing a criminal event. For example, while the ICC and international criminal law exists at an international level and International Humanitarian Law similarly exists in the spaces between and between nation-states. The real control influence of these laws and the court happens once a motivated individual is presented with a criminal opportunity that they fail to act upon because of the perceived deterrent value of the law and court action.

Deterrence theories clearly locate the real deterrent function of law and potential punishment not at the macro level of society, but at the micro level of perception. Even the earliest rational choice models (e.g., Bentham and Beccaria) focused not simply on the intensity of certainty, celerity, and proportionality of punishment but rather on the individual's perception of these elements. Although some rational choice theorists assume that offenders have a rather realistic perspective of punishment dimensions, much qualitative work done with active street offenders in the US shows the opposite (see Shover and Henderson 1992; Shover and Honaker 1995; Wright and Decker 1994). In our context, we would similarly be skeptical of the accuracy of the knowledge held by soldiers on the ground on international law, prosecution, and punishment. Regardless, anything that makes individuals on the ground in these situations believe that they are more likely to be caught or that the potential punishments outweigh the costs, should reduce the number of atrocity events. Such dynamics are the center of the ICC's claims concerning the influence that their prosecutions are having on certain events, especially the behavior of the LRA in Uganda.

An individual's perception of the legitimacy of law itself, both domestic and international, will serve as a strong mediator of the ability to law to control their behavior. Legitimacy gives power to the legal codes. However, as we have explored throughout this chapter specifically and the book itself generally, most committers of atrocities do not perceive either international or a given national law as legitimate and/or threat for prosecuting their behaviors.

REFERENCES

Adebajo, Adekeye and Chandra Lekha Sriram, eds. 2001. *Managing Armed Conflict in the 21st Century*. London: Frank Cass Publishers.
Adebajo, Adekeye and Christopher Landsberg. 2001. "The Heirs of Nkrumah: Africa's New Investments." Pugwash Occasional papers 2. Conference of Science and World Affairs. Retrieved January 17, 2008. www.pugwash.org/reports/rc/omo_africa.htm
Adhola, Yoga. 1994. *The Roots, Emergence, and Growth of the Uganda Peoples Congress, 1600–1985*. Joint State Government Commission, Commonwealth of Pennsylvania.
Africa News. 2000. "Case of 15 Congolese Women Buried Alive to be Probed." *All Africa, Inc.* February 17.
African Rights. 1994. *Rwanda: Who is killing? Who is dying? What is to be done?* A Discussion Paper. *Rwanda, Death Despair, Defiance*. London. May.
Agence France-Presse. 2000. "Rebels Behead 12 Women in Eastern Democratic Rebuplic of Congo." *Agence France-Presse*—English. February 1.
———. 1999. "Fifteen Women Buried Alive by Democratic Republic of Congo Rebels." *Agence France-Presse*—English. December 20.
Ager, Alistair, Wendy Ager, and Lynellyn Long. 1995. "The Differential Experience of Mozambican Refugee Women and Men." *Journal of Refugee Studies* 8 (3): 265–287.
Akers, R.L. 1977. *Deviant Behavior: A Social Learning Approach*. Belmont, CA: Wadsworth.
Amnesty International Press Release. 2005. AFR 54/059/2005. News Service No. 150.
———. 2004. AFR 54/058/2004. "The Wire." News Service. June.
An-Na'im, Abdullah A. 2004. "The Legal Protection of Human Rights in Africa: How to Do More with Less." In A. Sarat and T. Kearns, eds. *Human Rights: Concepts, Contests, Contingencies*. Ann Arbor: University of Michigan Press. 89–116.
———. 2003. "Introduction: Expanding Legal Protection of Human Rights in African Contexts." In Abdullah An-Na'im, ed. *Human Rights Under African Constitutions: Realizing the Promise for Ourselves*. 1–28.

Annan, Kofi. 2006. "UN Secretary General Discusses Darfur and Iran." *PBS Newshour* interview with Jim Lehrer, May 4. Retrieved January 17, 2008 from www.pbs.org/newshour/bb/international/jan-june06/annan_05-04.html

Apuuli, Kasaija P. 2004. "The International Criminal Court (ICC) and the Lord's Resistance Army (LRA) insurgency in Northern Uganda." *Criminal Law Forum* 15: 391–408.

Arkin, W. and Dobrofsky L. (1978). "Military Socialization and Masculinity." *Journal of Social Issues* 34 (1): 151–168.

Arvigan, T. and Honey M. 1982. *War in Uganda: The Legacy of Idi Amin*. London: Zed Press.

Arzt, Donna E. 2006. "Views on the Ground: The Local Perception of International Criminal Tribunals in the Former Yugoslavia and Sierra Leone." *Annals of the American Academy for Political and Social Science* 603 (1): 226–239.

Ascherson, Neal. July 1956. "The History of the Uganda National Congress." Unpublished notes written for the East African Institute for Social Research, Kampala, and deposited at the Library of Northwestern University, Evanston, Illinois, USA.

Associated Press. 2006a. "Riot Police Ready as Congo Election Season Begins: People Hope Vote Will Bring Peace After Civil War, Corrupt Leadership." *Associated Press*. June 30.

———. 2006b. "Group: Darfur Rapes on the Rise." *Associated Press*. August 24.

Barak, Gregg. 1990. "Crime, Criminology and Human Rights: Towards an Understanding of State Criminality." *The Journal of Human Justice* 2 (1): 11–28.

———.1991. *Crimes by the Capitalist State: An Introduction to State Criminality*. Albany, NY: State University of New York Press.

———. 2000. "Foreword." In Jeffrey Ian Ross, ed. *Varieties of State Crime and Its Control*. Monsey, NY: Criminal Justice Press. i–ix.

Barrett, Frank J. 1996. "The Organizational Construction of Hegemonic Masculinity: The Case of the US Navy." *Gender, Work and Organization* 3 (3): 129–142.

Bassiouni, M. Cherif. 2006. *Crimes of War: The Book*. Retrieved January 17, 2008 from www.crimesofwar.org/thebook/crimes-against-humanity.html

BBC. 2007a. UN Probing Democratic Republic of Congo Smuggling Claims. May 24.

———. 2007b. Pakistan Dismisses Democratic Republic of Congo Claim. May 26.

———. 2005. Hutu Militiamen Reported Harassing Eastern Democratic Republic of Congo Residents. February 2, 2005.

Behrend, Heike. 1998. "War in Northern Uganda." In Christopher Clapham, ed. *African Guerrillas*. Bloomington, IN: Indiana University Press. 107–118.

Berry, J.A. and Carol P. Berry. 1999. *Genocide in Rwanda: A Collective Memory*. Washington DC: Howard University Press.

Boyle, E.H. and J.W. Meyer. 2002. "Modern Law as a Secular and Global Model: Implications for the Sociology of Law." In Y. Dezalay and B.J. Garth, eds. *Global Prescriptions: The Production, Exportation, and Importation of a New Legal Orthodoxy*. Ann Arbor, MI: University of Michigan Press. 65–95.

Braeckman, C. 1994. *Rwanda, History of Genocide*. Paris: Fayard.

Brittain, Victoria. 2002. "Calvary of Women of Eastern Demoractic Republic of Congo (DRC)." *Review of African Political Economy* 93/94: 595–628.

Brookman, Fiona, Christopher W. Mullins, Trevor Bennet, and Richard Wright. 2007. "Gender, Motivation and the Accomplishment of Street Robbery." *The British Journal of Criminology* 47 (6): 861–884.

Broomhall, Bruce. 2003. *International Justice and the International Criminal Court: Between Sovereignty and the Rule of Law*. New York: Oxford University Press.

Bursik, Robert J. and Harold G. Grasmick. 1993. *Neighborhoods and Crime: The Dimensions of Effective Community Control*. Lexington, MA: Lexington Books.

Campbell, Catherine. 1992. "Learning to Kill? Masculinity, the Family and Violence in Natal." *Journal of Southern African Studies* 18 (3): 614–628.
Carroll, Rory. 2006. "Congo's Jungle Terrorists Disband." *Guardian Unlimited*. July 2.
Cassesse, Antonio. 2002. *The Rome Statute of the International Criminal Court: A Commentary*, Vol. I. New York: Oxford University Press.
Chamberlain, Muriel E. 1999. *Decolonization: The Fall of the EuropeanEmpires*, 2nd ed. Malden, MA: Blackwell Publishing.
Chambliss, W. 1993. *Making Law: The State, The Law, and Structural Contradictions*. Bloomington and Indianapolis: Indiana University Press.
———. 1989. "State Organized Crime." *Criminology* 27 (2): 183–208.
———. 1995. "Commentary by William J. Chambliss." *Society of Social Problems Newsletter* 26: 1–9.
Chang, Iris. 1997. *The Rape of Nanking: The Forgotten Holocaust of World War II*. New York: Basic Books.
Chossudousky, M. 1995. "Rwanda, Somalia, ex-Yougoslavia: Armed Conflicts, Génocide, Economic Responsibilities of the Institutions of Bretton Woods." In Banque *FMI, OMC: ça suffit!*, CADTM, Bruxelles.
Chossudousky, M. and Pierre Galand. 1996. "Le Génocide de 1994, L'usage de la dette extérieure du Rwanda (1990–1994). La responsabilité des bailleurs de fonds." Retrieved January 17, 2008 from www.globalresearch.ca/articles/CHO403F.html
Chretien, J.P. 1912. "The Revolt of Ndungutse." *Review Francaise Histoire* 59 (4): 645–680. Cited in Prunier, G. 1995. *The Rwandan Crisis: History of a Genocide*. New York: Columbia University Press.
Clohesy, W. and K. Kuraz. 2000. "Realizing Rights: The Role of NGOs in Universalizing Human Rights," Published in Working Paper Volume, Fourth Biennial Conference, International Society for Third Sector Research, Dublin, Ireland.
Cloward, Richard A. and Lloyd E. Ohlin. 1960. *Delinquency and Opportunity: A Theory of Delinquent Gangs*. New York: Free Press.
Coalition for International Justice. 2006. Survey (no longer available as organization—dismantled in March 2006). See also *Washington Post*, "Darfur's Real Death Toll." April 24, 2005, B06.
Collins, Carloe J. 1997. "Reconstructing the Congo." *Review of African Political Economy* 74: 591–600.
Committee on International Relations: Subcommittee on Africa, Global Human Rights and International Operations. 2005. *United Nations Organization Mission in the Democratic Republic of Congo: A Case for Peacekeeping Reform*. Washington DC: US Government Publishing Office. March 1.
Crowder, M. "The Second World War: Prelude to Decolonization in Africa." *Cambridge History of Africa, 1840–1975*. Vol. 8.
Davidson, Basil. 1994. *Modern Africa: A Social and Political History*. Harlow, England: Longman.
Destexhe, A. 1994. *Rwanda*. Brussels: Complexe.
Djungu-Simba, Charles. 2002. Democratic Republic of Congo: The war from the Perspective of the Congolese people. Geneva, Switzerland: United Nations High Commissioner for Refugees.
Doctors Without Borders. 2006. International Activity Report 2006: Democratic Republic of Congo.
Drumbl, Mark A. 2002. "Restorative Justice and Collective Responsibility: Lessons for and from the Rwandan Genocide." *Contemporary Justice Review* 5 (1): 5–22.

Egeland, Jan. 2006. *Speech by United Nations Undersecretary for Humanitarian Affairs.* Retrieved January 16, 2008 from www.genocideintervention.net/about/press/releases/2006/07/17/bipartisan-legislation-calls-for-special-envoy-to-darfur/

El-Bushra, Judy. 2003. "Fused in Combat: Gender relations and armed conflict." *Development in Practice* 13 (2/3): 252–265.

Epp, C.R. 1998. *The Rights Revolution: Lawyers, Activists, and Supreme Courts in Comparative Perspective.* Chicago: University of Chicago Press.

Erny, P. 1983. "The Spirit of Education in Rwanda." *Geneva-Africa* 21 (1): 26–54.

Ewans, Martin. 2002. *European Atrocity, African Catastrophe: Leopold II, the Congo Free State and It's Aftermath.* London: Routledge Curzon.

Fairhall, John. 1971. "Curfew in Uganda After Military Coup Topples Obote." January 25, Tuesday and January 26, 1971. *The Guardian. Nairobi.*

Falk, Peter. 1993. *Global Visions: Beyond the New World Order.* Boston: South End Press.

Finnstrom, Sverker. 2006. "Wars of the Past and War in the Present: The Lord's Resistance Movement/Army in Uganda." *Journal of the International African Institute* 76 (2): 200–220.

Franklin, John Hope. 1985. *George Washington Williams: A Biography.* Chicago: University of Chicago Press.

Friedrichs, D. 1992. "State Crime or Governmental Crime: Making Sense of the Conceptual Confusion." In Jeff Ross, ed. *Controlling State Crime.* New York, NY: Garland Publishing. 53–80

———. 2004. "White-Collar Crime in a Globalized World." Presentation at Western Michigan University.

Friedrichs, D. and J. Friedrichs. 2002. "The World Bank and Crimes of Globalization: A Case Study." *Social Justice* 29: 13–36.

Frulli, Micaela. 2001. "Are Crimes Against Humanity More Serious than War Crimes?" *European Journal of International Law* 12: 329–350.

Gapyisi, Emmanuel. 1995. "La fin d'un regime et la din d'une guerre." In Prunier, G. ed. *The Rwandan Crisis: History of a Genocide.* New York: Columbia University Press. 183.

Geis, Gilbert. 2007. *White Collar and Corporate Crime.* Upper Saddle River, NJ: Pearson.

Gertzel, Cherry. 1974. "Party and Locality in Northern Uganda, 1945–1962." London: The Athelone Press.

Gibson, James L. 2006. "Overcoming Apartheid: Can Truth Reconcile a Divided Nation?" *The Annals of the American Academy of Political and Social Science* 603: 82–109.

———. 2004. "Does Truth Lead to Reconciliation? Testing the Casual Assumptions of the South African Truth and Reconciliation Process." *American Journal of Political Science* 48 (2): 201–217.

———. 2002. "Truth, Justice and Reconciliation: Judging the Fairness of Amnesty in South Africa." *American Journal of Political Science* 46 (3): 540–556.

Global Security Report. 2006. "Uganda Civil War." Retrieved January 16, 2008 www.globalsecurity.org/military/world/war/uganda.htm

Glueck, Sheldon. 1944. *War Criminals: Their Prosecution and Punishment.* New York: Alfred A. Knopf.

Goldstone, Jack. 2004. "Response: Reasoning about History, Sociologically." *Sociological Methodology* 34 (1): 35–61.

Hagan, John and Scott Greer. 2002. "Making war criminal." *Criminology* 40 (2): 231–264.

Hagan, John, Wenona Rymond-Richmond, and Patricia Parker. 2005. "The Criminology of Genocide: The Death and Rape of Darfur." *Criminology* 43 (3): 525–562.

Hanssen, A. 1989. "Le De'senchantment de la cooperation, Enquete au pays des mille cooperants." In G. Prunier, ed. *The Rwandan Crisis: History of a Genocide.* New York: Columbia University Press. 394.

Hargreaves, John D. 1988. *Decolonization in Africa*. London: Longman.
Harris, Edward. 2006. "Congo Presidential Hopeful Claims Fraud." *Associated Press*. August 1.
Human Rights Watch. 2006a. *Democratic Republic of Congo: Army Abducts Civilians for Forced Labor*. New York: Human Rights Watch.
———. 2006b. *What Future? Street Children in the Democratic Republic of Congo*. New York: Human Rights Watch.
———. 2006c. *Democratic Republic of Congo: On the Brink*. New York: Human Rights Watch.
———. 2006d. *UPC Crimes in Ituri (2002–2003)*. New York: Human Rights Watch.
———. 2006e. "Democratic Republic Congo: Mai Mai Warlord Must Face Justice." May 17. New York: Human Rights Watch.
———. 2005a. "Sexual Violence and Its Consequences among Displaced Persons in Darfur and Chad." New York: Human Rights Watch.
———. 2005b. "Targeting The Fur: Mass Killings in Darfur." A Human Rights Watch Briefing Paper January 21.
———. 2005c. *Seeking Justice: The Prosecution of Sexual Violence in the Congo War*. New York: Human Rights Watch.
———. 2005d. *The Curse of Gold: Democratic Republic of Congo*. New York: Human Rights Watch.
———. 2004a. "Sudan-Darfur in Flames: Atrocities in Western Sudan." April, 16 (5)(a). New York: Human Rights Watch.
———. 2004b. "Empty Promises?" A Human Rights Briefing Paper. New York: Human Rights Watch.
———. 2004c. *Child Solider Use 2003: Uganda*. New York: Human Rights Watch.
———. 2003a. *Uganda: Stolen Children: Abduction and Recruitment in Northern Uganda*. New York: Human Rights Watch.
———. 2003b. *Uganda: Abducted and Abused: Renewed Conflict in Northern Uganda*. New York: Human Rights Watch.
———. 2003c. *Ituri: Covered in Blood: Ethnically Targeted Violence in Northeastern DR Congo*. New York: Human Rights Watch.
———. 2002. *The War within the War: Sexual Violence Against Women and Girls in Eastern Congo*. New York: Human Rights Watch.
———. 1999. "Uganda Historical Background Report." Retrieved January 16, 2008 from www.hrw.org/reports/1999/uganda/Uganweb-06.htm
———. 1997. *The Scars of Death: Children Abducted by the Lord's Resistance Army in Uganda*. New York: Human Rights Watch.
International Monetary Fund. 1999. *The IMF's Enhanced Structural Adjustment Facility (ESAF): Is It Working?* Retrieved January 16, 2008 from www.imf.org/external/pubs/ft/esaf/exr/index.htm
Isango, Eddy. 2006a. "Congo Arrests Guards in Alleged Coup Plot." *Associated Press*. May 24.
———. 2006b. "Mayhem in Congo as Vote Hearing Starts." *Associated Press*. November 21.
IRIN. 2006a. DRC: Mayi-Mayi Warlord Surrenders in Katanga. UN Office of Coordination of Humanitarian Affairs. May 12.
———. 2006b. DRC: From Protection to Insurgency—History of the Mayi-Mayi. UN Office of Coordination of Humanitarian Affairs. March 16.
———. 2006c. DRC: Interview with Army Col Louis Siatilo in Katanga. UN Office of Coordination of Humanitarian Affairs. February 13.
———. 2006d. DRC: The Peculiar Terror that is Northern Katanga. UN Office of Coordination of Humanitarian Affairs. February 13.

IRIN. 2006e. DRC: The Story of Kibwe Mwepwe, a Mayi-Mayi. UN Office of Coordination of Humanitarian Affairs. January 24.

———. 2004a. DRC: Fighters Commit Atrocities Against Women and also Men. UN Office of Coordination of Humanitarian Affairs. September 1.

———. 2004b. DRC: The Twa now Retract Cannibalism Charge. UN Office of Coordination of Humanitarian Affairs. September 14.

Jackson, Stephen. 2002. "Making a Killing: Criminality and Coping in the Kivu War Economy." *Review of African Political Economy* 93/94: 517–536.

Jacobs, Bruce and Richard Wright. 2006. *Street Justice: Retaliation in the Criminal Underworld.* New York: Cambridge University Press.

Jacobson, Ruth. 1999. "Complicating 'Complexity': Integrating Gender into the Analysis of the Mozambican Conflict." *Third World Quarterly* 20 (1): 175–187.

Jafari, Jamal. 2005. "Word Games: The UN and Genocide in Darfur." Retrieved January 16, 2008 from www.jurist.law.pitt.edu/forumy/2005/03/word-games-un-and-genocide-in-darfur.php

Jankowski, Martin Sanchez. 1991. *Islands in the Street: Gangs and American Urban Society.* Berkeley, CA: University of California Press.

Jorgensen, N. 2000. *The Responsibility of States for International Crimes.* Oxford: Oxford University Press.

Kangura. 1994. "Who Will Survive the March War?" *Kangura* January. 551.

Kasibante, George. 2006. *Africa's Greatest Bloodbath: The World Beyond Media Publication.* US Global Peace Policy Bureau.

Kauzlarich, D. and Ronald Kramer. 1998. *Crimes of the American Nuclear State: At Home and Abroad.* Boston: Northeastern University Press.

Kauzlarich, D., R.A. Matthews, and W. J. Miller. 2001. "Toward A Victimology of State Crime." *Critical Criminology: An International Journal* 10 (3): 173–194.

Keen, David. 2001. "War and Peace: What's the Difference?" In Adekeye Adebajo and Chandra Lekha Sriram, eds. *Managing Armed Conflicts in the Twenty First Century.* London: Frank Cass. 1–22.

Klug, Heinz. 2005. "Transnational Human Rights: Exploring the Persistence and Globalization of Human Rights." *Annual Review of Law and Social Science* 1: 85–103.

Kramer, R. 1982. "Corporate Crime: An Organizational Perspective." In Wickman and Tom Daily, eds. *White Collar and Economic Crime.* Lexington, KY: Lexington Books. 75–94.

———. 1990a. "State-Corporate Crime." Presented at the North Central Sociological Association and the Southern Sociological Association.

———. 1990b. "State-corporate Crime: A Case Study of the Space Shuttle Challenger Explosion." Presented at the Edwin Sutherland Conference on White Collar Crime: 50 Years of Research and Beyond, Indiana University.

———. 1990c. "The Concept of State-Corporate Crime." Presented at the Society for the Study of Social Problems, Washington, DC.

———. 1992. "The Space Shuttle Challenger Explosion: A Case Study of State-Corporate Crime." In K. Schlegel and D. Weisburd, eds. *White Collar Crime Reconsidered.* Boston: Northeastern University Press. 212–241.

———. 1995. "Exploring State Criminality: The Invasion of Panama." *Journal of Criminal Justice and Popular Culture* 3 (2): 43–52.

Kramer, R. and R. Michalowski. 1990a. "Toward an Integrated Theory of State-corporate Crime." Presented at the American Society of Criminology, Baltimore, MD.

Kramer, R., R. Michalowski, and D. Rothe. 2005. "The Supreme International Crime: How the US War in Iraq Threatens the Rule of Law." *Social Justice* 32: 2.

Kramer, R. and R. Michalowski. 2006. *State-Corporate Crime: Wrongdoing At The Intersection Of Business And Government.* ed. Ron Kramer and Raymond J. Michalowski. Piscataway, NJ: Rutgers University Press.

———. 2005. "War, Aggression, and State Crime: A Criminological Analysis of the Invasion and Occupation of Iraq." *British Journal of Criminology* 45 (4): 446–469.

Kristoff, Nicholas. 2005. "The Secret Genocide." *New York Times* Archive. February 23. Retrieved January 16, 2008 from www.sudantribune.com/article.php3?id_article=8204

Le Billon, Philippe. 2005. "Fuelling Wars: Natural Resources and Armed Conflict." *Adelphi Paper* 373. New York: Routledge.

Lemkin, Raphael. 1944. *Axis Rule in Occupied Europe.* Washington, DC: Carnegie Endowment for International Peace.

Lobban, R. 2004. "Complexities of Darfur." *Sudan Tribune.* August 3. A1.

Logiest, G. 1988. *Mission of Rwanda.* Brussels: Didier Hatier.

Low, D.A. 1962. "Political Parties in Uganda, 1949–1962." London: Athlone Press.

Low, D.A. 1967. "Buganda in Modern History." Berkely and Los Angeles: University of California Press.

Maquet, J.J. 1961. *The Premises of Inequality in Rwanda.* London: Oxford University Press.

Maton, J. 1994. Développement économique et social au Rwanda entre 1980 et 1993. Le dixième décile en face de l'apocalypse, Université de Gand, Faculté de Sciences économiques, 43.

Matthews, Rick A. 2006. "State-Corporate Crime in Nazi Germany." In R. Michalowski and R. Kramer, ed. *Corporate Crime: Wrongdoing at the Intersection of Business and Government.* New Brunswick, NJ: Rutgers University Press. 181–211.

Max, Arthur. 2006. "War Crimes Prosecutor Indicts Warlord." *Associated Press.* August 28.

McCormick, James. 2000. "Human Rights and the Clinton Administration: American Policy at the Dawn of a New Century." In Robert Patman, ed. *Universal Human Rights.* Basingstoke: Macmillan Press and New York: St. Martin's Press. 114–134.

Melver, Linda. 2004. *Conspiracy to Murder: The Rwandan Genocide.* London and New York: Verso.

Mendez, Juan. 2006. *United Nations Press Conference on Prevention of Genocide.* April 7.

Merton, Robert K. 1938. Social Structure and Anomie." *American Sociological Review* 3: 672–682.

Messner, Steven F. and Richard Rosenfeld. 2007. *Crime and the American Dream.* 4th ed. Belmont, CA: Wadsworth.

Mettraux, Guenael. 2005. *International Crimes and the Ad Hoc Tribunals.* London: Oxford University Press.

Michalowski, R. and R. Kramer. 1987. "The Space Between the Laws: The Problem of Corporate Crime in a Transnational Context." *Social Problems* 34: 34–53.

Michalowski, R. 1985. *Order, Law and Crime.* New York: Random House.

Moniter, The. 2001. Kampala News. Quoted in *Conciliation Resources.* 2002: 1. Accord. Retrieved January 16, 2008 from www.c-r.org/our-work/accord/northern-uganda/profiles.php

Mujaju, A.B. 1987. "The Gold Allegations in Uganda." *African Affairs* 87. October.

Mullins, Christopher W. and Dawn L. Rothe. 2007. "The Forgotten Ones: The Darfuri Genocide." *Critical Criminology* 15 (2): 135–158.

Mullins, Christopher W. and D. Kauzlarich. 2000. "The Ghost Dance: A Criminological Examination." *Social Pathology* 6 (4): 264–283.

Mullins, Christopher W., D. Kauzlarich, and Dawn L. Rothe. 2004. "The International Criminal Court and the Control of State Crime: Problems and Prospects." *The Critical Criminology* 12: 285–308.

Mullins, Christopher W. and Dawn L. Rothe. 2006. "On the Legitimacy of International Law: Reflections on Toronto." *The Critical Criminology* 15 (2): 135–158.

Mullins, Christopher W., Richard T. Wright, and Bruce A. Jacobs. "Gender, Streetlife, and Criminal Retaliation." *Criminology* 42 (4): 911–940.

Musa, A.H. 2003. in *Al-Khartoum*, March 4, 2003.

Museveni, Yoweri. 1990. "Theoretical Justification of NRM Struggle." In *Mission to Freedom: Uganda Resistance News 1981–1985* (Kampala: Directorate of Information and Mass Mobilization, NRM Secretariat, 1990) 3.

Mutesa, E. 1967. *The Desecration of My Kingdom*. London: Constable.

Mwenda, Andrew M. and Roger Tangri. 2005. Patronage, Politics, Donor Reforms, and Regime Consolidation in Uganda. *African Affairs* 104 (416): 449–467.

Mutibwa, Phares. 1992. *Uganda Since Independence: A Story of Unfulfilled Hopes*. Trenton, NJ: Africa World Press.

New York Times. January 26, 2007. "Uganda news." Retrieved January 27, 2007 from www.topics.nytimes.com/top/news/international/countriesandterritories/uganda/index.html

Ndagijimana, F.L. 1990. *The Face of Africa. The Problems of Rwandan Refugees. L'Afrique face a ses Defis. Le probleme des refugies rwandais*. Geneva: Arunga.

Orentlicher, Diane. 2006. *Crimes of War: The Book*. Retrieved January 16, 2008 from www.crimesofwar.org/thebook/genocide.html

Perrow, Charles. 1986. *Complex Organizations: A Critical Essay*. 3rd ed. New York: McGraw Hill.

Phom, P., Patrick Vinck, Marieke Wierda, Eric Stover, and Adrian di Giovanni. 2005. *Forgotten Voices: A Population Based Survey on Attitudes About Peace and Justice in Northern Uganda*. The International Center for Transitional Justice and the Human Rights Center, Berkely, CA.

Polgreen, Lydia. 2007. "A Darfur Rebel Alliance could Upend Sudan." *The International Herald Tribune* A1: 2. April 14.

———. 2006. "4 Months after DPA, Darfur Heads Toward Military Confrontation." *Sudan Times*. September 5. Retrieved January 16, 2008 from www. sudantribune.com/imprimable.php3?id_artcile=17368

Power, S. 2004. "Dying in Darfur." *The New Yorker*. August 30. Retrieved January 16, 2008 from www.newyorker.com/archive/2004/08/30/040830fa_fact1?currentPage=2

Pronk, Jan. 2004. In *United Nations Special Report: Envoy to Darfur. News Service*. Archived News. November 2. Retrieved from www.un.org

Prunier, Gerard. 2005. *Darfur: The Ambiguous Genocide*. Ithica, NY: Cornell University Press.

———. 2004. "Rebel Movements and Proxy Warfare: Uganda, Sudan, and the Congo (1986–1999)." *African Affairs* 103/412: 359–383.

———. 1995. *The Rwandan Crisis: History of a Genocide*. New York: Columbia University Press.

Ragin, Charles. 1987. *The Comparative Method*. Berkeley, CA: University of California Press.

Rajagopal, Balakrishnan. 2003. *International Law from Below: Development, Social Movements and Third World Resistance*. Cambridge: Cambridge University Press.

Reader, John. 1997. *Africa: A Biography of a Continent*. New York: Vintage.

Reeves, Eric. 2004. "Failure to Mount a Humanitarian Intervention in Darfur: Historical Context for Dramatically Escalating Insecurity." Retrieved January 16, 2008 from www.genocidewatch.org/SudanFailuretoMountaHumanitarianInterventioninDarfur30nov2004.htm

Reno, William. 2006. "Congo: From State Collapse to 'Absolutism' to State Failure." *Third World Quarterly* 27 (1): 43–56.

Renzetti, Claire. 2002. "Women's Experiences of Intimate Violent Victimization in Four Philadelphia Public Housing Developments." Paper presented at the Annual Meeting of the Society for the Study of Social Problems, Chicago, IL. August.

Rodriguez, Claudia. 2006. "Sexual Violence in South Kiva, Congo." *Forced Migration Review* 27: 45–46.
Rone, Jerome. 2005. "Uganda: Army and Rebels Commit Atrocities." New York: Human Rights Watch.
Ross, J. 2000. *Varieties of State Crime and It's Control*. Monsey, NY: Criminal Justice Press.
———1995. *Controlling State Crime: An Introduction*. New York: Garland Publishing.
Rothe, Dawn. 2006. "The Masquerade of Abu Ghraib: State Crime, Torture, and International Law." Western Michigan University Dissertation.
Rothe, Dawn and Christopher W. Mullins. 2006a. *The International Criminal Court: Symbolic Gestures and the Generation of Global Social Control*. Ann Arbor, MI: Lexington Books.
———. 2006b. "The International Criminal Court and United States Opposition." *Crime, Law and Social Change* 45: 201–226.
———. 2007a. "Darfur and the International Legal Realm: Genocide or Crimes Against Humanity?" *Humanity and Society*. 31(1):83–107.
———. 2007b. "International Community: Legitimizing a Moral Collective Consciousness." *Humanity and Society* 30: 3.
Rothe, Dawn and David Friedrichs. 2006. "The State of the Criminology of State Crime." *Social Justice* 33 (1).
Rothe, Dawn, Stephen Muzzatti, and Christopher W. Mullins. 2006. "Crime on the High Seas: Crimes of Globalization and the Sinking of the Senegalese Ferry Le Joola." *Critical Criminology* 14 (2): 159–180.
Sadat, Leila Nadya and S. Richard Carden. 2000. "The New International Criminal Court: An Uneasy Revolution." *Georgetown Law Review* 88: 381–474.
Saint-Exupery, Patrick. 1994. "Rwanda: The Assassins Remember the massacres." Quoted in Prunier, G. 2005. *The Rwandan Crisis: History of a Genocide*. New York, Columbia University Press.
Samset, Ingrid. 2002. "Conflict of Interests or Interests in Conflict? Diamonds and War in the DRC." *Review of African Political Economy* 93/94: 463–480.
Sands, Phillip. 2005. *Lawless World: America and the Making and Breaking of Global Rules*. London: Allen Lane.
Santhymurthy, T.V. 1986. "The Political Development of Uganda: 1900–1986." Aldershot, England: Gowers Publishing Company.
Schatzberg, Michael G. 1991. *Mobutu or Chaos? The United States and Zaire, 1960–1990*. Lanham, NY: University Press of America.
Shaw, Clifford and Henry D. McKay. 1942. *Juvenile Delinquency and Urban Areas*. Chicago, IL: University of Chicago Press.
Shaw, Rosalind. 2005. *Rethinking Truth and Reconciliation Commissions: Lessons from Sierra Leone*. Washington DC: United States Institute of Peace.
Shelden, R., S. Tracy, and W. Brown. 2004. *Youth Gangs in American Society*. 3rd ed. Belmont, CA: Wadsworth.
Short, Phillip. 1971. "Amin's Uganda." *Transition* no. 40 (December), 48–55, doi:10.2307/2934129.
Sideris, Tina. 2003. "War, Gender and Culture: Mozambican Women Refugees." *Social Science and Medicine* 56: 713–724.
Silverstein, K. 2005. "Official Pariah Sudan Valuable to America's War on Terrorism." *Los Angeles Times*. April 29.
Simpson, Sally. 2002. *Corporate Crime, Law and Social Control*. New York: Cambridge University Press.
Sutherland, Edwin. 1949. *White Collar Crime*. New York: Dryden Press.

Takirambudde, Peter. 2005. Cited in Eric Reeves, "Genocide in Darfur." *Sudan Tribune*, September 2. Retrieved April 5, 2006 from www.sudantribune.com/article.php3?id_article=11445- 46k

Taylor, Jenny. 2005. "Taking Spirituality Seriously: Northern Uganda and Britian's 'Break the Silence' Campaign." *The Round Table* 94 (382): 559–574.

Telarama. 1994. Quoted in Prunier, G. 1995. *The Rwandan Crisis: History of a Genocide.* New York: Columbia University Press. 254.

Thomas, W.I. with Dorothy Thomas. 1928. *The Child in America: Behavior Problems and Programs.* New York: Knopf.

Toussaint, E. 1999. *Your Money or Your Life!: Tyranny of Global Finance.* London: Pluto Press.

Tunnell, K.D. 1993. *Political Crime in Contemporary America.* New York, NY: Garland Publications.

Turk, A. 1982. *Political Criminality.* Beverly Hills, LA: Sage.

Ugandan Democratic Coalition. 1994. *Who are behind the Rwanda Crisis.* Langley Park, MD: UDC Newsletter.

UN Office for the Coordination of Humanitarian Affairs. 2006. *Humanitarian News and Analysis Uganda.* Retrieved January 16, 2008 from www.irinnews.org/webspecials/ RightsAndReconciliation/54272.asp

United Nations News Service. 2006. "Press Release." Retrieved January 16, 2008 from www.un.org/News/ossg/sg/stories/statments_full.asp?statID=39 also available as secondary source www.irinnews.org/report.asp?ReportID=50910&SelectRegion=East_Africa&SelectCountry=SUDAN

United Nations, UNSC. Monthly Report of the Secretary General on Darfur. 2005/821, 2005/719.

———. 2005. "News Service." December 29, 2005. Retrieved January 5, 2006 from www.un.org

———. 2004. "Special Report: Envoy to Darfur." *News Service.* January 2005.

United Nations Special Advisor Mendez. 2006. "Statement on Prevention of Genocide."

Van Acker, Frank. (2004). "Uganda and the Lord's Resistance Army: The New Order No One Ordered." *African Affairs* 103: 335–357.

Vlassenroot, Koen. 2002. "Citizenship, Identity Formation and Conflict in South Kivu: The Case of the Banyamulenge." *Review of African Political Economy* 93/94: 499–516.

Vlassenroot, Koen and Timothy Raeymaekers. 2004. "The Politics of Rebellion and Intervention in Ituri: The Emergence of a New Political Complex?" *African Affairs* 103/412: 385–412.

Von Glabn, Gerhard and James Larry Taulbee. 2007. *Law Among Nations: An Introduction to Public International Law.* New York: Pearson Longman.

Waal, A.D. 1989. *Famine that Kills: Darfur 1984–1985.* Oxford: Clarendon Press. 50.

Wairague, Francis, K. 2004. "The proliferation of Small Arms and their Role in Escalating the Conflicts in East Africa." In Nhemam Alfred, ed. *The Quest for Peace in Africa: Transformation, Democracy and Public Policy.* Addis Ababa: Ossera. 107–121.

Warburg, G. 2003. *Islam, Sectarianism and Politics in Sudan since the Mahdiyya.* Madison, WI: University of Wisconsin Press.

Weber, Max. 1946. *From Max Weber.* Ed. and trans. Hans Gerth and C. Wright Mills. New York: Oxford University Press.

———. 1963. *The Sociology of Religion.* Trans. Ephraim Fischoff. Boston, MA: Beacon Press.

Williams, George Washington. 1890. A Report upon the Congo-State and County to the President of the United States of American. Reprinted in Franklin. John Hope. 1985. *George Washington Williams: A Biography.* Chicago: University of Chicago Press.

Wright, Richard, Fiona Brookman, and Trevor Bennett. 2006. "The Foreground Dynamics of Street Robbery in Britain." *British Journal of Criminology* 46 (1): 1–15.

Treaties

The Covenant of the League of Nations
Declaration Renouncing the Use, in times of War, of Explosive Projectiles Under 400 Grammes Weight. 1868. St. Petersburg.
International Declaration concerning the Laws and Customs of War. 1874. Brussels.
Hague Convention, 1907.
United Nations General Assembly.
Nuremberg Charter, 1945.
1946 United Nations General Assembly Resolution 95: 1.
1946 United nations Resolution 260 A (III).
Universal Declaration of Human Rights 1948.
Convention on the Prevention and Punishment of the Crime of Genocide of 1948.
General Assembly Resolution 260 A (III), 1948.
The United Nations Convention for the Amelioration of the Condition of the Wounded and Sick in Armed Forces in the Field. 1949. San Francisco.
International Covenant on Civil and Political Rights of 1966.
The International Covenant on Social and Economic Rights of 1966.
1974. Declaration of the Establishment of a New International Economic Order. Resolution 3201.
The Convention on the Elimination of All Forms of Discrimination against Women of 1981.
The Convention against Torture and Other Cruel, Inhuman, or Degrading Treatment or Punishment of 1984.
The Convention on the Rights of the Child of 1989.
The Rome Statute of the International Criminal Court.
United Nations Resolution 1596, 2005.

Legal Cases, Documents, and Laws

Charter of the International Criminal Tribunal for Rwanda, 1994.
Charter of the International Criminal Tribunal for Yugoslavia, 1993.
Democratic Republic of Congo vs. Uganda. International Court of Justice. 2005.
International Criminal Court Prosecutor Opening Remarks. 2007.
The Hague. February 27. ICC-OTP-20070227-208-En.
International Commission of Inquiry Rwanda. 1959.
Legal Notice No. 1 of 1986 (Transitional government NRA).
Report of the Comission of Inquiry Human Right Violations in Rwanda. 1992.
Prosecutor vs. Akayesu. Trial Chamber (ICTR), September 2, 1998, para. 497; para. 505–506.
Prosecutor vs. Goran Jelisic. Appeals Chamber. Judgement (ICTY). July 5, 2001.
Prosecutor vs. Kayishema and Ruzindana. Trial Chamber (ICTR). May 21, 1999, para. 93, 527.
Prosecutor vs. Musema. Trial Chamber (ICTY). January 27, 2000, para. 157.

Prosecutor vs. Rutaganda. Trial Chamber (ICTR). December 6, 1999, para. 52.
International Criminal Court Arrest Warrants. 2005.
International Criminal Court. Warrant of Arrest: Thomas Lubanga Dyilo. February 10.
International Criminal Court. First Appearance, Thomas Lubanga Dyilo. March 20.
International Criminal Court Background to Situation in Uganda. 2004.
United Nations Security Council Commission Report. 2004, 2005, 2006.